KT-223-689

FIFTY YEARS OF CORONATION ST.™

50

FIFTY YEARS OF CORONATION ST.™

Tim Randall

itv STUDIOS
Home Entertainment

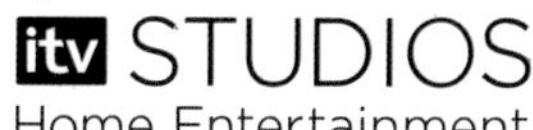

headline

This book is dedicated to the cast and crew of *Coronation Street*, past and present.

In memory of John Croome (1930–2009), a steadfast fan whose family knew never to phone him when *Corrie* was on.

Coronation Street is an ITV Studios Production
© ITV Studios Ltd 2010.
This book is produced under licence from ITV Studios Home Entertainment.

The right of Tim Randall to be identified as the Author of the Work has been asserted by him in accordance with the Copyright, Designs and Patents Act 1988.

First published in 2010
by HEADLINE PUBLISHING GROUP

1

Apart from any use permitted under UK copyright law, this publication may only be reproduced, stored, or transmitted, in any form, or by any means, with prior permission in writing of the publishers or, in the case of reprographic production, in accordance with the terms of licences issued by the Copyright Licensing Agency.

Every effort has been made to fulfil requirements with regard to reproducing copyright material. The author and publisher will be glad to rectify any omissions at the earliest opportunity.

Cataloguing in Publication Data is available from the British Library

ISBN 978 0 7553 1846 9

Design by Perfect Bound Ltd
Picture Research by Dave Woodward
All images used courtesy of ITV Studios except
page 276 © BAFTA/Richard Kendal
Manufactured in China by Butler, Tanner and Dennis Ltd
in conjunction with Beijing ShengTong Printing Co. Ltd

Headline's policy is to use papers that are natural, renewable and recyclable products and made from wood grown in sustainable forests. The logging and manufacturing processes are expected to conform to the environmental regulations of the country of origin.

HEADLINE PUBLISHING GROUP
An Hachette UK Company
338 Euston Road
London NW1 3BH

www.headline.co.uk
www.hachette.co.uk

itv STUDIOS
Home Entertainment

Special thanks to: Tony Warren, AJ Read, Helen Nugent, Dave Woodward, Amanda Weisberg, Alison Sinclair, Emma Tait, Stuart King, Judi Hayfield, Kieran Roberts, Dan Newman, David Crook, Kim Crowther, Dominic Khouri, Sam Walker, Phil Collinson, Kate Ashcroft, Mel Hutchwright, Bryan Kirkwood, Helena Caldon, Janice Troup, Andy Baker, Wendy Granditer, Jo Whitford, Sarah Moolla, Martin Sterling, Jo Baggott, Deirdre O'Brien, Jo Dipple, Vicky Johnson, Mark Horner, Kevin Morgan and Naheed Sanusi.

Contents

Foreword

2010 – *Coronation Street's* fiftieth year – has seen the programme become available for the first time on the brand-new ITV HD channel (actors shuddered at the thought of the intense scrutiny of the new system), the outdoor set on the back lot refurbished, the opening titles redesigned and the theme music re-recorded for only the third time in its history. As I listened to this latest version my mind went right back to the very first time I heard it...

All eyes are on Tony as he rehearses Margot Bryant, Violet Carson and Lynne Carol.

It was 1960 again and I was in executive producer Harry Elton's office. He was a huge and genial bear of a Canadian, brought over to Manchester to discover British writing talent. I was a former boy actor who had outgrown his talent by getting tall. Now I was trying to hang on in show-business by attempting to write scripts. It was Harry who turned me into the boy the newspapers called 'Britain's Youngest Scriptwriter'. First he commissioned freelance scripts from me for episodes of an established television series called *Shadow Squad*. Then he got me a job inside the building writing trailers, 'So you can really learn what television's about.' Eventually, Harry persuaded Granada to put me under contract as a writer at £30 a week, which seemed a lot of money to a twenty-three-year-old in 1960, and in that role I rebelled against the conventional shows I was meant to be writing and came up with something called *Florizel Street*.

As we listened to Eric Spear's haunting theme music that very first time, we were joined by some of the support team who had grown up around this new idea. Altogether there were three Harrys there: along with Harry Elton there was H.V. Kershaw, soon to be the show's first series editor, and Harry Latham our regular producer. At the age of eighteen I had auditioned for him as an actor. 'Too tall,' had been his comment, 'and much too young-looking for your height.' But if it hadn't been for depressing reactions like these I would not have ended up in that office listening to that new theme music. There were also two women casting directors who were determined to give Manchester actors a fair chance as until then, anybody playing a sizeable role had automatically been imported from London; Derek Bennett, a go-ahead young director who sported the first cropped hairstyle any of us had ever seen, and Denis Parkin, the designer, who had already toured the back streets of Salford with me on a search for authenticity. The whole room was alive with anticipation.

Alas, not all our convictions were shared by the Granada board of directors and their programme planning committee. The character our bosses disliked the most was Ena Sharples – they thought she was straight from music hall – and we were having our own problems finding an actress to play the part. I was even told I might have to get rid of her altogether. Fortunately I thought of Violet Carson, the formidable dowager who had once threatened to smack my bottom in a BBC radio studio during a break in a *Children's Hour* rehearsal. Even when we found her, one of the most powerful executives of all was heard to say: 'But Harry, what are we going to do about that face?' Within a year, a headline in *Variety* – the number-one American show-business newspaper – was describing the same scowl as belonging to 'The Second Best-Known Woman in Britain'.

Elsie Tanner exploded into our lives at one of the very earliest auditions. As Pat Phoenix started to read the script for us, something extraordinary was happening: I was hearing the lines delivered in exactly the same way they had sounded in my head when I was writing them. I had found my actress and she had found her author. Even then it was as though we both knew we had found a very special conspirator. From the word go we were laughing and arguing. It was to be like that right until the end.

The show caused a lot of people to produce some unexpected credentials. I had always thought of Harry Latham as rather grand, but this was before he said: 'I know what I'm talking about because I come from the back end of the Goldhawk Road.' The world was still unpleasantly snobbish at the end of the 1950s but in next-to-no time people who had previously kept their origins in the shadows were able to come out and say, 'I come from a Coronation Street' and a complete and friendly picture would fall into place – a cause for pride. Of course life on the cobbles has got a bit more dramatic since then…

Since 1960, there have been three Coronation Street sets. The very first was made from painted canvas with cobbles stencilled onto the studio floor. The next was constructed outside – a place of lath and plaster that always shivered in high winds. Finally, in 1982, Denis Parkin was allowed to build the real thing out on the Granada back lot. A street constructed from recycled Lancashire bricks and paved with rescued cobblestones. There had been a frantic rush to get it finished in time for our biggest-ever VIP event.

And here she came, the Queen of England, turning the corner by the Rovers Return, where we were all lined up to meet her – the survivors of that original meeting in Harry's office. That was the same sunlit morning the Queen asked me the question that nearly had me stumped.

'Where is the real Coronation Street?'

'Well it may sound a bit crowy, Ma'am,' I ventured (where had the word 'crowy' come from?), 'but it's wherever you want it to be in your own heart.'

This book is for all those people who have a place reserved in their own affections for *Coronation Street*. You are the ones who have made the show the success it is today. So thank you, wherever you are – thank you very much.

Tony Warren MBE
Creator of *Coronation Street*

1960s

Over the decades much has been written about the creation of *Coronation Street*. And even now, fifty years on from those humble beginnings, it remains impossible to underestimate just how revolutionary the *Street* was – bringing to the nation working-class characters, a region, and a regional accent previously unseen on the small screen.

'We hit the screen with colossal impact,' remembers William Roache. 'People forget there was no such thing as a soap when we started. We were a cutting-edge drama and literally within the first few weeks were thrown up into this stratosphere and that was it, we never looked back.'

The show was the brainchild of former child actor and twenty-three-year-old screenwriter, Tony Warren. Warren was initially contracted by Granada TV to adapt the *Biggles* adventures for television, but from the start he made it very clear that daredevil pilots weren't his bag. He remembers: 'I was hopeless at it. I begged to be allowed to write about something I understood, and what I knew about was theatre and the north of England.' Whilst the top brass weren't overly keen on the concept of a drama about ordinary people, a point in Warren's favour was Granada's unfulfilled commitment to reflect life in the north-west area in its programming.

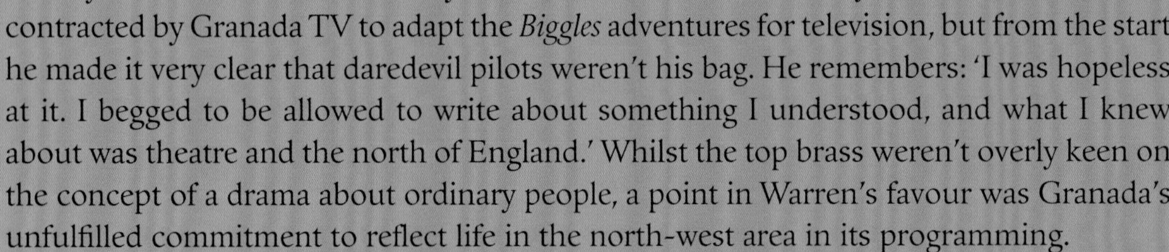

The premise for the series was based on an idea that had already been rejected twice by the BBC, with the titles *Our Street* and *Where No Birds Sing*. By the time he was reworking the proposal for Granada, the series had been retitled *Florizel Street* and, famously, for added realism Warren had visited local graveyards and noted down the names on the headstones for the street's residents. He outlined the programme in a memo in 1959: 'A fascinating freemasonry, a volume of unwritten rules. These are the driving forces behind life in a working-class street in the north of England. The purpose of *Florizel Street* is to examine a community of this nature and to entertain.' He added, 'Not only could we reflect the region, we could make the very accent fashionable.'

Starmaker: Tony Warren with Violet Carson.

In the beginning... the lineup gather for an early publicity shot.

Becoming Elsie: Pat Phoenix in the make-up chair.

Legend has it that *Florizel Street* became *Coronation Street* weeks before its launch when Agnes, a Granada tea lady, pointed out that Florizel sounded less like a drama serial and more like a pungent disinfectant. The name was promptly changed (*Jubilee Street* was another short-lived option) and *Coronation Street* went into production for a short thirteen-episode run.

The first ever episode – which Warren wrote overnight on his bedroom floor in Swinton – was broadcast live on Friday 9 December 1960 with a cast of twenty actors, and when regional audiences recognised their own lives reflected in a TV drama for the first time they sent the show soaring to the top of the ratings. It was fully networked in May 1961 and by the end of that year had become the most popular programme on British television. The Street itself was originally nestled on an indoor set (with the cobbles painted on the studio floor), but by 1968 the show had been deemed enough of a success to warrant a more realistic outdoor location. The familiar set was erected on an old railway siding near the studios, allowing the Mancunian drizzle to fall on Coronation Street for the very first time.

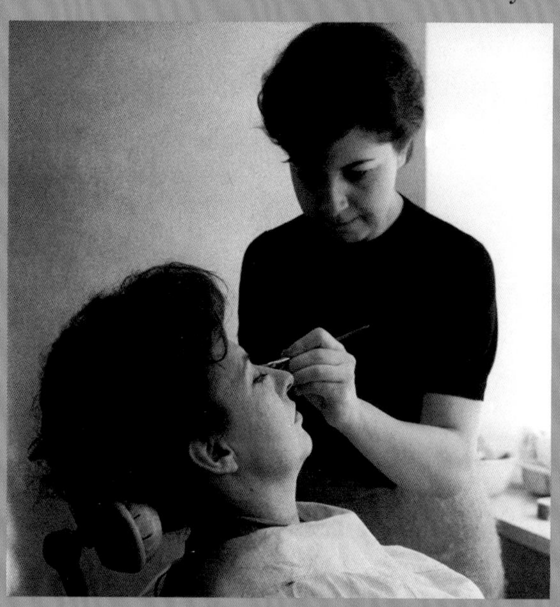

Even though the show mirrored real life, after the debut episode aired one TV critic bemoaned that 'in this day and age no one mends their bicycle in front of the living-room fire', as demonstrated by Frank Barlow, much to the disapproval of his snooty student son, Ken. Following a postbag of complaints, in the next issue the paper was forced to publish a page full of readers' letters insisting that was exactly where they did mend their bikes.

Perhaps most surprising of all is that the *Daily Mirror*, that champion of the working classes, didn't get the show at first: 'The programme is doomed from the outset with its dreary signature tune and grim scene of terraced houses and smoking chimneys,' wrote its critic. But another TV reviewer, the *Manchester Guardian*'s Mary Crozier, was much more in tune with popular tastes when she predicted the *Street* would run 'forever' – and she hasn't been proved wrong yet.

Although *Coronation Street* was on air for less than a month in 1960, it was clear that it had started as it meant to go on. By the end of December there had already been a police alert on the street, an unexpected pregnancy, a stroke, a robbery, a runaway and an untimely death. Plenty to keep the local gossips' tongues wagging...

Shy widow Florrie Lindley had her work cut out when she took over at the corner shop from previous owner, Elsie Lappin. For a start her second customer was grim-faced pensioner Ena Sharples (*see page 16*), who marched in and proceeded to give the bemused newcomer a grilling on her place of worship, her marital status and her burial plans (advising her against the crematorium), all whilst ordering iced fancies and a bottle of bleach on the slate. 'You've no need to worry – I'm not thinking of running away!' barked Ena, grabbing her purchases and heading for the door.

Secondly, just as Florrie began to settle in she was apprehended by the police, having been caught committing the serious crime of selling firelighters after seven in the evening. Embarrassed, the timid shop owner was only given a £1 fine, but when her name appeared in the local newspaper after they reported the incident she became consumed with worry that her new neighbours would shun her. Of course they didn't, but five years later it turned out

'There's some very peculiar people in this street. 'Ave you come across a Mrs Tanner yet? Watch her. She's a bad'un.'

Ena to Florrie

'Best years of me life, the Blackout. Every time I think of it, it reminds me of Yankee whisky.'

Elsie

that Florrie was harbouring a much more gossip-worthy secret – she wasn't a widow at all. The locals were nearly as shocked as she was when her estranged husband, Norman, turned up at the shop demanding a reconciliation.

Meanwhile, down-on-her-luck good-time girl Elsie Tanner (*see page 20*) found herself with a houseful again when her daughter, Linda Cheveski, reappeared at Number 11 having left her hard-working Polish husband, Ivan. At first Linda refused to be drawn on why she had left, but when Ivan showed up looking for her in the Rovers, Linda revealed that she had discovered she was pregnant and had just panicked. The couple were reunited and Ivan was as thrilled as Elsie about the prospective new addition to the family.

But the glamorous gran-to-be wasn't quite so chuffed when her layabout son Dennis, having been released from prison, turned up with a stash of cash he claimed he'd won on the dogs. Elsie feared the worst when she heard a local robbery had taken place at the same time Dennis was supposedly backing a winner. However, she was relieved when upstanding neighbour Harry Hewitt came to Dennis's rescue and told the police he'd witnessed his big win.

Newcomer Florrie sets up shop.

Linda makes a surprise appearance at Number 11.

Frank and Ken pile on the sauce at the Barlows'.

Ena and lay preacher Swindley fail to see eye to eye.

Elsie refuses estranged husband Arnold's request for a divorce.

'If I had my way, I'd just like to go like me mother did... She just sat up, broke wind and died.'

Ena

Over at Number 3, Ken (*see page 10*) and Frank Barlow's father–son relationship was deteriorating fast, as postman Frank continued to ridicule his snooty student son for his middle-class pretensions. Indeed, ex-serviceman Frank was furious when Ken announced he intended to go on a 'Ban The Bomb' march, and relations were not improved later when Ken brought his posh activist girlfriend, Susan Cunningham, home for the first time. It was obvious from the start of the visit that Ken was ashamed of his surroundings, and that for Ken, Susan represented all he was striving for – class; something he was unlikely to find in his backstreet terrace. Over dinner, Ken got sniffy as he watched his dad pick up the sauce bottle and help himself to some more. 'Don't they do that at college then?' retorted Frank. 'I bet they don't eat in their shirt sleeves either...?'

Elsewhere, teetotal lay preacher Leonard Swindley caught Glad Tidings Mission Hall caretaker Ena enjoying a surreptitious milk stout in the Rovers – which she indignantly insisted was for medicinal purposes. But the stress of the humiliation was so great that Ena collapsed in the vestry and was taken to Weatherfield Hospital suffering a stroke.

There was more medical drama a week later when the year ended in tragedy. After weeks of complaining of head pains, May Hardman died alone on New Year's Eve in the hallway of Number 13, having suffered a brain tumour.

It was a case of coach-trip wars when two rival outings were planned for the same day; the Street's pensioners had fancied gawking at the bright lights of the Blackpool Illuminations, whereas the Rovers regulars had a more laid-back trip to Morecambe in mind. In the end it was Emily who suggested the trips merge, a plan agreed on in principle by Ena (heading up the OAP delegation) on the proviso that the chosen destination was Blackpool – or there'd be trouble.

Once there, both Ena and Minnie visited a fortune-teller, although Ena scoffed at her reading, which suggested she was about to go on a very long journey. However, this prediction came spookily true when she managed to miss the coach home and had to return to Weatherfield on the back of a potato lorry. Meanwhile, an excited Minnie was told she'd receive a gift from the skies, which she did – a slate dropped off the roof of Number 13 and hit her on the head.

It was the men in her life that were to cause heartache for Elsie throughout 1961 – starting with a blast from the past, none other than her estranged husband Arnold, whom she hadn't set eyes on for fifteen years. Arnold turned up in Weatherfield to demand a divorce in order to marry his girlfriend, Norah. At first an indignant Elsie refused, but when Arnold threatened to divorce her on grounds of adultery (due to a fling she'd had in the war), Elsie knew she'd been cornered and reluctantly agreed.

The arrival of Dennis's latest girlfriend, Eunice, didn't help to lift Elsie's mood either – especially when she found out that Eunice was a stripper going by the stage name of La Composita. Part of her act involved a pet python, which had nearly scared Elsie to death when she had nosily opened the mysterious box Eunice had brought with her so she could see what was inside.

Ken Barlow

Played by **William Roache**

From the very beginning, fresh-faced student and idealist Ken Barlow was geared up to ditch working-class Weatherfield and take on the world. But despite his best attempts he's never made it any further than Rosamund Street. Indeed, as recently as 2009 Ken was still fantasising about making a run for it, but at the very last moment he chickened out of a new life aboard his artsy lover Martha's barge. Perhaps it had finally dawned on him that Weatherfield was where he belonged after all.

Unlike his alter-ego, as the only remaining cast member from the first episode, William Roache couldn't be more at home on the nation's favourite backstreet, and this year he officially becomes the world's longest-serving soap character, celebrating his own five-decade anniversary as *Coronation Street*'s crusading ladies man.

'I'm just as passionate about *Coronation Street* now as I was when we started. I've given my life to it and it's wonderful to see this resurgence in its fiftieth anniversary.

'I originally only signed up for thirteen episodes, but from the day we exploded onto the screen there was a feeling that this was something special and it was almost assumed even then that the show would go on and on.

'In the last few years it feels as though we've come full circle, which I think is very interesting indeed. Suddenly everybody wants to be on *Coronation Street* and we've had all these wonderful guest artists like Sir Ian McKellen and June Whitfield coming in, which is lovely for us.'

There was one blip in the early Eighties when William questioned his future as Ken, but since then he hasn't given retiring a second thought.

'I did consider leaving at around twenty years in because I felt the character wasn't going anywhere. I didn't want to leave particularly, but Ken had gone from being the young juvenile lead to a different age bracket and they didn't know quite what to do with him. The problem was why does Ken stay there, and we decided it was mainly his failings with his women that have kept him on the Street.

'It was the Ken, Mike and Deirdre love triangle that revitalised everything for me. I put a lot of frustration and anger into that storyline which I think really galvanised it and made the writers realise that Ken might be a nice liberal sort of guy, but he stands by his convictions and he's got guts. Before that storyline there was an attempt to make him into a sort of nerdy Roy Cropper type and I fought that, because it wasn't right.

50 CORONATION ST. ICON

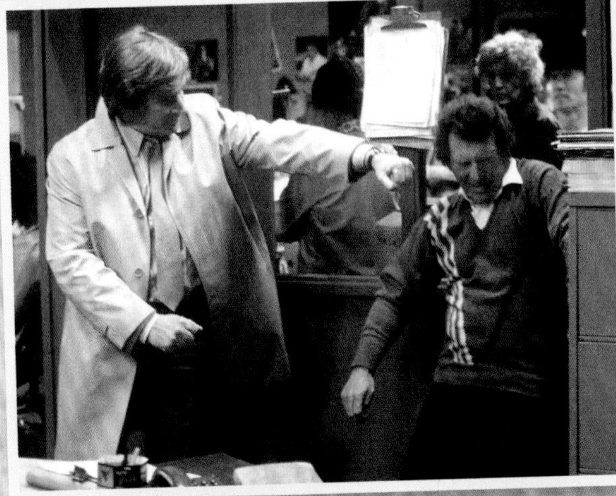

- Student Ken attempts to impress Ida and David with his reading matter.
- Newlyweds Ken and Valerie inspect their stash of gifts.
- Ken's left hook wins him the latest round of Barlow versus Baldwin.
- Deirdre lays down the law.
- Second time lucky? Ken and Deirdre tie the knot.
- Like father like son? Ken and Peter.

'He's supposed to be a bright man, but as long as I've known him he's blundered from one mess to the next.'

Alf on Ken

'Ken's a well-meaning guy who likes to think he's the voice of Weatherfield. He's a failed novelist, failed pretty well at everything and that's why he's stuck in this little backwater. But I think he really values Deirdre now and his wonderful dysfunctional family around him – a daughter who's a murderer and a son who's an alcoholic bigamist. And then there's poor Ken in the middle of it, trying to be normal and keep the peace and hold it all together.'

Born in Derbyshire, from the age of seven William was sent to boarding school in North Wales, where coincidentally he met Jack Howarth (Albert Tatlock). 'Synchronicity is a very strange thing. On my first day at school a boy was put in charge of me, and it was Jack Howarth's son. I remember that he always had a cane with an ivory top on it and we had a little chat. Then I never met him again until the first day of *Coronation Street*, and he remembered me.'

Despite William's three years in repertory theatre, he confesses nothing could prepare him for the terror of live television drama. 'When we did the most recent live episode for our anniversary in 2000 people were saying to me: "It's all right for you, you've done it before." And I thought, "Yeah, forty years ago..." In the Sixties the days of the actual live transmissions were quite nerve-wracking and extremely frightening. Even some commercials were done live back then – I remember once cutting to the other side of the studio and a guy with cornflakes standing there doing an advert!

'Occasionally you do feel nostalgic and I often stop and have a look at the old pictures. There's one on the wall outside my dressing room that was taken on the day of the very first episode and you look to see who is actually still alive. There's not much else that reminds me of those early days now, although on the Barlows' set the sideboard and the table and chairs are all from episode one and they do take me back. Sometimes I look at that sideboard and think: "My God, you've been here for fifty years as well..."'

Occupations: Retired schoolteacher, taxi driver, warehouse executive, community officer, journalist, Freshco trolley-pusher and Roy's Rolls fryer-upper.
On screen: 1960–
Defining moment: In 1986 Ken discovers arch-rival Mike is dating his daughter Susan – he marches into the factory, punches Baldwin to the ground and storms out.

Elsie dishes out tough love to Dennis.

Nor was Elsie having much luck in her own romantic affairs. First she dated Arthur Dewhurst, a glum-faced policeman who she eventually dumped for being too possessive. Next there was a brief fling with travelling salesman Walter Fletcher, and then she met an old naval shipmate of Len Fairclough's, Bill Gregory, at the cheery wedding of Harry Hewitt to sweet-natured Rovers barmaid Concepta Riley, at St Theresa's Church. There was an immediate attraction between the pair but Bill had conveniently neglected to mention to Elsie that he was already married.

When Elsie received an anonymous letter warning her that her relationship with Bill could jeopardise her divorce from Arnold, she suspected battleaxe Ena of sending it and had a huge public row with her on the cobbles. By the time she'd received a note from Arnold revealing it was Norah who'd written the poison-pen letter, it had all got too much for Elsie and she phoned Bill and told him to keep his distance.

OVERHEARD

Elsie accuses Ena of sending a poison-pen letter, 1961.

IN THE STREET. ENA AND ELSIE ARE IN THE MIDDLE OF A ROW. THE ASSEMBLED RESIDENTS (INCLUDING MINNIE, MARTHA, ANNIE, DOREEN, LEN, ALBERT AND DENNIS) TAKE IN THE SHOW.

ENA: (WAGGING HER FINGER AT ELSIE) You never will be any good and you never have been any good. It's a well-known fact people have been talking about you for years.

ELSIE: Oh, I'd expect you to know something like that. Every lying bit of gossip that goes about. What you don't know you make up. We don't need sewers round here, we've got Ena Sharples!

ENA: By gum there's something wrong with a woman that can't hold on to her husband.

ELSIE: At least mine wasn't carried out feet first!

ENA: What do you mean by that? What do mean by that, eh? (TO THE CROWD) Are you listening to this? I shall want you as witnesses after this!

ELSIE: I've listened to you talking as long as I can. I've only stood back out of respect for your age. But this time I'm going to land you one, so help me!

DENNIS HOLDS ELSIE BACK.

ENA: (TAKING THE HIGH GROUND). That's right. Go on. Strike a poor old defenceless woman. That's just about your level, Elsie Tanner. But before you raise yer hand and damn yerself forever, if you haven't already done it, you'll listen to me for a minute or two. I know all about that letter and personally I haven't the slightest doubt that everything in it is nowt but God's own truth.

ELSIE LUNGES FOR HER, BUT DENNIS TIGHTENS HIS GRIP.

You think on this, Elsie Tanner. I know plenty about you. I know plenty about you that you don't think I know. I could write a full-length book about you, let alone a letter. But if I had written it... if I had written it, it wouldn't have come anonymous. Oh no. I've never been afraid to stand behind me own beliefs. If I had written the flamin' thing it would've had Ena Sharples in big black letters at the bottom of it and well you know it. Now go on, stand there and deny it!

ELSIE FALTERS. SHE KNOWS ENA IS RIGHT.

ELSIE: (THE FIGHT HAS GONE OUT OF HER) Dennis, take me home.

THE CROWD CLEARS. ENA IS VISIBLY SHAKEN. ALBERT REMAINS SUPPORTIVELY BY HER SIDE ON THE PAVEMENT.

ENA: (DRAINED AND DESPONDENT) By gum, every street has it's own Aunt Sally. Talk til you're blue in the face. But if there's owt that goes wrong round here I know which way the finger points...

A LONELY FIGURE, SHE CROSSES THE ROAD TO THE MISSION.

There was a brief respite from all the drama for Elsie when her daughter Linda gave birth to a beautiful baby boy (the proud parents named him Paul), but her celebratory mood was cut short when Linda and husband Ivan announced they were emigrating to Canada, leaving Elsie at home for a miserable, teary and lonely Christmas.

For a short while there were good times to be had at the Barlows' too – Frank's promotion at the Post Office meant that kindly Ida could finally give up her back-breaking job at the Imperial Hotel, where she'd spent years scrubbing away as a lowly kitchen cleaner. But as the buoyed-up couple began to plan their first holiday in twenty years, tragedy struck. In September, Ida was knocked down and killed by a bus.

Dutifully putting his family first, Ken turned down a good job in Surrey in order to return home to look after his grieving father. After an unhappy period working in the personnel department of Amalgamated Steel, he took a temporary job as a postman, before settling on a permanent teaching post at Bessie Street School.

- Linda and Ivan make themselves at home at Number 11.
- Postman Frank bags a promotion.
- A shocked Frank needs a stiff drink after Ida is killed.

'He might be a walkin' flamin' dictionary, but he hasn't the guts of a louse.'

Len on Ken

Meanwhile, a red-faced Ena was forced to apologise after discovering a planning notice outlining the demolition of Coronation Street. The news led her shocked neighbours to organise an emergency residents' meeting in a bid to save the street. But it turned out that blind-as-a-bat Ena had misread the notice and it was Coronation Terrace that was to be knocked down. To get their own back, the piqued locals briefly sent Ena to Coventry...

By the time Ken wed hairdresser Valerie Tatlock at St Mary's Church on a sweltering August afternoon in 1962, all was harmonious on the Street, even though back in January Ken had been persona non grata, thanks to an article he'd written for a left-wing magazine titled: 'The Student and The Working Class'.

Elsie and Ena suspected Ken was up to something when they heard he'd been tapping the residents for information about themselves. Pensioner Albert Tatlock (*see page 50*) was horrified by the published article, as was Frank Barlow, who rowed with Ken, ashamed of his disloyalty to his class, and ordered his son not to show it to anyone. But it was too late – the local paper had already printed a report on the controversial article with the headline: 'Ex-Student Shams Neighbours!' It continued: 'Kenneth Barlow, 24-year-old schoolmaster of 3 Coronation Street jeered at the simple pleasures of his homely neighbours in a scathing 2,000-word attack in a left-wing political review. Summing up the attitude of the people he lives and works among, Barlow described them

1960s Births

Paul (Linda & Ivan Cheveski)	12 June 1961
Christopher (Concepta & Harry Hewitt)	6 August 1962
Susan Ida (Valerie & Ken Barlow)	5 April 1965
Peter (Valerie & Ken Barlow)	5 April 1965

Ena Sharples

Played by **Violet Carson**

Based on Tony Warren's grandmother, who was 'a big lady with a strong character', Ena Sharples was an outspoken and dominating presence. A hairnet-wearing harridan and keeper of the Street's moral values, she presided disdainfully over the goings on in the Rovers from the vantage point of the snug, aided and abetted by cohorts Minnie Caldwell and Martha Longhurst. Occasionally a gentler side did break through her battleship-like exterior, such as the time she kept a tireless vigil at Minnie's hospital bedside, and over the years she softened (not that she'd ever admit it) towards her arch rival, the scandalous Elsie Tanner.

Meanwhile, behind the scenes at Granada Violet Carson was equally vociferous, as William Roache remembers:

'She was very much the matriarch of the show, there's no question about that. I loved Vi, she was one of these beautiful, strong, fair-minded, lovely women with a nice sense of humour – but you didn't mess with her. Any problems with the management and she'd be straight up there telling them we're not having that – just as Ena would've done.'

Teatime with Albert and Alf.

Putting the world to rights alongside Minnie and Martha.

A rare heart-to-heart with Elsie.

Unlike the rest of the original cast, Violet was already an established BBC radio star before she appeared on *Corrie*, well known for her work with Wilfred Pickles on the popular series, *Have A Go*. But it was in 1951, while recording an episode of *Children's Hour*, that she was to meet someone who would later propel her to a whole new level of stardom – twelve-year-old child actor Tony Warren.

'The first thing I remember her saying about me was: "If that child doesn't shut up I'll smack his bottom!"' recalls Tony, laughing at the memory.

'We had quite a prickly relationship, but she mellowed with the years and I suppose so did I. Yes, I handed her a great part, but my God how she rewarded me with a wonderful performance.

'A year or so before her death in 1983 Violet wrote to me and said, "This wretched anaemia means I come but slowly to paper, but soon I will come to Manchester and visit my friends and that, my darling, means you." So that was lovely, because it meant we were all right in the end.'

Occupation: Caretaker at the Mission and the Community Centre.
On Screen: 1960–1980
Defining moment: The row in 1965 when she inherits Number 11 and threatens to evict Elsie is so vigorous that she accidentally smashes a window with her handbag.

Fresh-faced Ken and Val tie the knot with Uncle Albert's blessing.

as lazy-minded, politically ignorant, starved of a real culture and stubbornly prejudiced against any advance in human insight and scientific progress.'

Len Fairclough in particular took Ken's article personally. Unapologetic as ever, Ken stood up to the residents, but when he attempted to explain his viewpoint a furious Len punched him in the jaw and the pair ended up battering each other in a full-scale brawl in the Rovers.

Harry and Concepta became the proud owners of an athletic-looking greyhound, 'Lucky Lolita', and a Coronation Street outing by minibus to the White City track was organised for her first race. To cheers from the residents, Lucky Lolita romped home in first place and later that evening everyone celebrated by spending their winnings in the Rovers. As a result, for the hound's second outing every penny they could scrape together was staked – including Elsie's entire holiday fund. But despite the fact that Harry (much to Concepta's horror) had been feeding the dog the finest port and steak money could buy, it turned out Lolita wasn't so lucky after all and she came in last. An unlucky Elsie was then forced to holiday in gloomy Weatherfield instead.

Annie offers her support to a distraught Harry and Concepta.

Elsie searches for a job under the watchful eye of Len.

Elsewhere, the Hewitts celebrated their first wedding anniversary and vowed to make more of an effort with Lucille (Harry's daughter from his previous marriage) to ensure she didn't feel sidelined by the arrival of baby Christopher. But as they prepared for their anniversary party, Christopher was kidnapped from outside Gamma Garments where Lucille had briefly left him whilst running an errand for Rovers landlady Annie Walker (*see page 33*).

The police were soon on the scene. Concepta, meanwhile, had also disappeared, but she was later found by Florrie – tearily searching the streets for her baby son. While the Hewitts were hounded by news-hungry journalists, the residents helped the police scour the neighbourhood and frogmen drained the canal. It was thanks to the combined efforts of sensible-shoed Emily Nugent (*see page 26*) and feisty Elsie that an unharmed Christopher was tracked down to the home of confused local woman, Joan Akers, who revealed that her own baby had died, which was why she'd stolen little Christopher.

The community pulled together again that year when the Post Office decided there were too many 'Coronation Streets' in

'When they come to bury Mrs Tanner, there'll probably be two men fighting at the graveside.'

Annie

Weatherfield and that some of them should be renamed. When the residents discovered their road was to be bizarrely rebranded as 'Florida Street', they flipped. Albert started a petition to send to the town hall, but an incandescent Ena set her sights higher than the local council and went straight to the top, writing to Prince Philip instead. It may have just been a coincidence, but in the end the street's name was saved!

Fed up with being treated like a servant while her husband boozed it up in the Rovers, in 1963 Len's wife Nellie left him for good, taking their son Stanley with her. Not that Len seemed especially devastated by this, and instead he saw it as the perfect opportunity to further his burgeoning friendship with Elsie. The pair would often spend their evenings socialising together, but Elsie made sure that everything was above board and woe betide any gossips (specifically Ena) who suggested there was anything more than companionship to their liaisons.

However, there was an obvious chemistry between the pair, and when their relationship inevitably threatened to become more intimate – on occasions such as their romantic night out at the Builders' Federation Dance – Elsie cooled things. After all, Len was still married to Nellie. However, in August that year Nellie finally agreed to divorce Len and he wasted no time in asking Elsie to marry him in three months' time on Bonfire Night, when his divorce would become absolute. Much to Len's disappointment, Elsie didn't jump at the offer. Instead she asked for time to mull it over, explaining that neither of them had been success stories when it came to their previous attempts at marriage. Despite her son Dennis and even a bossy Ena advising her to go for it, in the end Elsie declined Len's offer – saying she felt that marriage would ruin their friendship.

Meanwhile, the darts team's annual outing to New Brighton wasn't Albert's finest hour. Nor was it a moment the GPO manager and future Mayor of Weatherfield, Alf Roberts (*see page 75*), would ever want to be reminded about. They both remembered little about how, after their coach broke down, they'd ended up being charged with assaulting a police officer who'd found a drunken Albert clinging to a lamp post for dear life.

Elsie Tanner

Played by **Patricia Phoenix**

There's no doubt that cleavage-heavy, scarlet woman Elsie Tanner was the most gossiped about woman in Weatherfield, but off-screen Britain's very first queen of soap, the glamorous Pat Phoenix, was also the talk of the town.

William Roache, who appeared with Pat in *Corrie*'s very first episode, remembers his co-star with affection: 'She was a wonderfully extravagant and generous person, and in that episode she brought to life a character that reached out and touched the hearts of the nation and helped cement *Coronation Street* into its place in history.'

Her career began as a child actor on the BBC's *Children's Hour*, but after nearly eighteen years in rep and the occasional film role, success came late in life for Pat. She'd been out of work for a year and was considering giving up on acting altogether when she auditioned for the part that was to make her a household name.

Street creator and close friend Tony Warren explains: 'Pat had tatted around in rep and on tour for years and what she brought to the show was something not really seen much on television in those days – great star quality. When she came on it seemed as though they'd turned the lights up a little more brightly.'

Party-loving Pat's own life often mirrored Elsie's – they'd both been born into poor working-class, Mancunian backgrounds, and despite the difficulties life threw at them, they'd remained determined, indomitable survivors. Like warm-hearted Elsie, Pat also married three times. Her sassy alter ego tied the knot with businessman Alan Howard in 1970 and the actor who played him, Alan Browning, became Pat's real-life husband in 1972, until his death seven years later.

In 1983 the much-loved soap legend made headline news and shocked fans (and the show's producers) when she revealed she was quitting the *Street* for good. Three years later she made headlines again with the announcement that she was suffering from incurable lung cancer. She died in September 1986, shortly after marrying fellow actor, Tony Booth.

'We were great friends right until the end and I was a witness at her deathbed wedding,' adds Tony Warren. 'As a friend she was fiercely loyal, frequently impossible, and I wouldn't have missed knowing her for anything.'

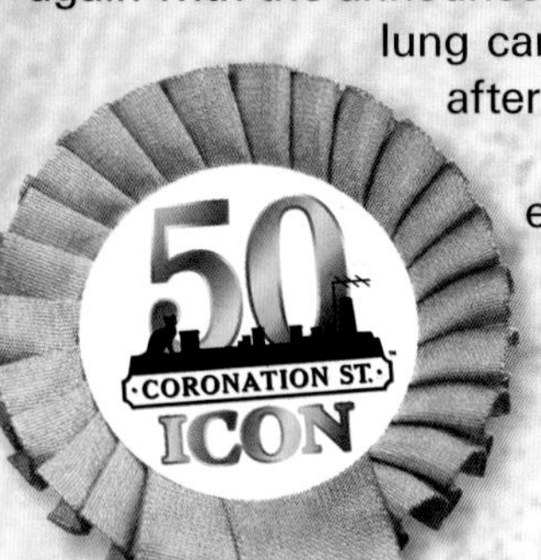

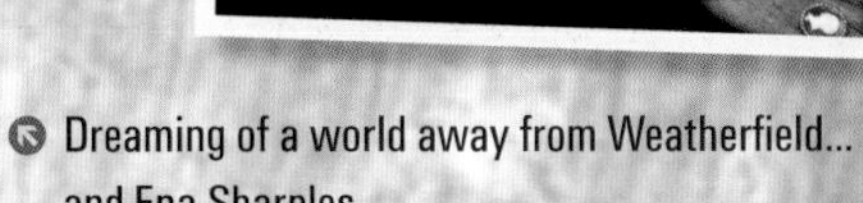

Dreaming of a world away from Weatherfield... and Ena Sharples.

With husband number three, the dashing Alan Howard.

Occupations: Croupier, florist, Miami Modes shop assistant, factory supervisor, machinist, café worker and artist's model.
On screen: 1960–1973, 1976–1984
Defining moment: Returning to Coronaton Street after only six weeks living in America with new husband Steve.

Dodgy wide-boy Neil Crossley became manager of clothing shop Gamma Garments – helping himself to the takings in the process – and began a fling with a loved-up Sheila Birtles, who worked down the road at Ellison's Raincoat Factory. When Neil callously dumped the factory girl, telling her she was just a bit of fun, Sheila became depressed. She was then sacked from her job because of her unreliability and so she decided to take her own life with an overdose. However, this scene was never aired, as only days before the episode was due to be screened the story was leaked, causing uproar in the press and complaints from viewers. What followed was a hasty rewrite and instead Sheila merely suffered a breakdown before leaving Weatherfield to move back home to her worried parents in Rawtenstall. Three years later a recovered Sheila reappeared in the Street for a brief fling with old flame Jerry Booth.

1963

They both seemed to have conveniently forgotten that in the early hours of the morning a policeman had asked them to quieten down and Albert had responded by knocking off his helmet while a plastered Alf tried to punch him. The pair were charged in court the next day – while a mortified Alf was fined £10, Albert managed to get away with a lesser £5 penalty, due to his OAP status.

There was more out-of-character behaviour in March when widowed Frank started dating factory girl Christine Hardman, which had the gossips literally frothing at the mouth with disapproval. Ena pointed out that foolish Frank was old enough to be Christine's father, which was true – she'd actually been at school with Ken and there had even been a brief flirtation between the pair in their youth. So perhaps it wasn't a surprise that Ken didn't exactly approve of his dad's new relationship, and when the couple became engaged he distanced himself from his father.

While Frank couldn't believe his luck at having a girl like Christine on his arm, Christine wasn't quite so sure about the benefits of dating Frank. She liked him, but didn't love him, and it soon became apparent that their age difference meant they had little in common. Much as it broke her heart, Christine decided to be honest with Frank and called off the engagement. Frank was upset but understood, and in order to get over the disappointment he quit the Post Office and opened his very own DIY shop in Victoria Street instead.

1960s Marriages

Joan Walker & Gordon Davies	8 March 1961
Concepta Riley & Harry Hewitt	1 October 1961
Christine Hardman & Colin Appleby	20 June 1962
Valerie Tatlock & Ken Barlow	4 August 1962
Myra Dickinson & Jerry Booth	19 October 1963
Irma Ogden & David Barlow	8 December 1965
Elsie Tanner & Steve Tanner	4 September 1967
Jenny Sutton & Dennis Tanner	29 May 1968
Audrey Bright & Dickie Fleming	15 July 1968

⊙ Milk-stout-supping Ena lays down the law to Minnie and Martha.

⊙ Emily's emotions are a tangled mess thanks to Swindley.

That Christmas Dennis showed his community-spirited side when he decided to entertain the gathered neighbours with a full-scale live version of *This Is Your Life* at the Mission Hall. As the news spread around the Street, the big question on everyone's lips was who was going to be the recipient of this honour. While Emily fretted it could be her, Elsie gave her son strict orders not to invite any of her former boyfriends if her disastrous love life was to be the focus of the evening's entertainment.

In fact, the mystery victim turned out to be Annie, who was clearly in her element as the star of the show. Guests reminiscing on stage included her children Joan and Billy (who arrived late), husband Jack and the three pensioners of the snug, Ena, Minnie Caldwell (*see page 36*) and Martha Longhurst, who were announced off-stage by Ena intoning their oft-used catchphrase: 'Three milk stouts please'. Annie's gracious smile faltered slightly when Ena disputed Minnie's recollection that Annie had given the regulars a free drink when the Walkers had moved into the Rovers in 1939, but her mood perked up again when her friend from the Operatic Society, Mr Nuttall, was introduced and they performed a coquettish duet for the audience.

However, Annie's thrill at so much undivided attention being directed at her good self was dented somewhat by the appearance of Edgar Stubbins, the elderly owner of the horse she had ridden when she'd graced the 1933 Clitheroe Co-Op Pageant Of The Ages as Lady Godiva – dressed only in a body-stocking and a long blond wig! He recalled: 'I remember we lost the procession three times. I mean, when you're leading a horse with a naked woman on it, well, you're not going to spend much time looking where you're going, are you?'

Down the road at Gamma Garments Leonard Swindley had always been a rather pompous man, but there's no accounting for taste and Emily was smitten. For Emily, the daily grind at Gamma was made all the more bearable by his stumpy presence and she firmly believed that one day he would ask for her hand in marriage. In the end, with her patience running out, Emily decided to ask him instead – it was a leap year, after all. She proposed over a romantic home-cooked meal, but instead of accepting, a flustered Leonard flatly refused her offer, made his excuses and left.

'The time to get worried about Emily Nugent is when something isn't troubling her.'

Ena

Mortified, Emily felt she could no longer work alongside him and resigned from Gamma Garments. Such was her humiliation she even considered leaving Weatherfield for good, but a few days later Leonard had a change of heart and bought Emily an engagement ring for £25. The couple set a date in July 1964, but

as their wedding plans gathered momentum, Emily started to have doubts, especially at the idea of being intimate with Leonard. Emily confided in Ken that deep down she knew Leonard didn't really love her, and by the eve of the wedding she was definitely getting cold feet.

The next day, as a nervous Leonard waited uncomfortably at the altar, Emily told Jack Walker (who was due to give her away) that she couldn't go through with the union because she knew it was a mistake and, much to both participants' relief, the wedding was cancelled. They'd both realised they weren't right for each other and while Leonard headed off for their North Wales honeymoon alone, Emily returned their wedding presents before travelling to Wakefield for a few days to get over her embarrassment at all the fuss she'd caused.

At the Rovers, an over-imaginative Annie had put two and two together and got five when she saw their bank account was overdrawn and that her husband had been sending regular cheques to a mysterious Mrs Nicholls. Suspecting Jack of having an affair, she disappeared without telling him. Later that day, Jack discovered that Annie had found out about Mrs Nicholls and telephoned their daughter, Joan, assuming Annie would be staying with her. She wasn't.

'It's a travesty of the marriage service. Leonard Swindley has never loved, honoured or obeyed anybody in his life apart from himself.'

Ena

Service with a smile from the welcoming Walkers.

TOP FIVE Corrie Pets

From broody budgies to pampered pooches, sometimes it isn't only the residents creating the drama...

BOBBY

owned by Minnie Caldwell The pensioner's life revolved around her adored tabby cat. When Bobby disappeared he was replaced with a stray found on the viaduct and Minnie named him Sunny Jim, her nickname for her surrogate son and lodger, Jed Stone. But, unable to remember her new cat's monicker, in 1969 Minnie reverted to calling him Bobby.

HARRY/ HARRIET

owned by Mavis Riley Harry became Harriet in 1982 when Mavis's much-loved budgie laid an egg, immediately bringing issues of gender to the fore. But the shock of moving from The Kabin flat to Number 4 was all too much for Harriet and she died in 1990. Her replacement was a runaway budgie called Boris, which Mavis imaginatively renamed Harry.

ECCLES

owned by Blanche Hunt In 2006 Blanche returned from her friend Lena's funeral with a bequest – Lena's dog Lady Freckles. Renamed Eccles (thanks to Amy's inability to pronounce the full name) the border terrier took an instant dislike to Ken, but the pair eventually bonded and in 2009 Eccles was instrumental in Ken's affair with Martha, as they first met when she was fished out of the canal by the barge-living actress.

'He's the best mate I ever had. He never picked on me or shouted at me. Always wagged his tail when he saw us. He wanted to be with me and I wanted to be with him.'

SCHMEICHEL

owned by Chesney Battersby-Brown Chesney's adored Great Dane underwent a life-saving operation when he was accidentally run over by a bus driven by Claire in 2005. He caused chaos when he climbed into a bath with Les and Cilla, and in 2008 he was removed by the RSPCA when Chesney was taken into care. But there were wagging tails all round when they were later reunited.

LEANNE

owned by Simon Barlow Named after his dad's girlfriend, Leanne the rabbit wasn't long for this world. When he died in 2009 Peter debated replacing him, but Blanche insisted that Simon should be told the truth. As Peter gently broke the news, his son asked if Leanne was in heaven with his mum. The rabbit was later buried in a moving ceremony in the Websters' garden.

Emily Bishop

Played by Eileen Derbyshire

When bovver-booted activist Emily Bishop found herself splashed across the front pages of the *Weatherfield Gazette* for spending the night up a tree while protesting at the redevelopment of the Red Rec, the locals could've been forgiven for thinking they were hallucinating. But the sensible-shoed pensioner had always stood up for what she believed in – back in 1971 she organised a human barricade to picket against the proposed new warehouse (and was covered in sand from a dumper in the process) and three years later she even threw a brick through councillor Len Fairclough's window when she discovered plans to demolish the Street.

So when her new-age, eco-warrior nephew, Geoffrey 'Spider' Nugent, pitched up in 1997 Emily discovered a kindred spirit with a passion for just causes. Together they saved the Red Rec and she went on to join him in the PLO (Prawn Liberation Organisation) to rescue the Norwegian Prawn from Firman's Freezers supermarket.

Meanwhile, Eileen Derbyshire has always preferred a quieter life and, much to her own amusement, she was once labelled the reclusive 'Garbo of the soaps' by *The Times* newspaper.

'Several people have told me I've been called that, but I'm not a recluse at all...' laughs Eileen. 'A recluse implies I barely leave the house and when I do it is in the middle of the night disguised with some kind of shawl over my head. It's just that I don't really like the publicity side of things or big awards ceremonies. Strangely, even as a child I never liked big parties and if there was any kind of gathering I'd always much prefer for them to happen spontaneously and to have fun out of the blue.

'Also, I just don't think I'd be terribly good at doing interviews and red carpets – I mean, you look at someone like Julie Goodyear or Barbara Windsor, they love it and they take a joy in it, whereas I would be terrible at them. I just like to do the job and go home, and thankfully the powers that be at Granada have been very kind and have let me off much of it.'

50 CORONATION ST. ICON

Falling for photographer husband-to-be Ernest.

Happiness before the heartache: Arnold turns out to be a bigamist.

Percy gives Emily food for thought.

Emily becomes an eco-warrior alongside Toyah, Roy and Spider.

Page-turning in the Kabin with Norris.

Mild-mannered Miss Nugent made her debut on the cobbles in early 1961 (she wasn't furnished with a Christian name until a year later), clashing with Ena Sharples, caretaker of the Glad Tidings Mission Hall, over clearing up after services.

'I was asked to come into Granada and they said: "We're doing this little series and it seems to be taking off. It's fully cast now, unfortunately, and the only part we've got at the moment is this shy religious woman who goes to the local mission hall and helps at the local drapers shop. It isn't much of a character, so perhaps you'd rather wait for something better as part of a new family?" They said it would only be a week's work but I agreed to do it – a bird in the hand and all that and I didn't want to be out of work. Talk about a momentous decision, because I can't imagine my life without *Coronation Street* now, quite honestly. There was such a camaraderie on set back then, because you were all bound together by the terror of doing it live. At one time the very sound of the signature tune used to give me awful butterflies because I'd be so terrified.'

'You have done something in your life if you'll venture to let me say so. Something very important in this world. You've been an example – an example of decency and right-mindedness.'

Percy to Emily

Since then the sherry-sipping churchgoer has married photographer Ernest Bishop, only to be widowed when he was killed during a factory wages raid, and then her faith was questioned decades later in 2006 when Ernest's now reformed killer, Ed Jackson, returned and sought her forgiveness. In 1964 she jilted her Gamma Garments' boss Leonard 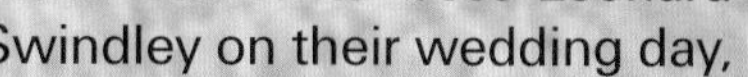Swindley on their wedding day, and in 1980 she married again, but second husband, pet-shop owner Arnold Swain, turned out to be a disturbed bigamist. Over the years her loyal band of lodgers have included surrogate son Curly Watts, curmudgeonly pensioner Percy Sudgen, and her current tenant, Norris Cole. In 2009 she became fond of Ramsay Clegg, Norris's half-brother, who was visiting from Australia, and she was heartbroken when he died.

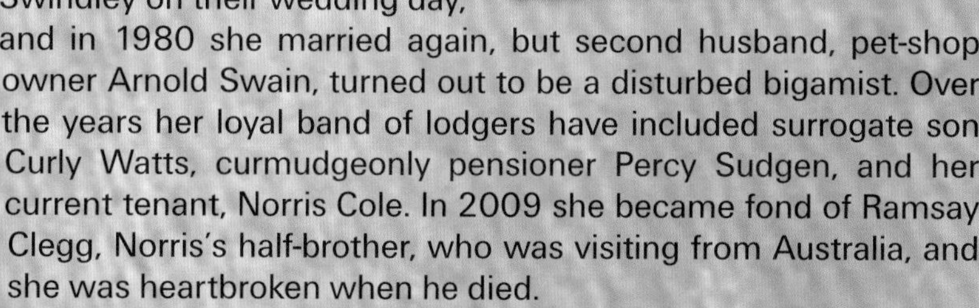

'Emily has been a solemn soul but she has had her comic moments as well. Ultimately we are very different people; she's a much neater, sensible sort of a woman, whereas my life can be quite chaotic.'

After training at the Northern School of Music, Eileen taught speech and drama before following her acting dream. The veteran star is now *Coronation Street*'s second-longest-serving cast member, but she is barely recognisable out of her character's coppered 'shampoo and set' hairpiece and fussy high-necked blouses.

'Nonetheless, sometimes people do spot me and say the strangest things which make me laugh – when it was in black and white viewers would stop you in the street and tell you how much better you looked in colour. But it's my poor husband who suffers the most because he's even been called Mr Emily. Poor Tom! But I think he's got used to it by now...'

Occupations: Former shop assistant, secretary, accounts clerk, café employee and charity worker.
On screen: 1961–
Defining moment: In 2003 evil Richard Hillman tries to murder investor Emily for her cash by clubbing her over the head with a crowbar.

Whether it was Hilda's high-pitched warbling or her waspish attempts to spur her Stanley into action, the decibel levels at Number 13 were never the same again when the Ogdens arrived in Coronation Street. Surprisingly, the Ogdens were the Street's very first home-owners, with their £200 deposit scraped together from one of Stan's lucrative spells as a long-distance lorry driver. In fact, they'd paid off their mortgage altogether by 1965, thanks to Hilda's no-nonsense frugality. The bickering couple were quick to make an impact, none more so than when – in a bid to earn an easy fiver – a nervous Stan endured a brief stint as a wrestler after his manager, Tickler Murphy, arranged his first (and last) bout at the Viaduct Sporting Club with real-life wrestling professional, Ian Campbell. Predictably, 'Oggie The Terrible' proved to be no match for the Scottish twenty-stoner, and he conceded defeat after being unceremoniously flung out of the ring and into Hilda's lap.

Worried, Jack called the police and asked them to trace his missing wife, but later he received a phone call saying Annie was staying at the Egremont Hotel under her maiden name – she'd broken down in tears in the hotel reception, forcing another guest to contact Jack and tell him where she was. Jack panicked that Annie might have left him for good, but it was an earwigging Ena who took control of the situation and headed straight over to the hotel to drag Annie home. Embarrassed, Annie feared Jack wouldn't want her back, but Ena explained he'd gone to pieces without her.

Back at the Rovers, Jack revealed to Annie that their son Billy had been sacked from his garage job and he'd merely been paying Billy's rent to his landlady, Mrs Nicholls. Clearly more relieved than she'd intended to let on, Annie was for once sheepish about her behaviour and apologised to Jack.

Front of house, life at the Rovers was never the same again after 13 May, when the snug's most formidable threesome, Martha, Minnie and Ena, unexpectedly lost one of its members. There had been no indication that Martha was feeling unwell. In fact, in the days that led up to her death she'd been feeling positively spritely, having just been invited to go abroad for the first time to help look after her grandchildren on holiday. She was all pumped up for her trip to Torremolinos and proud as punch to be in possession of her first-ever passport. However, she kept her plans a secret from Ena until the last minute for fear of her stoney-faced friend's disapproval.

Days before she was due to leave there was a celebration in the Rovers – Frank had sold his DIY shop to Summitt Supermarkets for a healthy £6,000 and, having already splashed out on a new car (a white Zodiac), he was now treating the regulars to a glass of bubbly. At first everyone was chuffed for him, but as the evening went on they became increasingly annoyed as Frank drunkenly lorded his new-found wealth over them and even managed to wind up the usually placid Jack by treating the Rovers as if he owned it.

Martha was partying with the rest of them, but all of a sudden she began to feel ill. She moved away from the others and sat alone in the snug with a glass of sherry, still proudly clutching her passport. As the regulars gathered around Ena, who was tinkling the ivories for a rendition of 'Down At The Old Bull And Bush', a weary Martha loosened her collar, removed her glasses and briefly cradled her head in her hands before collapsing onto the table. Soon after she was discovered by Jack, having suffered a sudden heart attack.

Shell-shocked by her friend's death and for the first time looking her age, Ena herself later laid Martha out in the vestry. When absent Minnie returned from holiday she broke down when she heard the terrible news. However, the women managed a rueful smile when they discovered a recording amongst Martha's things that their late friend and a youthful suitor had made long ago in Blackpool, in which he declared his undying love for her. For such a peevish character, it seemed Martha had managed to have some fun in her life after all...

'She weren't the biggest comedian we've ever had round here, but she was good company for me.'

Ena on Martha

Swindley leads the mourners at Martha's graveside.

OVERHEARD

Martha Longhurst passes away unexpectedly in the snug, 1964.

THE ROVERS IS PACKED. FRANK CELEBRATES THE SALE OF HIS SHOP AND THE DRINKS ARE ON HIM. THE PARTY IS IN FULL SWING.

LEN: (EXUBERANT, TO ENA) How about you having a little tinkle on the piano, darlin'?

ENA: I beg your pardon. I'll have you know that I reserve my musical talents for songs of praise, Len Fairclough, not a public-bar orgy.

LEN: Look, luv, this isn't Gomorrah you know, Mrs Sharples. All we want is a little bit of music to spread a bit of happiness. Come on!

ENA: No, I'm not playing owt till I've wet me palate. You come to a party...

LEN: Leave that to me...(SHOUTS) Oi! Double large champagne for Mrs Sharples!

MARTHA: (TO JERRY AND MYRA, PROUD AS PUNCH) Have you seen a passport in your life, have you? It's for my Spanish 'oliday.

ENA SITS DOWN AT THE STOOL IN FRONT OF THE PIANO. FRANK FILLS ENA'S GLASS.

ENA: Right, what do you want? I suppose Martha'll be wantin' a Paso Doble.

ENA STARTS SINGING AND PLAYS THE PIANO.

LEN: (CONDUCTING) All together now. (TO MISS NUGENT) Just pretend it's the Messiah darlin'.

THE REGULARS SING ALONG TO 'MOONLIGHT BAY'.

'I was smiling away on Moonlight Bay...'

MARTHA, FEELING OUT OF SORTS, SITS AWAY FROM THE GROUP WITH A GLASS OF SHERRY AND THE PASSPORT. SHE REMOVES HER SPECTACLES. SHE CRADLES HER HEAD IN HER HANDS AND SLUMPS ONTO THE TABLE.

'You've stolen my heart, but please don't go away...'

THE SINGING GETS LOUDER. MYRA – LOOKING IN THE DIRECTION OF MARTHA – RAISES HER EYEBROWS AND NUDGES JERRY, THINKING SHE HAS NODDED OFF IN THE MIDDLE OF A PARTY.

JACK: (ALSO SPOTTING MARTHA ALONE) All right, Mrs Longhurst? By gum, you'll have to get used to supping wine in Spain, you know. When I was in the army we called at the...

HE STOPS AND GENTLY SHAKES MARTHA. CONCERNED, HE FETCHES ANNIE, WHO IS FOLLOWED BY LEN.

ANNIE: (ALARMED) Jack, get the doctor.

THE SINGING TAILS OFF. ENA STOPS PLAYING.

LEN: She's dead.

ENA, UNBELIEVING, AS THOUGH SHE'S BEEN HIT TO THE HEART, WALKS SLOWLY TO THE SNUG. THE OTHERS SILENTLY FOLLOW.

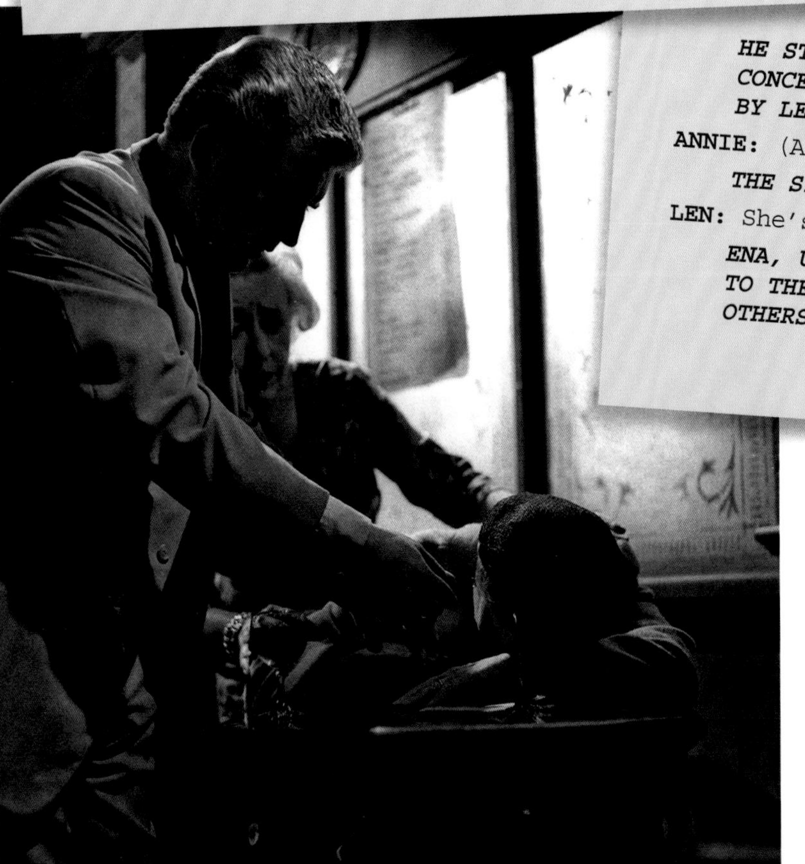

There was a turnaround in fortunes for Ena in 1965 when she found out Mrs Briggs, the owner of the Street's buildings, had died and left her one of the houses in her will. Ena was tempted when Mr Wormold, the Street's landlord, offered to buy it from her for £350, but when she discovered the house in question was Number 11, i.e. the home of Elsie, Ena saw it as the perfect opportunity to lord it over her sparring partner.

Gobsmacked is the only word to describe Elsie's reaction when she found out the identity of her new landlady, and a battle of wills ensued. Elsie demanded some much-needed repairs to the house, so Ena decided to raise the rent to pay for them. When Elsie objected, Ena gave her notice to quit. Now a woman of property, Ena wasn't especially bothered when she heard the Mission had been threatened with demolition – she would simply evict the Tanners and move into Number 11 herself.

New landlady Ena lords it over her sitting tenant Elsie.

The unimpressed residents gave Ena the cold shoulder when word spread that she was putting the Tanners out onto the street and, hatching a plan, Elsie asked Len to fix things in Number 11 so it looked like the place was a death trap and not worth living in. The next day Ena inspected the state of the property, complete with DIY damp patches hastily created by Dennis. Elsie insisted the house was falling to pieces, but Ena could see through her play-acting and told Minnie she intended to live there and was unimpressed by Elsie's attempts to hoodwink her.

When Ena gave Elsie her notice in writing, a livid Elsie went for her in the snug and the fight spilled out into the street. Ena barked at Elsie that she wouldn't be throwing her out if she wasn't being thrown out of her own home at the Mission. She made a swing for Elsie with her handbag, but she missed and smashed one of Number 11's windows instead. A ruffled Leonard attempted to separate the warring women by revealing the Mission had been given a reprieve and Ena's accommodation there was safe. As a result, Ena sold the deeds of Number 11 to Mr Wormold for £350, but showing her softer side, made him agree to do the repairs for Elsie as a condition of the sale.

'She's t'worst actress since Jean Harlow.'

Ena on Elsie

1960s Deaths

May Hardman (brain tumour)	31 December 1960
Ida Barlow (killed by a bus)	11 September 1961
Martha Longhurst (heart attack)	13 May 1964
Vera Lomax (brain tumour)	11 January 1967
Harry Hewitt (crushed under van)	4 September 1967
Steve Tanner (pushed down stairs)	28 September 1968

Lovers Irma and David savour a rare moment alone.

'You're the same as the Ogdens underneath and you know it. You were born 'ere, Coronation Street, a two-up, two-down terrace with a backyard and an outside lav. Our dad was a postman and our mam was a cleaner in a hotel. Not much to be proud about in that, is there?'

David to Ken

In 1965 fun-loving Irma Ogden became Weatherfield's very first WAG when she started dating professional footballer David Barlow, who had just returned from a club down south after suffering a leg injury. Their first night out together was at an arty jazz club, but Irma didn't fit in and they rowed – she bawled at him that she was cheap and common and if he didn't like that he should find someone else. Eventually they made up and Irma was chuffed when David was offered a two-year contract as player-coach with Weatherfield Athletic on an impressive wage of £35 a week. He took the post and asked Irma to marry him by getting down on one knee and revealing a diamond engagement ring.

The lead-up to the wedding wasn't straightforward; while father of the bride Stan (*see page 45*) worried how he was going to pay for it all, David's brother Ken openly voiced his disapproval, saying he thought the Ogdens were common. A furious David was quick to retort that his brother had little to be snooty about.

Things went from bad to worse when Stan caught David hiding in Irma's bedroom and he slapped his daughter around the face. She then refused to speak to her father or even eat in the same room as him. At the end of her tether with the pair of them, Hilda (*see page 40*) put her foot down, insisting they were both to blame and ordered them to kiss and make up.

Annie Walker

Played by **Doris Speed**

With her delusions of grandeur, landlady Annie Walker was forever trying to take the Rovers upmarket – whether it was turning it into a French pavement café or her failed attempt at a cocktail hour (which she conceded was like 'feeding strawberries to pigs'). But despite her hoity-toity nature, Annie was held in deep affection by the residents – rather like Doris Speed who was much loved by her fellow cast members, despite her withering looks that could freeze ice at fifty paces.

'I'd been there six months before she called me to her dressing room – which was like being granted an audience with royalty – and told me I could stop addressing her as Miss Speed and could now call her Doris. Before I could even thank her she'd already dismissed me from the room!' remembers Julie Goodyear. 'But I came to adore Doris, and thankfully she adored me back.'

Betty Driver agrees: 'Doris was very like she was on screen and at first I think she thought she was from the upper classes and I was just a cheap variety act. Once we were meant to sit on a couch side by side before a funeral scene and she said: "Darling, are you going to be moving around a lot?" I said: "I shouldn't think so, Doris, we're burying Cyril so I shan't be dancing." She said: "Oh good, I want to pin my script on you because I haven't learnt it." I said: "You are joking?" But she wasn't and it was pinned to my shoulder, my arm and my leg. She always used to do that – she was a little devil but, oh God I loved her.'

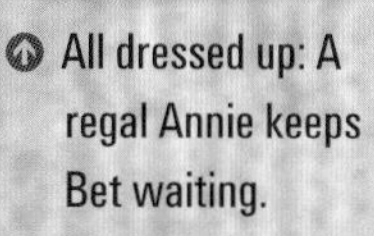

All dressed up: A regal Annie keeps Bet waiting.

Motherly love in the back-room with Billy.

Following the sudden death of her loyal husband Jack in 1970, Annie continued at the Rovers for another thirteen years until Doris fell ill and Billy Walker informed the regulars that their landlady had retired to Derby. To her horror, the *Daily Mirror* revealed the actress (who had made her music-hall debut aged three) was eighty-four years old and not sixty-nine as she'd claimed. She died ten years later in a Manchester nursing home.

'I first knew Doris when I was a little boy in *Children's Hour* and the part of Annie Walker was written very much with her in mind,' reveals Tony Warren. 'Doris had a fur coat and she called it "Tony" because she said without me she'd never have got one!'

Occupation: Rovers Return landlady.
On screen: 1960–1983
Defining moment: In 1967 Annie accuses Elsie of having an affair with her husband Jack and rows with her in the street – she's red-faced when it becomes clear he's been hanging out with Albert Tatlock instead.

David and Irma prepare to celebrate tying the knot.

As the weeks passed, David and Irma grew tired of the sniping between their families and made plans to marry in secret, only for the taxi driver taking them to the Ridgeway Street Registry Office to inadvertently leak their plans to Len. Len suggested the Street's residents gatecrash the Barlows' reception and booked a table for eleven at the Greenvale Hotel, where the couple had planned to celebrate alone. The newlyweds were delighted by the surprise and proud dad Stan made a speech which had both Irma and Hilda in bits.

The newly married Barlows moved into an upmarket new block of flats on Sandy Lane, but David's football career was cut short by a knee injury and he became depressed. After receiving £300 in compensation from the club, Irma came up with an ultimatum for David – to buy the corner shop or she was leaving. So David put all his money into buying the shop and the couple settled

In March the colour drained from Ken's already pallid face when Val told him they were expecting not one, but two, bundles of joy. When gossip-monger Ena found out this juicy titbit she couldn't wait to spread the news, offending Albert in the process, who was perturbed that as a close family member he was the last to know. To pacify him, Val asked her uncle to be godfather, which perked up the old soldier no end. As was the norm in the Sixties, while a hospitalised Val sweated it out, enduring hours of labour, father-to-be Ken waited nervously for news while supping ale in the Rovers. The couple decided on Peter and Susan Ida (after Ken's late mother) as names and the delighted residents popped open the champagne to celebrate the birth of Coronation Street's first-ever set of twins.

into life behind the counter. They weren't shopkeepers for long, though, three years later, David was offered the chance to play for an Australian football team and the couple decided to emigrate for a new life down under, where Irma gave birth to their son, Darren.

Meanwhile, just when Elsie also thought her children had finally flown the nest for good, both Dennis and Linda slunk back to Number 11 in 1966, bringing with them a trauma-filled few months for their long-suffering mum. It was Dennis who resurfaced first; he was on the run from Carlisle (where he'd been working at a holiday camp) with a couple of heavies on his trail for a £94 debt from a nightclub gambling scam. Genuinely terrified, he asked Len to lend him the money to pay them off, but as ever with Dennis, neither Len nor Elsie could work out if he was telling the truth. In the meantime, Elsie managed to get Dennis a job at the bookies and she began to take her jumpy son's story more seriously when she caught him nervously locking himself in at Number 11.

A few days later, two grizzly looking henchmen, Sid and Geordie, tracked Dennis down at the betting shop and gave him a week to pay up or he'd have to take the consequences. Bookie boss Dave Smith told Elsie he'd settle the debt if she promised to pay him back 'in kind'. Insulted, Elsie refused and stormed out of the shop.

Minnie Caldwell

Played by **Margot Bryant**

Everyone's ideal nan, sweet and gentle Minnie Caldwell was at her happiest when pampering her adored puss, Bobby, or doting on cheeky lodger Jed 'Sunny Jim' Stone – he called her Ma, while she treated him as the son she'd never had. Even when she was on the receiving end of her long-time friend Ena Sharples' caustic tongue, Minnie seemed dottily oblivious to the insults being dished out.

While put-upon pensioner Minnie wouldn't say boo to a goose, forthright Margot Bryant was legendary behind the scenes for being the complete antithesis of her cosy character.

Corrie creator Tony Warren recalls: 'Her language would've made a sailor blush. What you had to remember was Margot had waited in the wings. She'd understudied big stars in the West End, she'd danced in the chorus with Fred Astaire and had seen how big stars behaved. So when her opportunity came she seized it with both hands and in a very short time she was covered in mink and diamonds and was flying off for the weekend to see the latest musicals on Broadway. A friend of mine once asked why their plane was being held up on the tarmac, only to be told: "They're waiting for Minnie Caldwell."'

Hull-born Margot made her television debut in the play *My Mother Said*, and in 1950 she appeared in the film *Cure For Love*, which also featured future co-star Jack Howarth. She made her first *Coronation Street* appearance in episode two and played meek Minnie until her health deteriorated in 1976, forcing her to retire. She passed away twelve years later at the grand old age of ninety.

'You certainly didn't mess with her,' reminisces William Roache. 'She looked like this frail little old lady but in fact she was very frightening. I remember once someone asked what she'd be if she wasn't an actor and she said a pirate. Go out to a restaurant and she'd be swearing and asking for the manager at the slightest thing. Margot loved shocking people, but I still liked her because I always thought, even when she was telling the rudest of jokes, using the worst of swear words or just being really horrible, there was still a mischievous and playful twinkle in her eye.'

For once Minnie has the ear of Ena and Martha.

Surrogate son Jed gives Minnie more to worry about.

The cat-loving pensioner alongside best friend Ena.

Occupation: Retired mill worker.
On screen: 1960–1976
Defining moment: In 1969 skint Minnie is so ashamed of her £10 bookie debt that she flees Weatherfield, but she is discovered by Ena – in hospital suffering from pneumonia after sleeping rough.

Ivan and Linda's shouting matches are the final straw for Elsie.

When Ena saw the thugs reappear on the Street to beat up Dennis she went to find back up; Dave refused to help, but Len was soon on the scene, as was Elsie, who lashed out at them with a cast-iron poker. The scuffle got out of hand when the thugs turned on Elsie, and in the end it was Len who called a halt to the proceedings by coughing up the £94 himself. As part of the deal he gave Dennis a job in the yard to make sure he got his money back. But, predictably with Dennis involved, things didn't go to plan and several weeks later he quit the yard after setting fire to Len's kitchen with a blowtorch while decorating.

In October, the glum-faced trio of Linda, Ivan and Elsie's five-year-old grandson, Paul, moved back to Weatherfield having been living in Canada. From the word go Elsie was suspicious of Linda's supposed homesickness, and after some serious probing, her sheepish daughter admitted she'd had an affair in Canada and that's why they'd returned to England. However, Elsie's main concern was Paul's happiness and, sick to the back teeth of Linda and Ivan's constant rowing, she made arrangements to see a solicitor in order to get custody of her grandson.

Full of Christmas spirit, Ken and Val organised a festive fancy dress bash at the Mission – sending the residents into a frenzy of anticipation as to who would go as who. The Barlows decided on Lawrence of Arabia and Nell Gwyn, while Dennis was Batman – as was Len, much to Dennis's annoyance. Other highlights included Minnie as Old Mother Riley and Elsie as a glamorous Flamenco dancer (cue builder Jerry, dressed as Robin, making the obligatory maracas gag). Annie surprised no one by making a grand entrance dressed up to the nines as Elizabeth I, leading Hilda to gawp: 'What's she gorrup as, a flippin' Christmas tree?' Len respectfully laid down his Batman cape and a regal Annie walked over it saying, 'Thank you, Sir Walter'. When Jerry's Robin won the Best-Dressed prize Annie forced a smile, although she was convinced she'd been robbed. However, just as she was about to turn on her queenly heels and leave, it was announced there was also an award for Best-Dressed Female, and feigning false modesty that they could possibly think her costume was better than anyone else's, Mrs Walker happily accepted her prize of chocolate liqueurs.

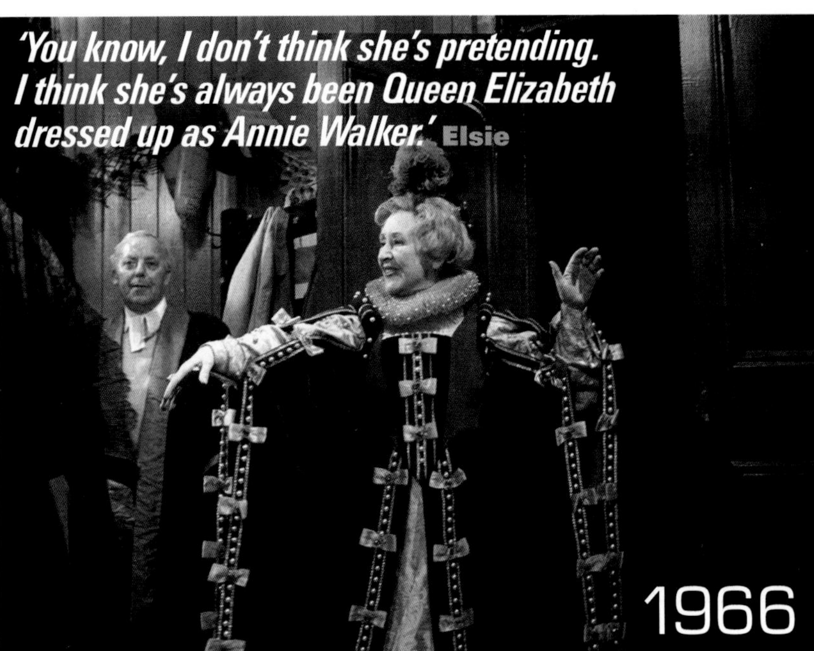

'You know, I don't think she's pretending. I think she's always been Queen Elizabeth dressed up as Annie Walker.' **Elsie**

1966

When Paul went missing the warring family blamed themselves and they were relieved to discover that after falling into the canal while playing on the path, he'd been pulled out of the water by a quick-thinking passer-by. After a short stay at the infirmary with pneumonia, Paul made a full recovery and moved with his reconciled parents to Birmingham for a fresh start. Meanwhile, a conman had posed as Paul's heroic rescuer and was given a reward by Elsie, but he was exposed as an imposter by Dave, who produced Paul's cap, proving it was the bookie who had rescued Paul and that maybe he wasn't such a sleaze-ball after all.

Elsewhere, everyone was stunned when Ena was charged with shoplifting in the Pick-A-Snip Supermarket. She and Minnie had been hauled into the manager's office and confronted with the unpaid items – two tins of salmon. Ena steadfastly protested her innocence and her friends rallied round. Minnie and Ken

'Once upon a time I used to enjoy scratchin' Elsie Tanner's eyes out – I'd get more pleasure than listening to the Queen's Christmas Day message.'

Ena

accompanied her to court where she pleaded not guilty to theft but refused point blank to give her age until the magistrate threatened her with obstructing the court. Much to her distress she was found guilty, fined and given a conditional discharge.

Overnight a distressed Ena seemed to have lost some of her fight, and just when she thought things couldn't get any more deflating, her gutsy daughter Vera turned up to spend Christmas with her. The pair had never seen eye to eye, so when Vera complained of constantly feeling tired and ill, Ena accused her of malingering. But after giving her the once over, a doctor revealed to Ena that Vera had a brain tumour and only a month to live. A crushed Ena opted not to tell her daughter what was wrong and did her best to care for her. Vera became suspicious of her mother's sudden concern, but when Ena suggested her change of heart was down to Christmas spirit, her daughter scoffed that there'd be another Christmas next year, although she didn't suppose she'd be invited to that one. By now Ena was close to breaking point and tearfully turned away from her daughter, knowing she was unlikely to see next month, never mind next Christmas. A few days later, in the vestry, Vera died in her mother's arms.

↑ Absent-minded Ena's stash of tinned salmon looks fishy.

↓ Ena shows her softer side to dying daughter Vera.

Hilda Ogden

Played by **Jean Alexander**

Despite the fact her pinny, headscarf and curlers hadn't been seen on the cobbles for eighteen years, in 2005 Hilda Ogden was voted the UK's favourite soap character of all time in a survey of readers of *TV Times* magazine. Another impressive accolade bestowed on Hilda came from a 1982 poll that saw her picked as the fourth most recognisable woman in Britain after the Queen Mother, Queen Elizabeth II and Diana, Princess of Wales. Not bad company for a hardworking scrubber whose grafting never seemed to get her anywhere.

'Hilda would have loved that and I am honoured people still remember her so fondly. I suppose the viewers recognised her type, and on location on the backstreets of Manchester I've happened upon a few Hildas myself who could've come straight off the *Coronation Street* set.'

'The day Hilda Ogden is the last person to know anything I'll do a somersault over the town hall.'

Elsie

Jean had already popped up in two episodes as Mrs Webb, a boarding house landlady, and even with ten years of stage experience in repertory across the North West under her belt, arriving on the *Coronation Street* set in 1964 was still daunting for the Liverpool-born performer who'd spent five years as a library assistant before following her dream of becoming an actress.

'It was a bit scary because the only person I knew was Eileen Derbyshire, as we'd been in weekly rep together in Southport in the Fifties. So it was nice to have a friendly face there, but you quickly find out with the *Street* that other people aren't watching to see what you're doing; they're too busy getting on with their own bit of acting, so there really is nothing to be nervous about.'

Hilda had married lethargic husband Stan in 1943 for better or worse. But it was usually for the worse...

'They would bicker between themselves but no one else dared raise a finger or a say word against either of them or they'd both be up in arms. Hers was a life of disappointment, so it was my idea that the middle flying duck on her famous 'muriel' should always be taking a nose-dive. Each time Hilda went past she would try to push it up straight, but it always fell down again. Which summed up her life really. They did live at Number 13 after all.'

50 Coronation St. Icon

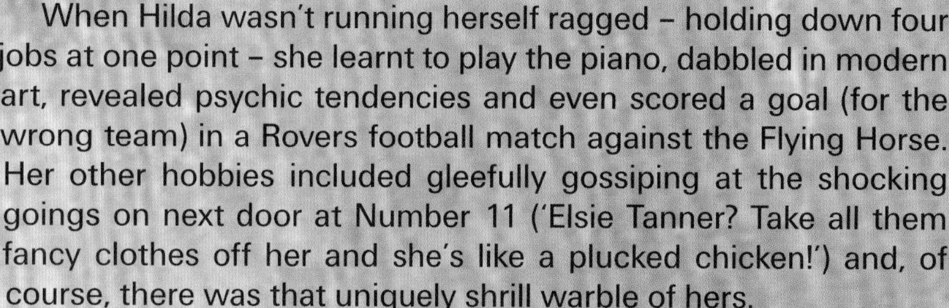

When Hilda wasn't running herself ragged – holding down four jobs at one point – she learnt to play the piano, dabbled in modern art, revealed psychic tendencies and even scored a goal (for the wrong team) in a Rovers football match against the Flying Horse. Her other hobbies included gleefully gossiping at the shocking goings on next door at Number 11 ('Elsie Tanner? Take all them fancy clothes off her and she's like a plucked chicken!') and, of course, there was that uniquely shrill warble of hers.

'I'd been in it a couple of months and the script said: "Hilda is out of shot in the backyard pegging out washing and singing". So I just started singing the sort of songs that Hilda would know, that were from my own era actually, and the crew fell about laughing. They all thought it was hysterical, so after that whenever they wrote in "Hilda sings", they'd never state the song and they'd just leave that to me.'

Hilda sticks her nose into Mrs Walker's business.

Stan tries to worm his way out of trouble yet again.

Elsie lets rip at her disapproving next-door neighbour.

Clairvoyant Hilda predicts the future from her tea leaves.

Hilda comes to terms with life on her own.

The residents wish her luck as they wave her goodbye.

While living with Stan was never easy, Hilda couldn't contemplate life without him. When he died in 1984 Hilda was shattered, and Jean's portrayal of grieving Hilda had the nation reaching for their hankies and won her the much-respected Royal Television Society's Best Performance Award. Three years later, the actress decided to quit while she was ahead and Hilda's farewell on Christmas Day remains the highest-rated episode of *Coronation Street* ever. Nearly 27 million viewers tuned in to see her head off for a new life as housekeeper to Dr Lowther in the Derbyshire countryside.

For the last twenty years Jean has been putting her comic timing to good use as money-grabbing junk-shop owner Auntie Wainwright in the long-running BBC comedy *Last Of The Summer Wine*, and she insists she won't be reappearing on the cobbles any time soon.

'It'd be a complete mistake to go back. And Hilda would be a different person now because she has achieved the status she'd wanted all her life – to be the doctor's housekeeper and have her own apartment in his house. She'd have smartened herself up no end. But I admire the current cast very much because it must be very hectic now doing the *Street* for five episodes a week. I still watch and keep an eye on it, mainly because I want to make sure my friends there are still alive and on their feet!'

Occupations: Cleaner and general busybody.
On screen: 1964–1987
Defining moment: With the slogan 'Be a mistress as well as a wife, and your husband will still be your boyfriend', she wins a luxury second honeymoon competition in 1977.

Disaster quite literally struck Weatherfield in 1967 when a goods train derailed from the top of the viaduct and came crashing into the heart of Coronation Street. The residents watched on, horrified, as they tried to work out whom amongst their number was missing. Annie feared Jack was under the rubble, but much to her relief he turned up unharmed, as did her ward Lucille Hewitt, who had been lodging with the Walkers since Harry and Concepta's move to Ireland. Ena was nowhere to be seen, though, and when the body of a local girl, Sonia Peters, was pulled out from the wreckage by the police, the locals began to fear the worst. However, just as the shattered viaduct began to teeter, a heroic David found Ena alive but unconscious under the debris and she was rushed to hospital.

'Cuts, bruises and a broken arm? If that woman were dropped off Blackpool Tower I swear she'd bounce!'

Elsie on Ena

While Jack comforted Minnie, at the Infirmary Elsie pretended to be Ena's daughter and discovered that against all the odds Ena had only suffered a few bruises and a broken arm, which made her chortle at Ena's invincibility. The pair had a touching moment when Ena admitted that for once she approved of Elsie's latest gentleman friend, showing that despite their differences there was an underlying respect between the strong-willed women. The

'Elsie Tanner's a loud-mouthed, pig-headed, painted tramp with a bust-ful o'brassiere and nowt on top. And with the right man on her arm she'd turn into the best wife a lad could wish for.'

Ena

next day, bored of being fussed over by nurses and still suffering from bruises and shock, Ena discharged herself, turned up at the Rovers and ordered a milk stout.

The gentleman friend Ena had been referring to was handsome American serviceman Steve Tanner, an old flame of Elsie's who had recently been posted at the nearby Warrington base. It seemed happiness had finally come knocking for Elsie, and when Steve proposed over a romantic meal at the Roebuck Inn in Cheshire, she readily accepted.

The couple married near the air base at St Stephen's Methodist Church, Warrington, and as they prepared to leave for their honeymoon in Lisbon, a radiant Elsie turned and threw her bouquet into the gathered crowd – only for it to be caught by a red-faced Ena! But their marriage wasn't to last, and by the following year Elsie had left Steve, saying their relationship was a twenty-year-old dream and they'd been foolish to think it would work after all this time. Steve did return to Weatherfield a few months later to give their marriage another go, but he was found dead in his flat and Len became briefly implicated in his murder, having never made any secret of his dislike for the man. The real culprit was not revealed until many years later.

Over at Number 11, with the house to himself Dennis saw Elsie's absence as the perfect opportunity to make some extra cash. He decided to take in circus acts as lodgers, starting with a noisy female bagpipe band, who were followed by a somersaulting double

◀ ◀ A goods train derailment leaves Ena's life hanging in the balance.

▼ Elsie can't resist a man in uniform and takes the plunge with Steve Tanner.

1967

There was no way Annie was going to allow Lucille to attend a football match without a chaperone, so the Rovers landlady insisted on accompanying her in order to see first-hand the hooliganism she'd heard took place at such events. But once there, Annie began to thoroughly enjoy herself and didn't see a hint of bad behaviour. It was off the pitch on the way home that the problems started. When a couple of rival fans provoked Annie by sneering at Manchester City's ball control, she retaliated by indignantly grabbing one of their rattles and slinging it over her shoulder, only for it to smash a chip-shop window. Stunned, Annie was arrested for football hooliganism and when the police found a toilet roll in her handbag, planted by another supporter, it looked like she was going to be banged to rights. Luckily for her the charges were dropped when Len explained what had happened – but she still had to pay for the broken window.

act, The Pinelli Brothers. They arrived with their fussy mother Mrs Cook, whose constant changing of the sleeping arrangements made Dennis wish he'd never had the lodging idea in the first place, especially when he ended up sleeping on the sofa.

For Len the arrival of his estranged son Stanley was a chance to build bridges, but unfortunately Stanley wasn't interested. He was too full of resentment towards his father for the way he had treated his mother, Nellie. When mouthy Stanley made his first appearance in the Rovers, the regulars were shocked by the lack of respect he showed towards his father and he annoyed everyone with his superiority complex. Even Len found Stanley hard going, and against his better judgement he allowed him to smoke in a bid to appease the angry young man.

But still the guilt remained for Len. He felt he'd let his son down in the past and now was the time to make it up to him. He pulled a few strings to get him a place at Granston Technical College, but Stanley couldn't have cared less. In fact, all that interested the young lad was being as sullen as humanly possible, and in a last-ditch

The arrival of his estranged son Stanley means trouble for Len.

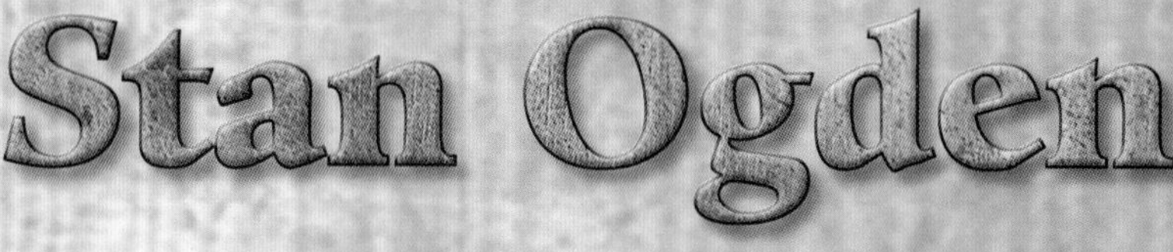

Stan Ogden

Played by **Bernard Youens**

Dubbed 'the greatest living Englishman' by the 'Stan Ogden Appreciation Society of Newton Abbot', there was much to admire about Stan's bumbling ability to avoid work at all cost and his seemingly jinxed attempts to make an easy buck. Within his first year on the Street he'd been sacked from a chauffeur's job for using the Rolls Royce out of hours, endured his one and only fight as a professional wrestler, and nearly got Jack Walker arrested for opening after hours when he secretly stopped the pub clock to ensure more drinking time.

Indeed, the Rovers was Stan's spiritual home – a peaceful haven away from Hilda's mithering – and when his attendance at the boozer turned out to be something of a record, the brewery rewarded his loyalty with free beer for a week.

Unlike 'rough around the edges' Stan, repertory theatre actor Bernard Youens was renowned for his honeyed vocal tones and in 1956 became a continuity announcer at Granada. Initially he turned down the opportunity to audition for new TV serial *Coronation Street*, preferring instead to stick with the security of his announcer's role. But in 1964, with the *Street* now a solid hit, he was cast alongside screen wife Jean Alexander as long-suffering layabout, Stan.

Throughout his later life Bernard ('Bunny' to his friends) suffered with his health and endured severe arthritis in his knees. A series of heart attacks and strokes left his speech badly impaired, but he carried on playing the role that made him famous until March 1984. He passed away in his sleep in August of the same year.

'My admiration for him as an actor was enormous,' remembers Jean Alexander. 'We'd never met before our audition but we were a team right from the word go. Initially we were only signed for a three-month try-out, then we got a six-month contract and after we'd been there nearly a year Bun said to me, "Do you think we'll be stopping?" We didn't have a clue back then if we'd be stopping or going, but it all worked out in the end, didn't it?'

- Stan downs a pint with gusto at Elsie's wedding.
- 'Oggie the Terrible' wrestles for his life.
- Plotting yet another money-making scam with Eddie.

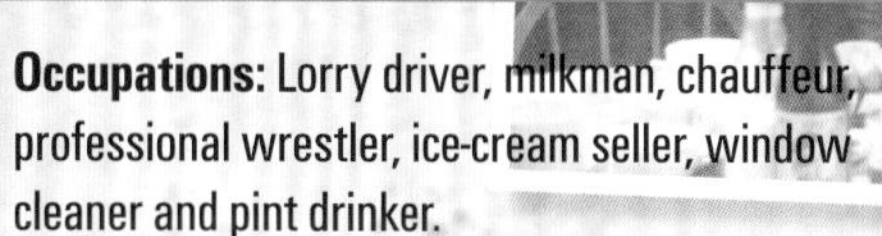

Occupations: Lorry driver, milkman, chauffeur, professional wrestler, ice-cream seller, window cleaner and pint drinker.
On screen: 1964–1984
Defining moment: Bravely rescuing Minnie Caldwell from the clutches of deranged murderer Joe Donnelli in 1970.

OVERHEARD

Annie falsely accuses Elsie of having an affair with Jack, 1967

ANNIE MARCHES PURPOSEFULLY DOWN THE STREET WITH ENA AND MINNIE IN TOW. SHE RAPS ON THE KNOCKER OF NUMBER 11. ELSIE ANSWERS. DAVID ALSO WITNESSES THE SCENE AND HILDA LOOKS DOWN ON THE ACTION FROM AN OPEN WINDOW NEXT DOOR.

ANNIE: Mrs Tanner!

ELSIE: That is the name, luv.

ANNIE: Would you mind giving me my husband back?

ELSIE LOOKS STARTLED AND THEN LAUGHS.

ELSIE: Now what would Jack Walker be doing in my house?

ANNIE: I shudder to think.

ELSIE: This can't be true. You are talking about Jack? Our Jack Walker?

ANNIE: Oh yes. Except that I've not ever considered it a case of mutual ownership. Do you deny that my husband is in your house?

ELSIE: (BAFFLED) Have you been at the cherry brandy?

ANNIE: And that he's been sleeping there – I use the word loosely – for the last week.

ELSIE: Now, look, Mrs Walker. A joke is a joke...

ANNIE: I'm not laughing.

ELSIE: You wanna try it some time.

ANNIE: Insults are of no avail, Mrs Tanner.

ELSIE: (AT THE END OF HER TETHER) I wouldn't lower myself. Don't you blame me if you can't hang on to your husband.

ANNIE: I blame you for enticing him away!

HILDA: (SHOUTING SMUGLY FROM HER BEDROOM WINDOW) I'd just like to see her try and entice my Stan, that's all.

ELSIE: (YELLING BACK AT HER) I wouldn't have to try very hard. No wonder he went back on the lorries...

ANNIE: (TO HILDA) You take no notice, dear, at least you don't flaunt your body half way out of your frock.

ELSIE: (RUEFULLY) Ha! Only cos' she's got nowt to flaunt. That's why.

ANNIE: (IGNORING HER) Jack Walker! Will you come out of there!

ELSIE: If he's got any sense he'll be a hundred miles away from here by now. He wants a medal, you know, living with her all these years.

ANNIE: Yes, well, your husband threw the towel in pretty quickly, didn't he? Mind you, it's not every man that wants a wife with the morals of an alley cat.

ELSIE: And it's not every feller that wants a clapped-out mill hand with delusions of grandeur for a wife. And you bleach yer hair!

ANNIE: Jack Walker! For the last time will you come out of there!

ELSIE: (UTTERLY EXASPERATED) How the hell can he come out when he's not flamin' in there to start with?

THE FRONT DOOR OPENS. JACK SAUNTERS OUT, IGNORES EVERYONE AND HEADS TOWARDS THE ROVERS. HE HAS MISCHIEVOUSLY SNEAKED INTO ELSIE'S THROUGH THE BACK DOOR, HAVING BEEN ALERTED BY ALBERT. THE CROWD ARE OPEN-MOUTHED WITH SURPRISE. NONE MORE SO THAN ELSIE.

DAVID: (GRINNING) The fruity monkey!

It's surely only Hilda who could convince herself that vampish Elsie was having an affair with her sloth-like husband, Stan, but when Stan gave Elsie a driving lesson which resulted in them staying out all night, she was certain they'd been up to no good. In fact what had actually happened was that Elsie's car had run out of petrol and they'd spent the night stranded on the moors. With Stan and Elsie's absence still unexplained, Annie enjoyed teasing a vexed Hilda about what Stan and Elsie could've been up to in the moonlight, insisting there was no smoke without fire. By the time Stan sheepishly showed his face, Hilda was practically spitting blood, and while he lamely protested his innocence a fired up (and boozed up) Hilda laid into Elsie in the street, accusing her of having to nab other women's fellas because she couldn't hold on to one of her own. When Hilda proudly declared that, unlike promiscuous Elsie, she'd stayed with one man for all these years, Elsie spat back: 'It's no wonder, because no other man ever looked twice at you!'

'Drop dead Stan. And then get up and do it again!'

Hilda

attempt at revenge he tried to burn down Len's yard. Unfortunately for him, he did this while still inside, and as the flames began to engulf him, he panicked when the door wouldn't open.

Len managed to smash the door down, but as he tried to pull Stanley from the fire he himself became trapped. Thankfully, a passing workman managed to save both of them and they were taken to hospital. When Stanley was discharged, he broke down fearing Len might not survive, knowing it was all his fault. When Len's condition improved, a shame-faced Stanley told his dad the fire had been an accident and in the short time remaining before Stanley headed back to school in Nottingham, Len and his son finally began to bond.

In 1968 Ena was finally forced to leave the home she had lived in for as long as anyone could remember when the Mission was demolished, along with Ellison's Raincoat Factory, to make way for a new block of flats. She was suitably outraged to be offered a place at an old people's home and chose instead to lodge with a friend in St Anne's, followed by a brief stint at Number 5 with Minnie, a living arrangement that was never going to work as they constantly got on each other's nerves. When the spanking new maisonettes were finished, Ena relented and moved into a purpose-built, OAP, ground-floor flat, and she was chuffed to bits

TOP FIVE Weatherfield Pop Stars

These musical maestros had everyone dancing in the street...

Peter Noone
Before enjoying worldwide fame as the lead singer of Herman's Hermits, Peter made a name for himself in 1961 as Len's schoolboy son, Stanley.

Davy Jones
At the tender age of fifteen, the Manchester-born future frontman of The Monkees appeared in 1961 as Ena's grandson, Colin Lomax.

Kym Marsh
Michelle Connor appeared briefly in 2006 trouncing a jealous Liz McDonald for the position of lead singer in Vernon Tomlin's band. Later that year she returned as a regular character with a messed-up family of her own.

Keith Duffy
The Boyzone heart-throb arrived in Weatherfield in 2002 as Peter Barlow's naval pal, Ciaran McCarthy. He remained in the show for three years before leaving, but he made a welcome return to the cobbles in 2010.

Status Quo
In 2005 Les Battersby came face-to-face with his idols – who promptly battered him as payback for an incident twenty years earlier. To avoid legal action they performed at his wedding to Cilla.

when she realised it had been built on the exact spot where the vestry had stood.

There was a heavy police presence in Weatherfield at the end of July thanks to a prisoner on the loose, who had escaped while being transferred to Weatherfield nick. The unlucky resident who ended up being confronted by the convict was Val, who was at home with the twins while Ken indulged his thespian tendencies at a Weatherfield Amateur Dramatics rehearsal. While some of the locals gathered in the Rovers for company, not wanting to be on their own with a dangerous criminal on the loose, Val became a sitting target and the man – Frank Riley – forced his way into the maisonette.

Terrified, Val told him she didn't have any children and was home alone, but he knew she was lying when Peter woke up and a frightened Val began to fear for the twins' lives as well as her own. She managed to alert neighbour Ena by banging a message on the central heating pipes, but it was Val he seemed most interested in, and after demanding she gave him money and clothes he then started caressing her face, saying there was something else he wanted from her...

A terrified Val is held hostage by escaped convict Frank Riley.

Albert Tatlock

Played by **Jack Howarth**

At sixty-five years old, instead of putting his feet up and retiring Jack Howarth took on the role that was to prove to be the pinnacle of his career. Grumpy, cloth-cap-wearing pensioner Albert Tatlock was held in great affection by the public – and by Ken Barlow, who had married his niece Valerie. When Val died tragically at the hands of her hairdryer, it seemed only natural that Ken should move into Number 1 with crusty Uncle Albert, who thought of him as the son he'd never had.

'Albert was a slightly gruff, eccentric, little potato-shaped man, and in some ways his character was a forerunner of Blanche, in that the rest of us would work really hard on a scene and then Jack would have one line at the end and completely steal it,' recalls William Roache.

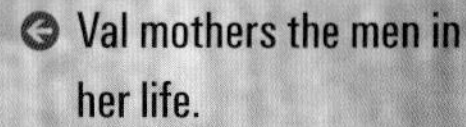

Val mothers the men in her life.

Drinking buddies Albert, Len and Frank.

Happy families at Number 1.

One of Jack's first jobs in showbusiness was selling programmes at Rochdale's Theatre Royal. After serving in France during the First World War, Jack toured the country before settling in Colwyn Bay, where he ran his own repertory theatre for the next twelve years. During the Second World War, he played most of the male roles himself due to the shortage of men at the time. In 1984, two months after his last appearance on the *Street*, the veteran actor died of kidney failure at the grand old age of 88.

William continues: 'I loved Jack dearly. He was a lovely man, but if you said anything nice to Jack he'd burst into tears and he always said he wouldn't be able to cope with a *This Is Your Life*. But, however reluctantly, he did manage to get through his episode in the end.'

Thelma Barlow – alias Mavis Riley – remembers with fondness Jack's penchant for tea and cake. 'Whenever the tea trolley appeared he would always walk over, grab a couple of cream cakes and stuff them in his pockets. Some of the young lads, like Graham Haberfield [who played Jerry Booth] and Nev Buswell [Ray Langton], were really naughty and would then go up to him and say, "How do you do then Jack?" and slap his pockets. We always used to wonder what kind of sticky mess was inside those trouser pockets...'

Occupations: Retired town hall clerk, community centre caretaker and lollipop man.
On screen: 1960–1984
Defining moment: In 1973 he suggests marrying Minnie to save on their living costs – but they get on each other's nerves and the engagement is called off.

Val promised she wouldn't raise the alarm if Riley left her alone but by now the convict could see the police gathering outside – alerted by Ena – and Val shuddered when he produced an iron crow bar and brandished it at her menacingly. Ken had also reappeared and begged the police to let him try to speak to Riley, but the cops insisted he kept his distance. As Riley made a move to leave, using Val as his shield, the police burst in through the kitchen window and overpowered him. Sobbing with relief, Val assured Ken and the police that Riley hadn't touch her. A WPC then told Val that Riley was a convicted rapist – it looked like she'd had a very lucky escape.

Elsewhere, it was love at first sight for Dennis when he set eyes on sweet-natured hippy Jenny Sutton, who was squatting in the Street. He even followed her to her native London when she unexpectedly left Weatherfield. Later in the year Dennis and Jenny returned to Number 11 claiming they'd married – they hadn't, it was merely a ruse Dennis had come up with to ensure his mum Elsie would allow them to sleep under her roof together. But of course Elsie could read her son like a book and saw through the lie. While Dennis moved back in with his mother and got a job as a salesman, Jenny was forced to lodge with Minnie. Eventually, Dennis and Jenny announced they were to marry for real and Elsie began to warm to her soon-to-be daughter-in-law.

Lovebirds Dennis and Jenny take to the floor.

When it came to the results of the brewery's 'Perfect Landlady Competition', Annie was in no doubt whatsoever that the best woman had won, as she'd nabbed the crown for herself. The prize was a holiday for two to Majorca. However, hubby Jack had to stay behind to run the pub so Annie was open to offers as to who she should choose as her travel companion. Never someone who was backward at coming forward, Ena volunteered her services and much to everyone's astonishment – including Ena's – Annie agreed to take her. On her return Ena thanked the landlady by spreading gossip that Annie had stayed on in Majorca 'because of a man', whereas in fact Annie was negotiating with the brewery to take over the running of a bar on the island. Unfortunately for the Walker's sun-kissed dreams, the brewery turned them down due to Jack's advancing years.

The wedding at the Weatherfield Registry Office went without a hitch. His emotional best mate, builder Jerry Booth, was best man and Albert was given the responsibility of choosing a gift on behalf of the Rovers regulars. After careful consideration he'd chosen an imposing stuffed stag's head with a massive set of antlers for them to hang on their bedroom wall. While a horrified Annie tactfully commented that at least he'd chosen something unique, Ena was less impressed and barked at a miffed Albert she'd never seen such a daft wedding present.

A solemn Dennis and Jenny say, 'I do'.

'I can never understand why the conversation in this bar gets so degrading when there's a wedding in the offing.'

Annie

Annie-isms: **when it came to thinly veiled disapproval, no one dished it out like the Rovers landlady...**

The only fly in the ointment was that after planning the big day Dennis had been instructed to be in Bristol for an important work meeting... on his wedding night. In typical Dennis style he'd failed to inform Jenny of this fact and nervously broke the news to her during his wedding speech. But instead of slapping him around the chops with her bouquet, Jenny was surprisingly supportive, impressed even, at this more mature side of Dennis. At the meeting his boss was also impressed by the sacrifice Dennis had made in order to further his career and offered him the position of area manager in Bristol. A week later the new Mr and Mrs Tanner moved there to start married life. Meanwhile, on her wedding night Jenny bedded down on Minnie's settee with only a cup of cocoa to keep her warm!

It was in 1969 that Betty Turpin (*see page 56*) bagged her first shift at the Rovers, and it was all thanks to her shopkeeper sister Maggie Clegg, who'd begged Jack to give Betty a trial in a bid to get her bossy sister from under her feet. From the moment no-nonsense Betty had arrived at the corner shop earlier in the year (with her policeman husband Cyril), she had got Maggie's back up by trying to run her younger sister's life as well as her business.

New girl in town: Betty arrives with husband Cyril.

The residents' day trip turns into a nightmare after a fatal coach crash.

From the word go there was a hostility between down-to-earth Betty and Annie, with all her airs and graces. After several months of tolerating each other behind the bar Annie sacked Betty, accusing her of stealing a brooch. Along with Hilda, who had also been accused of the theft, Betty threatened Annie with legal action unless she apologised and even drew up a notice to that effect and displayed it in the window of the corner shop for all to see. She then got a job at the Flying Horse, but returned to the Rovers after wringing a grovelling apology (and a gift) from Annie who had managed to locate her missing jewellery.

Earlier in the year Betty had been accused of another crime – then it had been adultery, and with Stan of all people. It was Stan's uncharacteristic lack of appetite that had first aroused Hilda's suspicions, and when she caught him whispering conspiratorially with Betty in the Rovers she became convinced they were having an affair. However, it turned out that Stan and Betty had secretly signed up for a slimming club called Fatties Anonymous, a fact that a relieved Hilda discovered when she followed the pair to a meeting. Her heart swelled with pride when she eavesdropped Stan explaining to the group that the reason he'd wanted to lose weight was to make himself more attractive to his wife.

In November Emily organised a day trip to the Lake District, but what was intended to be a fun day out soon turned into a horror story. Not long after they had departed, the coach company realised their driver had mistakenly taken the wrong vehicle and the cheerfully unaware group of Coronation Street day-trippers were in fact travelling on a bus with faulty brakes. The company made frantic calls to the police, but were unable to track down the coach as the driver had decided to take an alternative, more scenic route. There were ear-piercing screams as the coach careered off the road and smashed into a

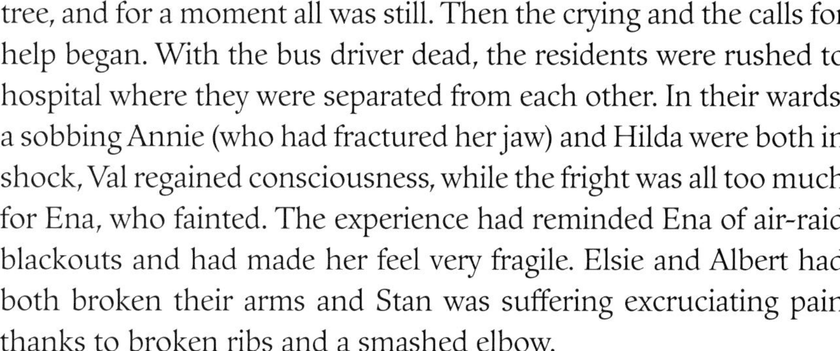

tree, and for a moment all was still. Then the crying and the calls for help began. With the bus driver dead, the residents were rushed to hospital where they were separated from each other. In their wards, a sobbing Annie (who had fractured her jaw) and Hilda were both in shock, Val regained consciousness, while the fright was all too much for Ena, who fainted. The experience had reminded Ena of air-raid blackouts and had made her feel very fragile. Elsie and Albert had both broken their arms and Stan was suffering excruciating pain thanks to broken ribs and a smashed elbow.

Ena, meanwhile, whose physical injuries once again merely consisted of bruises, kept an all-night vigil praying at the bedside of an unconscious Minnie, who was on the critical list having lost a severe amount of blood. When Minnie eventually came round Ena talked the doctors into letting her stay until her dear friend was discharged. Of the Street's residents it was Len's friend, the handsome builder Ray Langton, who'd topped the injury list, suffering a spinal injury that was to leave him paralysed from the waist down – fortunately only for four frustrating months. Newly diagnosed and not knowing if he'd recover, Ray was transferred to an orthopaedic hospital, and while the coach firm admitted liability for the crash, a crushed Ray told Ena he'd rather have died than be alive in this state.

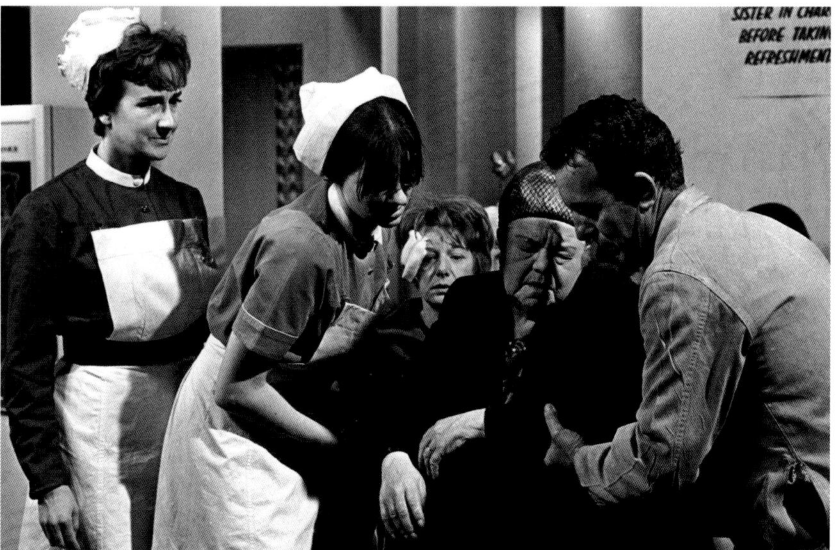

As the decade drew to a close the residents held a festive talent night, which saw Ken playing the trumpet, Minnie reciting 'The Owl and The Pussycat', and Irma (on a flying visit from Australia) doing her best Hylda Baker impersonation. However, the Seventies was about to bring the most unbearable heartache for the unsuspecting, fun-loving young mum…

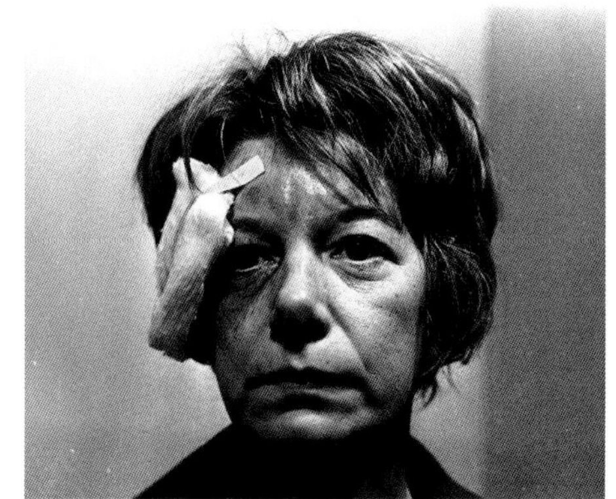

Betty Williams

Played by **Betty Driver**

No-nonsense barmaid Betty Williams has been sacked and reinstated, stormed out and been begged to return (often with a hefty pay rise) almost as many times as she's served the legendary hotpots that bear her name. Amongst these dramatic departures from the Rovers there was haughty Annie Walker firing her on the grounds of incompatibility, Betty herself stomping off in response to new landlady Vera Duckworth's demands that she cleaned as well as cooked, or the moment in 2009 when she was tersely dismissed by temporary manager Poppy Morales before being reinstalled by suitably remorseful landlord Steve McDonald.

In 2010 she was interviewed by the *Weatherfield Gazette*, who crowned her – at ninety – the oldest barmaid in the northwest. In the same year, showbiz veteran Betty Driver celebrated her own ninetieth milestone and confesses she never expected to still be pulling pints forty-one years on from her *Coronation Street* debut.

'The first time they asked me to come into Granada and read for them was in 1964 and they said: "We're casting a character called Hilda Ogden." Then they told me she was a cleaner and I said: "I don't do cleaners, I don't think I want to be her." And they said: "Well, you're not really suited anyway because she's supposed to be thin and whippety." And I said: "So I'm just too fat, is that it?"'

In 1965 she played canteen manageress Mrs Edgeley in *Corrie* spin-off *Pardon the Expression*, in which Arthur Lowe recreated his role of Leonard Swindley. But after she dislocated her hip and seriously injured her back in a scene that called for a judo throw, Betty decided to stop performing and instead opted to run a pub in Derbyshire with her sister, Freda.

'Arthur Lowe didn't stand near enough to me, so I had to bend too far down and I did my back in. Six weeks later I fell to the floor, paralysed. I'd given up the business when the *Coronation Street* producer Harry Kershaw came to see me and said: "Why don't you come and pull pints in the Rovers as well as here?" I talked it over with my sister and agreed to do it for what I thought was half a dozen episodes.

50 CORONATION ST. ICON

'Before I joined I had a throat operation, so by the time I got to the studio I was very nervous because I hadn't used my voice for six weeks. But Arthur Leslie [who played Jack Walker] was so wonderful with me. He said: "I'll stand by you and I won't leave your side while you're talking." He stood for the whole time with his hand on my back to give me confidence and I sailed through and never went wrong. I said: "You're an angel." He was the loveliest man I've ever met and it was such a shock when he died so suddenly.'

Ballsy Betty Turpin arrived in Weatherfield in 1969 with her policeman husband, Cyril, to help younger sister Maggie Clegg run the corner shop, but she soon transferred her loyalties to the Rovers. Cyril died of a heart attack in 1974, but Betty found romance again in 1995 at the Rovers VE Day celebrations when she was reunited with her first lover, Billy Williams, and they married. Unfortunately their happiness was cut short when Billy passed away two years later.

'There's no getting rid of her, is there? She should be written into the deeds of this place.'

Alec on Betty

'To me *Coronation Street* is just like a family, and I enjoy working with the youngsters because they keep me young. Looking back, Julie Goodyear is the best person I have worked opposite because I knew her every move and she knew mine. At the moment I really like Michelle Keegan, who plays Tina. When she cries, she's crying from the heart. She's a beautiful little actress.'

By the age of ten Betty was performing professionally, pushed onto the stage by her strong-willed mother to work the variety halls of the north of England. In the Thirties and Forties she became famous as a singer topping the bills she played on, and she also appeared on the radio in Henry Hall's *Guest Night* and had her own show, *A Date With Betty*. In addition she starred in several musical films, including *Penny Paradise* and *Let's Be Famous*.

With such a glittering career behind her the ever-popular actress can still see the funny side of being famed for serving pub grub:

'I've been in the business for eighty years and to finish my life famous for a bloody hotpot, well, it drives me mad! I can remember someone said: "Should we have a dish for the Rovers? How about hotpot?'" And I thought: "Oh God, I don't eat them myself and I can't cook." But I went home and asked my sister to give us a recipe because she was a lovely cook, so she wrote it down and we're still using the same one today!'

- At first Betty and Mrs Walker fail to see eye to eye.
- Bet and Betty get into another fine mess as Laurel and Hardy.
- Exasperated by secret son Gordon.
- Younger sister Maggie offers support at Cyril's burial.
- Wedded bliss with old flame Billy Williams.
- Friends reunited: Bet returns to Weatherfield.

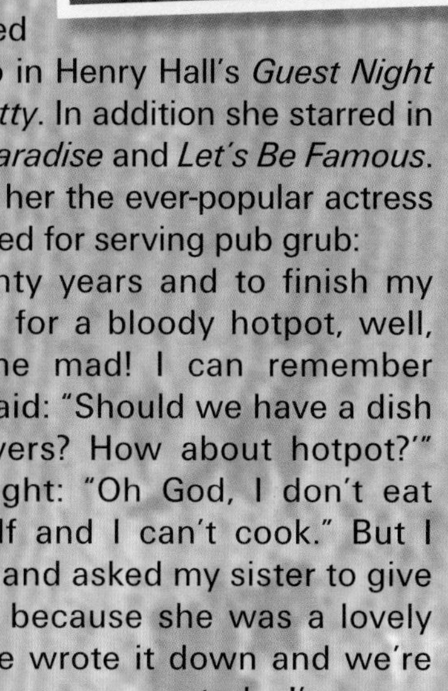

Current occupation: Senior barmaid.
On screen: 1969–
Defining moment: In 1974 it is revealed that Betty has an illegitimate son, Gordon Clegg, who has been raised by her sister Maggie as her own.

1970s

In 1970, *Room At The Top* author John Braine mused in the *TV Times* on the longevity of *Coronation Street* and concluded: 'The most important character in the *Street* is the Street itself. No matter who comes and goes, the Street remains.'

This proved to be true in a decade that saw the sudden deaths of two universally liked cast members; Arthur Leslie (genial landlord Jack Walker) suffered a heart attack and Graham Haberfield (shy guy Jerry Booth) died from heart failure caused by a liver condition at the tender age of thirty-four. But *Coronation Street* soldiered on and the baton was passed to the likes of Julie Goodyear, Anne Kirkbride and Barbara Knox – all of whom moved centre stage during the course of the Seventies.

By the time the *Street* had celebrated its 1000th episode on home shores in August 1970, it had also become popular overseas in territories as diverse as Thailand, Sweden, Australia and Nigeria, and proved to be an enormous hit in Canada and New Zealand, where it still has a loyal following. Quite how the Lancashire dialect (usually dubbed or subtitled) translated into native tongues is anyone's guess, but *Coronation Street*'s international drawing-power demonstrated one thing at least – that ordinary folk recognised ordinary folk the world over.

- From Coronation Street to Downing Street; the cast meet Harold Wilson.
- Happy Birthday! The regulars raise a glass to celebrate turning eighteen.
- Hanging around; Betty Driver and Jean Alexander get the giggles.

'At one point we were in about fourteen countries around the world, all of them just watching this little Manchester backstreet,' says William Roache. 'It was the universality of it that was so extraordinary.'

A strike at Granada stopped production for most of June 1970, and while colour had arrived in Weatherfield in late 1969, it reverted to monochrome between 1970 and 1971 due to further industrial action. Blackouts became a part of everyday life, and on Christmas Day 1974 the Street's residents amassed candles to illuminate the Rovers, where they all huddled to keep warm.

At the end of the decade, Street life came to an abrupt halt from 8 August until 24 October 1979 when the serial was taken off air as part of a bitter pay dispute by technicians across the ITV network. Meanwhile, viewers were left on tenterhooks to find out why, in the episode broadcast before the walk-out, Deirdre Langton had been reduced to tears by an unexpected letter from her estranged husband Ray in Holland.

When the show came back to life after its enforced seventy-seven-day hiatus, a special recap scene was screened before the opening titles, featuring Bet Lynch with Len Fairclough, who began: 'Welcome back! We've missed you. Now, I suppose I'd better remind you what was going on in our little street when you were last here...' And the reason for Deirdre's tears? Ray had asked her for a divorce.

There was heart-breaking tragedy across the globe from Coronation Street in 1970 when David Barlow was killed in a car crash with his son Darren. Hilda travelled to Australia (on a £600 flight paid for by bookies owner, Dave Smith) to bring her daughter, grieving widow Irma, home.

It was a crushing turn of events for Irma. She was so traumatised by the death of her twenty-seven-year-old husband and her toddler son that she even stole a stranger's baby. Fortunately, sympathetic new barmaid Bet Lynch (*see page 64*) and Emily quietly returned it before the alarm was raised. At the end of the year Irma began dating again, but she was horrified when her new boyfriend, American soldier Joe Donnelli, drunkenly confessed to her that he'd murdered Elsie's estranged husband Steve two years earlier, revealing that he'd pushed him down the stairs after a disagreement about a gambling debt.

Donnelli held Irma hostage in the flat at the corner shop. Irma managed to escape, though, when a group of locals came to the door and asked her to come to the pub. Joe slipped away and it was Minnie who found herself looking down the cold steel of a loaded gun barrel, as Donnelli held the timid pensioner and her cat Bobby hostage in the back room of Number 5. Stan was the unlikely hero of the hour, saving the day by breaking into the house and offering himself up as hostage, allowing Minnie to go free. However, Stan was unaware that the increasingly deranged soldier was armed and when Donnelli forced him to sing Christmas carols at gunpoint, Stan thought his days were numbered. The locals waited outside and feared the worst when they heard a gunshot ring out. But Stan emerged unscathed and revealed that he'd been unable to talk the crazed soldier out of turning the gun on himself.

Annie's world was also shattered that year when her beloved husband Jack had a heart attack and passed away while he was visiting their daughter Joan in Derbyshire. Accompanied by Lucille, a distraught Annie headed down to Joan's and the much-respected pub landlord's funeral was held there. The news of Jack's sudden death shocked the residents, but just as he would have wanted, the Rovers remained open in the days that followed.

1970s Deaths

David Barlow (car crash)	8 April 1970
Jack Walker (heart attack)	30 June 1970
Joe Donnelli (suicide)	21 December 1970
Valerie Barlow (electrocuted)	27 January 1971
Cyril Turpin (heart attack)	25 February 1974
Lynne Johnson (murdered by husband)	29 January 1975
Martin Downes (car crash)	9 July 1975
Frank Barlow (old age)	21 April 1975
Edna Gee (killed in fire)	1 October 1975
Jerry Booth (heart attack)	10 November 1975
Janet Barlow (suicide)	21 February 1977
Ernest Bishop (shot)	11 January 1978

Minnie tries to negotiate with gunman Joe Donnelli.

As the police gather outside, Stan bravely faces the barrel of a gun.

On her return from Derbyshire, despite her grief Annie continued to rule the roost behind the bar and applied to take over as the sole licensee of the Rovers Return. Her smooth-talking son Billy moved back to Weatherfield to keep an eye on his mother and thankfully the brewery was satisfied that with Billy around as her right-hand man Annie was more than capable of continuing as landlady.

'You won't have seen the new barmaid in the Rovers, will you? First time I saw her I thought it were a juke box.' Hilda on Bet

1970

The start of the new decade saw former launderette worker Bet begin her twenty-five-year stint at the Rovers – but she'd only got the job because Emily, who had been helping out behind the bar, felt serving ale in a public house didn't sit well with her more spiritual work at the Mission. Billy had promised his mum he'd find a new barmaid and had hired buxom Bet while Annie was out shopping. If Annie had got her own way Bet's first shift would have been her last; she commented on her return to the bar that Billy had to get rid of her as she was lowering the tone. She spluttered: 'Common? So much make-up she looks psychedelic...' But by the end of her first week it was clear that Bet's flirty, wise-cracking presence was good for business and Annie allowed her to stay on, on a purely temporary basis, of course...

Meanwhile, Elsie had begun dating suave businessman Alan Howard, but it took a while for them to realise their feelings for each other ran deep. When her old flame Bill Gregory reappeared and proposed after an eight-year absence, she turned him down for a second time and started to ponder more on her feelings for Alan. Maybe he meant more to her than she'd realised after all? But when Alan made it clear he only wanted to live with Elsie and wasn't looking to put a ring on her finger, she was furious and ended their relationship. Their separation didn't last long, though, as it became increasingly clear that they genuinely loved each other. So when Alan finally saw the light and proposed properly, a relieved Elsie happily accepted.

Stetson-wearing Elsie falls for suave Alan Howard.

The Howards get hitched with Len and Bet as their witnesses.

As this was her third attempt at wedded bliss she didn't want to make a fuss, so the couple tied the knot in a short but sweet service at Weatherfield Registry office in July 1970. However, she was touched when the residents gathered together in the Rovers for a surprise celebration with the newlyweds before they jetted off for their honeymoon in Paris. On their return Alan moved in with her at Number 11 and later the couple moved to Newcastle when Elsie was offered a job there in 1973. But typically for Elsie there wasn't to be a happy ever after and their relationship ended three years later when it turned out Alan was a boozer who drank away any money he earned. So Elsie returned to Weatherfield alone, with her tail between her legs.

'I've left home so many times me suitcases pack themselves every time I whistle.'

Elsie

There was trauma for barmaid Betty in 1970 when a customer at the Rovers took an unhealthy interest in her and ended up following her home. Startling Betty, the man identified himself as Keith Lucas and ranted that her copper husband Cyril had put him in prison three years ago and he was now looking for revenge. Soon Lucas was terrorising her on a daily basis, and with Cyril away on a week-long policing course, she feared for her own safety. Cyril was infuriated when he found out what his wife had been through in his absence and stormed off to find her stalker, attacking Lucas with a crow bar. It was only Len's intervention that prevented him killing the man. The next day Cyril was appalled at his own behaviour and handed in his notice, which was accepted. Len's evidence helped clear Cyril at a Police Disciplinary Enquiry and he was allowed to retire from the force with a full pension.

Bet Lynch

Played by **Julie Goodyear**

With her trademark beehive, big earrings and a penchant for leopard-skin print, blonde bombshell Bet Lynch sustained an impressive twenty-five years of pint-pulling service behind the bar at the Rovers Return. But four years before she took up residence at the pub, ballsy factory girl Bet's life on the *Street* had come to an abrupt end when she was written out after a six-week contract.

'I honestly believed that at the end of those six weeks they would beg me to stay, but the storyline finished and they just said thank you very much and goodbye. It was a terrible shock to catch the Number 4 bus back home to Heywood and unemployment. I was gutted because when I saw the first episode of *Coronation Street* in 1960, I knew it was for me. Call it a sixth sense, but I just knew I would end up there and it had taken me until 1966 to get in.'

Up until that point single-mum Julie had done anything to earn a crust – she trained as a shorthand typist, worked in an aircraft factory, sold washing machines and dabbled as a hand and feet model before signing up for extra work at Granada. When her *Corrie* contract wasn't renewed, she took the advice of mentor Pat Phoenix and went in search of some formal acting training.

'I went to Oldham Repertory Theatre and got a job there as an assistant stage manager, and I cleaned the gents' toilets. I hated it, but I learned the hard way what professionalism was all about. After a year I went back to Granada and said, "Right, I've got more experience, I'm ready," but they still didn't want me.'

Meanwhile, Julie bagged a small role in the ITV drama series *Family At War*, which was being directed by June Howson.

'At the end of filming June said to me: "Julie, I don't know if you'd be interested but I'm about to take over as producer on *Coronation Street*. Would you like to come in on a contract?" And lo and behold my first six-month contract came through in May 1970 on fifty quid an episode, which back then was like winning the lottery. And so it began...'

It was Billy Walker who'd employed brassy Bet at the Rovers, and his mum Annie had initially been appalled by the demeanour of her buxom new barmaid, but soon realised that the regulars loved her.

Mrs Walker advises Bet on the art of pint-pulling.

Bet and Betty are all smiles for the camera.

Sally joins Bet and Gloria for a brief stint behind the Rovers bar.

Leopardskin a-gogo; Bet takes a trip.

Queen Bet summons the Rovers troops.

The Gilroys give each other the silent treatment.

'You had to earn your stripes with the older members of the cast, people like the wonderful Doris Speed and Violet Carson. That's very much how it was then. You had to prove your professionalism, your timekeeping, your behaviour. It wasn't just what you gave on screen, it was an all-round thing. You learnt very quickly that you didn't speak until you were spoken to, and God help you if you sat in the wrong chair in the green room.

'But Betty Driver took me under her wing – she was like a second mum to me and the Rovers set became my home. In my work I'm an absolute perfectionist, my private life has always been in tatters, I'm hopeless at it, but work-wise – everything had to be right. When Bet became landlady I would inspect that set before I'd work on it. I would check the beer, the floor had to be clean, the hotpot had to be, please God, at least edible occasionally. I needed money in the till and I used to insist the set was fumigated at least once a year because it was in an old warehouse that was full of rats. In the summer months it'd get extremely hot so I'd have a shammy leather handy to throw around the back of my neck and you'd dry out in seconds. Every single detail I checked and it was as if I was running that pub both on screen and off it.'

By the time a divorced and cash-strapped Bet was forced to bid an emotional farewell to her beloved Rovers in 1995, she'd become the show's most famous and popular barmaid of all time.

'I'd go back and do it all again if I could, because it was wonderful,' states Julie, who was awarded the MBE in the 1996 New Year's Honours List for her services to drama and television. 'People loved Bet because they laughed with her and they cried with her. I did a lot of promotional work for the *Street* around the world and there were always Bets waiting to meet me wherever I went. Whether it was Canada, New Zealand, Australia, Hong Kong, they'd be there waiting for me with their shoulder pads and their big hair. They may not have always been women… but they were there!'

'Bet Lynch's place is behind a bar wearing a pair of daft earrings and very little else.'

Hilda

Occupations: Factory girl, Rovers barmaid and landlady.
On screen: 1966, 1970–1995, 2002, 2003
Defining moment: 'Me behind a bar, I'm in me element. It's like Santa in his grotto!' Bet convinces the brewery to make her the Rovers landlady in 1985.

The future was looking sunkissed and full of rum-filled possibilities for the Barlows in 1971, when Ken was offered a well-paid teaching job in Jamaica. But as the family prepared to emigrate, yet again Ken's attempts to distance himself from grimy, working-class Weatherfield were thwarted. A flustered Val was late getting ready for the going-away party that was being thrown for them by Annie in the Rovers, so Ken went ahead and waited for her in the pub. Back at the maisonette, Val's hairdryer was on the blink and she tried to fix it by tightening it with a screwdriver. But as she plugged it back into a faulty adaptor socket, sparks flew and Val was given a mammoth electric shock. As she fell to the ground she knocked an electric heater into a packing crate; it quickly lit and soon the whole room was ablaze.

After rushing out of the pub on hearing the bells of the fire engines, frantic Ken had to be held back by several firemen as he attempted to save Val himself. But it was too late – Val was rushed to Weatherfield Infirmary but was declared dead on arrival, electrocuted by the faulty socket. After Val's funeral the residents were at a loss as to how to help a devastated Ken; with the twins whisked away to Glasgow to stay with Val's family, Ken was officially a broken man and his new life in Jamaica was just a shattered dream.

The first Mrs Barlow is about to meet a tragic end.

Grieving widower Ken struggles with his loss.

The Rovers' landlady was not amused at the start of the year when she found herself accused of serving watered-down gin to her customers. Needless to say, the accusations were bad for business, and when the regulars started staying away, an outraged Annie had no choice but to give her staff a week's notice. Fearing prosecution and under threat of losing her licence, it was Len who saved the day when he overheard one of the draymen admitting he'd watered down the gin to get his own back on her son Billy, and the case was dropped.

The council later announced they intended to demolish the new flats built on the site of the old Mission, as the fire at the Barlows' had exposed structural faults in them. In their place a new community centre was to be built and Ena felt it was the obvious choice for her to take on the position of caretaker. She was interviewed for the job, but was affronted to discover a woman called Hetty Thorpe had pipped her to the post. That wasn't going to stop Ena pursuing the coveted position she felt was rightfully hers, though. Determined to ensure things went in her favour, she invited Hetty to tea and scared the living daylights out of the poor woman with tales of local hooligans and the decidedly rough neighbours. When Hetty fled in horror, Ena was duly recruited and felt she had finally come home when she moved into the caretaker's flat, which was on the site of her old home in the former Mission vestry.

'It's something to do with being born a Barlow or marrying a Barlow – life seems to have it in for us.'

Irma

When Ray and Irma discovered Stan regularly slept in his van during his shift as night-watchman at Hulmes Bakery, they decided to teach him a lesson. With Stan snoring away, oblivious to the world around him, Ray snuck into the van and drove it onto a wasteland, where Stan was picked up by the police. He was promptly sacked from the bakery and when Stan found out it was prankster Ray he had to thank for his new unemployed status, he made it quite clear that when he got his hands on the builder he would wring his neck. After finding a nervous-looking Ray hiding from him in the ladies' loo at the Rovers, Stan was offered a job at the builder's yard by way of an apology. However, Ray and Len would only allow Stan to do all the donkey work, which he didn't like at all. Exhausted, Stan felt he was being exploited and in protest formed his own union – the Stanley Ogden District Union, otherwise known as SODU!

The first event to be held at the community centre was a Flower Show and Fête, with Annie, Emily and Alf responsible for judging the homemade cakes, wine and beer respectively. An old flame of Hilda's, George Greenwood, was judging the flowers and veg, and much to Hilda's embarrassment he recognised Stan's colourful entry as an orchid stolen from the park. As the day progressed, Minnie and Ena became increasingly sloshed as they helped Alf judge the home-brew, Emily got tiddly on the wine and Len was horrified to discover he'd won the cake-decorating competition. In fact, his cheeky-chappie workmate Ray Langton had set him up, persuading Maggie Clegg to bake a cake which he'd then entered under Len's name. The day's overall winner was green-fingered Albert, who was proud as punch at winning the highly coveted Challenge Cup for his sweet peas, dahlias, geraniums and cabbages.

'When it comes to sticking the oar in, she's got the Boat Race knocked into a cocked hat.'

Alf on Ena

However, the next day it was scowls all round for Annie when a humorous cartoon of the judges at the event, drawn by an anonymous cartoonist, was published in the local paper. Horrified at the unflattering caricature of herself, she threatened legal action. Determined to find out who the culprit was, at first Annie assumed it was

❷ The flower-show judge questions the authenticity of Stan's potted plant.

⬆ A spinster no more: Emily finally becomes Mrs Ernest Bishop.

'arty' Ken and then accused Emily when Hilda pointed out that Miss Nugent wasn't featured in the cartoons herself. Emily reacted angrily to Annie's accusations, retorting that she would never do something in such poor taste. However, Emily later discovered who was to blame when she came across some cartoon sketches in Ernest Bishop's drawer at the local photographic studio, where she'd been working. At first she was appalled and ended their friendship, but eventually she forgave him and they became engaged.

Things were taking a turn for the worse for Emily, too, and it looked as if her engagement to Ernest would be called off when the mild-mannered photographer was arrested and jailed in Majorca while working there on an assignment. He had been accused of taking so-called pornographic shots, but Emily stood by him, knowing him to be innocent (which he was later proved to be).

Ernest and Emily were married at the Mawdesley Street Chapel on Easter Monday in 1972, with ditzy best friend Mavis Riley (*see page 70*) in attendance, Bet Lynch and Lucille Hewitt as bridesmaids and Len giving Emily away. But the day wasn't without its moments of tension, none more so than when, at the last minute, Ernest panicked and kept on driving around the block, deciding what to do for the best, while a nervous Emily was left waiting in the vestry. Thankfully he came to his senses, and after a reception at the Rovers and a walking holiday honeymoon in Edale, Derbyshire, they settled comfortably into married life at Number 3.

Mavis Wilton

Played by **Thelma Barlow**

Jealous Mavis Riley made her first appearance at good friend Emily Nugent's engagement party. That night she proceeded to get drunk on gin and bitterly carped to Bet Lynch and Betty Turpin that the soon-to-be Mrs Bishop had no right to get engaged before her, as Emily was much older. 'At least six months older,' she added, on the verge of tears.

But Mavis needn't have worried about being left on the shelf; later she was to find herself torn between two lovers and was even branded an unlikely Jezebel when Derek Wilton (played by Peter Baldwin) came home to find his love rival, Victor Pendlebury, furiously massaging her feet. As dithery as each other, both Mavis and Derek failed to turn up for their first wedding, but they were reunited several years later and second time around they made it down the aisle.

The Wiltons successfully tie the knot at the second attempt.

Mavis enjoys some budgie love.

Rita comforts a perturbed Mavis.

'I think Mavis's popularity was down to her vulnerability, really. All the teasing and leg pulling that went on from other characters brought out the protective side in the audience.'

Of course, the other great partnership of Mavis's life was with an often-exasperated Rita Sullivan. An unlikely double act, they were to spend over twenty years together behind the counter, until a widowed Mavis quit Weatherfield in 1997 to open a B&B in the Lake District. Being on The Kabin set had its perks: 'Everything in the sweet jars was real. Barbara [Knox] and I loved munching the Pontefract Cakes and we used to pinch them all the time.'

In the early 1980s, it was comedian Les Dennis's send-up of Mavis (alongside his comedy partner Dustin Gee as Vera Duckworth) on *Russ Abbott's Madhouse* that saw the twittering shop assistant become the impression of choice in playgrounds up and down the country.

'Suddenly everywhere I went people were doing Mavis impersonations. There was no escaping it. Little boys would shout it at me when I walked past, and once I was walking up Dean Street in Manchester and this huge great articulated lorry slowed down next to me and a big burly trucker leaned out and shouted "I don't really know" at me in the most effeminate voice possible. It was hilarious – although I doubt Mavis would've approved!'

50 CORONATION ST. ICON

Occupation: Shop assistant in The Kabin.
On screen: 1971, 1972, 1973–1997
Defining moment: Finally saying goodbye to spinsterhood by tying the knot (at the second attempt) with dozy Derek in 1988.

It's decision time for Rita and young Terry Bates.

Ken finally had a stroke of good luck and was appointed Deputy Head at Bessie Street School. However, there was soon a clash of personalities, thanks to the opposing teaching styles of no-nonsense headmaster Wilfred Perkins and Ken's more caring-sharing approach. When Ken started to take an interest in feisty Rita Bates (*see page 80*), the stepmother of disruptive pupil Terry, Perkins made his disapproval all too clear. Ken was clearly attracted to Mrs Bates, but Mrs Bates had her eye on butch builder Len Fairclough, so when Len discovered that Rita wasn't Mrs Bates at all and wasn't actually married to Terry's father, his interest perked up no end. Rita and a jealous Harry Bates did separate fleetingly, when he threw her out, but she soon went crawling back to him, worried about his children managing on their own without her.

Len thought that was the last he'd ever hear of Rita, but at the New Victoria Working Men's Club in June he was gobsmacked when she sauntered on stage, singing under her real name, Rita Littlewood. This time Len told a newly single Rita he wanted to get to know her better – they spent the night together and began dating.

Two months later, several of the women of Coronation Street – including Elsie, Emily and Lucille – were victims of a peeping Tom, and when Stan was discovered in suspicious circumstances he became the Number One suspect. Stan protested his innocence when the residents turned on him and, standing by her man, Hilda gave them a piece of her mind and spat on the Rovers floor to show her disgust at the way they were treating her husband. When the real peeping Tom was caught in the act by the police on Bessie Street, Stan's name was cleared and the locals apologised. He was soon back in the fold, though, and two months later he was the pride of the Street when he won a beer-drinking competition against Piggy Owen at the Flying Horse, as part of the Weatherfield Pub Olympics. Meanwhile, in the same competition Ena beat a nervous Flying Horse regular at dominoes, winning the game by intimidation – she glared at him so contemptuously that the poor chap mistakenly played the wrong domino.

'They named a sherry trifle after me at one labour club I played.'

Rita

- The flame-haired songstress belts out another tune.
- Len tells Rita he wants to get to know her better.
- Showstoppers Norma, Bet and Betty as the Andrews Sisters.
- A leggy Emily shows her fruitier side to Ray and Jerry.

At Christmas there was more memorable fun and games in the Rovers when the regulars took part in a 1940s-style variety show organised by Emily and Ernest. Perhaps unsurprisingly, Annie played the part of Britannia trilling 'There'll Always Be An England', Rita sang 'Lili Marlene' as a sultry Marlene Dietrich, and Bet, Betty and shop assistant Norma Ford harmonised as the Andrews Sisters. Ray Langton and Jerry palled-up as Flanagan & Allen, while Emily was an unlikely Carmen Miranda and suffered a wardrobe malfunction during her routine as she kept losing the bananas from her headdress!

'I've always wanted to be stormy, passionate and tempestuous. But you can't be. Not when you're born with a tidy mind.'

Emily

Fired up by the idea of a life on the ocean waves, warm-hearted builder Jerry laboured long and lovingly over the construction of an 11-foot sailing boat, which he named his very own Shangri-La. Len's premises were transformed into Weatherfield's first shipyard, and as the vessel took shape, yachting fever spread across the Street and everyone came in to admire the work in progress. Competition was fierce for the honour of crewing its maiden voyage, but Ray and an unlikely Stan were the lucky seamen to be recruited. With proud captain Jerry at the helm the trio took to the water – but the Shangri-La proved to be more Titanic than Noah's Ark and capsized within minutes, sinking like a stone.

Ken and his second wife Janet Reid had very different ideas about what their married life should entail – Ken wanted his twins, Peter and Susan, to live with them, whereas Janet made it quite clear she had no interest in becoming a full-time stepmother or housewife and that her career at the Department of Education was her priority. Despite differences from the off, the fraught couple had married while on holiday with Ken's children and threw a wedding reception at the Rovers on their return.

Life is one long spat for Ken and second wife Janet.

Alf Roberts

Played by **Bryan Mosley**

'He'd skin a flea then sell it a vest, would Alf Roberts,' was aggrieved customer Hilda Ogden's take on Weatherfield's penny-pinching yet cordial shopkeeper. Alf made his first appearance two months after the series began as a Post Office colleague of Frank Barlow; he went on to become a pillar of the community and a champion of old-fashioned values.

His first wife, Phyllis, died of cancer and his second marriage was cut short when corner-shop owner Renee was killed in a tragic car accident. After her death Alf inherited the business, which became his pride and joy, and flighty Audrey Potter – who would become his third wife in 1985 – set up a temporary hair salon in the back room.

Having served as a hardworking mayor and local councillor, Alf was delighted to be awarded an OBE at Buckingham Palace, and at one point there were even plans to rename Coronation Street in his honour – until the horrified residents opposed it.

Alf and Renee's happiness is short-lived.

Opposites attract: Alf and Audrey turn out to be the perfect match.

Audrey's all a-flutter at Alf's finery.

It was while he was on national service that Bryan Mosley began acting, and after touring in rep he secured big-screen roles in the likes of *A Kind Of Loving*, *Billy Liar* and *Get Carter* (in which he was catapulted to his death from the top of a multi-storey car park by Michael Caine). Bryan was also a highly respected fight director and fenced with Terence Stamp for his swashbuckling sword battle in *Far From The Madding Crowd*.

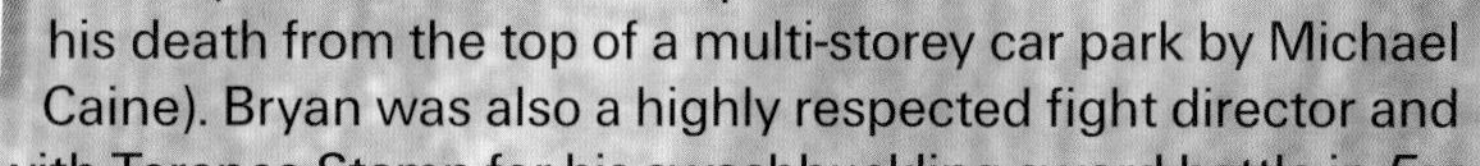

Sadly, in his later years Bryan was plagued by ill health, and he passed away in February 1999, less than six weeks after his trilby-hatted character had died of a heart attack at Nick Tilsley's birthday party.

'I'll say until my dying day that lovely Bryan didn't get the acting plaudits and the kudos he deserved,' comments his screen wife Sue Nicholls. 'Alf may not have been the most showy character, but he was an ordinary man and it's very difficult to play ordinary. Any of us, with due respect, can play over the top, do a funny walk or pull a silly face, but it's very difficult to play ordinary because people don't think you're acting. Bryan came into that category because he remained so wonderfully true to the character he played.'

Occupations: Post Office worker and shopkeeper.
On screen: 1961, 1962, 1963, 1967, 1971–1999
Defining moment: In 1980 Alf teaches Renee to drive but she stalls the car – as Alf gets out to take over at the wheel she is killed by an oncoming truck.

50 CORONATION ST. ICON

Sometime-club-singer Rita sold her very first newspaper in May when Len bought Biddulph's Cafe and Lending Library and rechristened it The Kabin. Rita had wanted it to be called 'Rita's', but stubborn Len had refused to give his girlfriend top billing. He did allow Rita the meaningless title of manageress, though, but when he snubbed her request for an assistant she told him where he could stick his job. Eventually Len capitulated and Rita took on a nervy Mavis as her right-hand woman – despite Mavis's bout of high-pitched hiccups throughout the job interview. As the weeks passed, the duo became increasingly puzzled by the steady flow of shifty looking male customers in search of glossy farming magazines. They later discovered the former owner had been selling illegal porn under the guise of the *Pig Producer's Monthly*!

Their marriage got off to a shaky start when Janet set her sights on a £12,000 detached house in Cheadle, but they lost the property because Ken was late paying the deposit. This lead to a furious row which culminated with Ken slapping a shell-shocked Janet around the face. Later in the year they rented Number 11 when Elsie and Alan moved to Newcastle, but with Janet still haughtily refusing to have any kind of relationship with the twins, it was a union doomed from the start. The following year Janet walked out on Ken, saying she found his lack of drive and ambition unappealing. Ironically, on the day she left he was offered a high-earning executive position at the warehouse.

Another doomed coupling occurred in 1973 when struggling pensioners Albert and Minnie became engaged. However, this was no love-match; Albert popped the question thinking that if he and Minnie lived in the same house they'd be financially better off. Dithery as ever, Minnie wanted to run the idea past Ena first, but Ena got the wrong end of the stick, thought Albert was proposing to her – and accepted!

Eventually, Minnie agreed to give Albert her hand in marriage, thinking she'd be glad of the company in her old age, but after three months of engagement the tetchy pensioners were already getting on each other's nerves. So when an exasperated Ena pointed out that as a married couple they would receive less hand-outs than they would individually, it seemed the perfect opportunity to call the whole thing off. Later, Minnie admitted

'The story of my life. Two marriages. Two kids. Several jobs. A variety of dreams and ambitions, some shattered, some just getting a bit tatty around the edges.'

Ken

'She bullies me. She's always bullied me... in the name of Christianity.'

Minnie on Ena

she didn't even like Albert very much, especially the way he slurped his tea out of his saucer.

Ena suffered two heart attacks that year, but even so she refused to move into an old people's home, saying she wanted to die on the Street. Not that she was going anywhere soon, as Ena was still a formidable figure, laying down the law on a daily basis. However, things did take a turn for the worse, health-wise, for one of the residents of the Street; Albert was accidentally gassed by his new stove at Number 1 and had to be rushed to hospital. A gas leak was suspected, so the residents were immediately evacuated from their homes and into the community centre. Minnie was frantic with worry when her cat Bobby couldn't be found, and Hilda began to fret about Stan's whereabouts. Meanwhile, Elsie was furious she'd been dragged from Number 11 in the middle of setting her hair and was convinced she looked a right sight.

The Mayor and his suitably regal Lady Mayoress.

At the hospital Ken kept vigil by Albert's bedside until the old man was out of danger. When the police gave the all-clear to the other residents of the Street and told them it was safe to return to their homes, it became apparent that Jerry was to blame for the scare as he'd taken out Albert's old stove and had attempted to replace it with a new model. Not one to hold a grudge, Albert refused an apologetic Jerry's offer of compensation. Meanwhile, Hilda had been so inspired about the day's dramatic events she decided to write a play about a gas leak and gave it to a bemused Ken to read.

In the meantime, newly elected Mayor of Weatherfield Alf Roberts asked Annie to be his Lady Mayoress, and she eagerly accepted, admitting it was a duty she'd been born to perform. As Lady Mayoress, Annie decided to invite visitors from Weatherfield's twin town of Charleville, France, to come and stay with the residents. Stan and Hilda opted for a woman, Rene Dubois – only she turned out to be a burly male lorry driver who became firm friends with Stan. The Bishops struggled with their Frenchman, Charles Follette, who spoke zero English, and Bet had high hopes of romance with the brooding Marcel Lebeque who was

French kissing in Weatherfield? Bet with Marcel Lebeque.

staying at the Rovers. Unfortunately for Bet, Marcel was married, but she was happy to let the regulars speculate that he and Bet had spent a passionate night together. On the visitors last soirée there was an exciting poker game in the pub between Stan, Rene and Marcel – but Bet wiped the floor with all of them and bagged the winnings.

A year later, as Betty was celebrating Len and Rita's engagement in the Rovers, the police called on her sister Maggie to inform her that Cyril had collapsed and died outside their home on his way to the function. It was up to Maggie to break the terrible news to Betty, which she did as best she could in the back room of the Rovers. When Annie found out she stopped the party and sent everyone home.

Over the next few days Betty became confused and distant and continued talking about Cyril as if he were still alive – she even called at the Rovers to tell Bet she couldn't work because she was going out for the day with Cyril. Meanwhile, Cyril's former boss called at Maggie's and told her that a muddled Betty was at his house, looking for her husband. At one point Betty had to be sedated. Maggie found it increasingly hard to cope with her widowed sister's unpredictability and decided it would be best to keep her away from the funeral. However, Betty surprised everyone by turning up at the churchyard, having finally come to terms with Cyril's death and now ready to grieve properly.

TOP FIVE Spooky Moments

Over the years many a ghostly presence has sent chills down the spines of the Weatherfield residents...

The ghost of Martha Longhurst, 1975

More than ten years after her death, having found a mysterious pair of thick black-rimmed glasses on the bar, Betty and Ena became convinced they'd seen Martha in the Rovers. Two months later, Alf was staying there when Annie was away and after closing was startled to find a half-empty milk stout bottle by Martha's old chair in the snug. The regulars tried to contact her on a ouija board but there was no response.

A woman possessed at Number 13, 1977

After a successful tea-leaf-reading session, Hilda held a seance at Number 13 with a dubious Bet, Elsie, Gail and Suzie in order to convince them she really did possess supernatural powers. But when Hilda went into a trance the table collapsed and she managed to scare everyone, including herself!

Poltergeist at The Kabin, 1979

A terrified Mavis heard bumps in the night and became convinced that psychic phenomena were haunting The Kabin flat. She called in Eddie to keep watch but he dozed off. The following night he heard them too and cowered with a trembling Mavis in her bedroom for safety. It turned out to be a budgie trapped behind the boarded-up fireplace.

The ghost of Ivy Brennan, 1996

After popping to the loo while visiting Don Brennan at Number 5, Vera sensed an eerie chill and was scared witless to be confronted by Ivy's ghost on the landing. She then believed the ghost of her best mate had followed her to the Rovers and was now haunting the pub. Meanwhile, landlord Jack sensed a business opportunity and had t-shirts made with 'Rovers Return – Try Our Spirits' on the front and 'Our Beers Are Out Of This World Too' on the back.

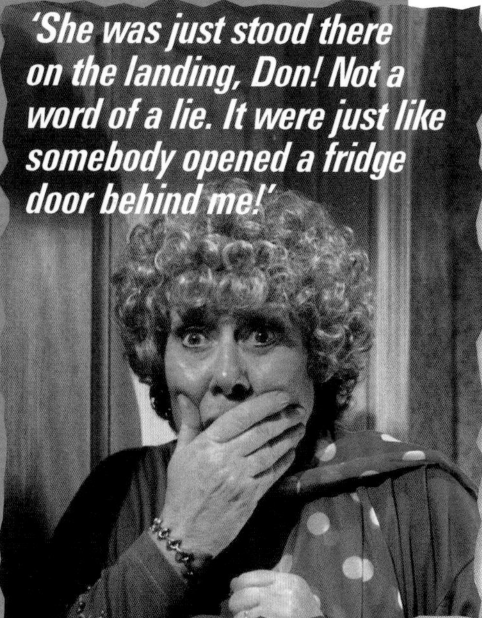

The ghost of Vera Lomax, 2004

Norris convinced himself that The Kabin was haunted when Emily told him that Vera Lomax, the daughter of Ena, had died of a brain tumour when the Glad Tidings Mission had stood on the site. He organised a seance in the stock-room, with a sceptical Rita, Blanche and Betty holding hands around the table in a bid to contact dead Vera's spirit. Everyone jumped when a box fell off a shelf, but they later discovered the 'haunting' had been caused by rising damp.

'Spirit of Vera Lomax, we ask that you commune with us and move among us. Signify your presence!'

Rita Sullivan

Played by **Barbara Knox**

What Rita Sullivan doesn't know about marking up papers and peddling penny chews isn't worth bothering about. However, back in the day it was exotic dancing that was the former showgirl's speciality, and in 1964 she popped up in the Rovers, fluttered her fake eyelashes and sweet-talked Dennis Tanner into giving her digs for the night.

'She was part of a double act – Rita Littlewood and her partner Sissy, they'd do exotic dancing and Sissy played the trombone. But Sissy had broken her arm so she wasn't there, and when Rita finds out Elsie's away she persuades Dennis Tanner to let her sleep in his mum's bed. The episode ended with Gordon Rollings [who played Minnie Caldwell's lodger, Charlie Moffitt] looking for wires in the loft and coming through the ceiling of the room she's sleeping in, practically falling into Rita's lap. Well, I thought this was marvellous and I was convinced I'd be called back to do more episodes. I didn't hear from them for years.'

In fact it was another eight years before Barbara was asked to return as Rita, this time with the name Mrs Bates, the mother of one of schoolteacher Ken Barlow's most troublesome pupils, Terry.

'Only one thing would worry me if I was Rita. Where could I get a hat to put on all that hair?'

Elsie

'I think Ken was expecting a meek little woman, and of course Rita comes into the school and reads him the riot act. In reality I had a cup and saucer in my hand that was shaking and rattling away because I was so nervous about doing a scene with William Roache. The cast of *Coronation Street* were like gods to me at that time,' remembers Barbara.

It turned out Rita wasn't actually married to Mr Bates, nor was she the mother of his children, leaving her free to pursue builder Len Fairclough, who couldn't take his eyes off her when she slinked onto the stage at the New Victoria Working Men's Club and crooned 'I Enjoy Being A Girl'.

'In those days you met the writers before you joined and they said 'Where do you think Rita works?' I said she'd be in the clubs because she's a flighty madam. So a few weeks later, God's honest truth, I got the script and it said: "Rita is discovered singing". I think I aged ten years. I phoned Harry Kershaw, who was the producer at the time, and said: "'Is this a joke? I was

50 CORONATION ST. ICON

thinking more of a hat-check girl or behind the bar? I'm not a singer!'"

Being an on-screen chanteuse opened up a whole new sideline for the actress, who was personally invited by conductor Carl Davis to sing with the Liverpool Philharmonic Orchestra and even recorded her own covers album in 1973, appropriately titled *On The Street Where I Live*.

Meanwhile, Len installed future wife Rita as manageress of his new business venture, a newsagent and tea room called The Kabin. In 1983 she was widowed, but nine years later she wed again, this time to terminally ill sweet salesman Ted Sullivan. In the intervening years came the relationship that nearly put Rita off men for life. With her sparkly shoulder-padded sweaters and unyielding helmet of red hair, Rita had always been a woman who knew her own mind – but she lost the plot completely thanks to the physical and mental abuse dished out to her by cheating, bullying boyfriend Alan Bradley. Thankfully he later met a nasty end courtesy of an oncoming Blackpool tram.

'My dressing room used to have bin liners full of letters from ladies going through the same thing. So many said: "It was like watching my own life." And they weren't all from little backstreets – there were doctors' wives, lawyers' wives, judges' wives. Her situation had hit a nerve with women all over the country.'

Such was the impact of the storyline that Barbara won the *TV Times* Best Actress Award in 1989, beating some pretty highbrow competition: 'I was up against some tremendous actresses, including Dame Judi Dench and Pauline Collins, so I really wasn't expecting to win. When they called out my name I went into shock, I really did. I remember the next day the Chairman of Granada, David Plowright, sent a huge bouquet of fifty red roses to congratulate me, which was lovely.'

In 2004 Barbara was honoured with a Lifetime Achievement accolade at The British Soap Awards and two years later won Best Partnership with her current Kabin side-kick, Malcolm Hebden, who plays Norris Cole.

'Every day I thank my lucky stars for the opportunities I've had. I find it fascinating to look back and think that all these wonderful experiences in my life have come out of me going into *Coronation Street* in 1964 for one little episode.'

- Rita vamps it up as Marlene Dietrich in a Rovers variety show.
- Another run-in for the Faircloughs.
- Happy families with Jenny and Alan Bradley?
- Service with a smile at the Kabin.
- Norris takes an instant dislike to Rita's Shi-Tzu, Mr Woo.

Occupations: Former exotic dancer, club singer and newsagent.
On screen: 1964, 1972–
Defining moment: In 1998 Rita nearly dies from carbon monoxide poisoning due to a faulty gas fire – old friend Alec Gilroy saves her and they briefly become engaged.

Later that year, Maggie married reformed alcoholic Ron Cooke and the couple decided to start a new life in Zaire. Battleaxe Granny Hopkins and her son Idris took over as the new corner-shop owners, making an enemy on their first day by refusing to give hopping mad Hilda any credit. With Maggie overseas, it was finally revealed that the sisters had been harbouring a deep, dark secret – that Maggie's son Gordon was actually the illegitimate son of the recently widowed Betty.

When Annie found out her thirty-six-year-old son Billy was dating gangly nineteen-year-old Deirdre Hunt (*see page 96*), the Rovers grande-dame reacted by taking to her bed, aghast at Deirdre's unsuitability. When the pair announced their engagement, Annie was horrified at the prospect of Deirdre as a daughter-in-law and gasped, 'But she's just a secretary at a backstreet plumbers.' Genuinely upset, she became convinced that Deirdre's tenacious mother, Blanche (*see page 199*), had encouraged her teenage daughter to snare her son. The revelation that Billy was to foot the bill of his wedding only added to Annie's woes, and the icing on the

Recently engaged Deirdre turns to Blanche for support.

When it came to planning that year's RADA (Rovers Amateur Dramatic Association) production, organisers Emily and Ernest had very different ideas. While arty Ernest favoured (much to the residents' bemusement) an erotic contemporary play called *Sand*, a victorious Emily won everyone over with her suggestion of Oscar Wilde's *The Importance Of Being Earnest*, setting her heart on playing the imperious Lady Bracknell herself. However, director Ernest insisted that role went to a grateful Annie, whilst Deirdre was cast as Gwendolen and Ken won the part of Algernon. It looked like poor Emily was destined to remain backstage, until Rita stormed out after some over-critical rehearsal feedback from Ernest, leaving her to take over the role of Miss Prism herself. The production was a roaring success, apart from Annie ruining her expensively hired costume by sitting on a freshly painted piece of scenery, and Mavis (who'd been working backstage) mistakenly walking into the wrong dressing room and being confronted by the stark-naked male members of the cast!

cake was when she returned to the pub with her brand new wedding outfit to discover Blanche's outfit was exactly the same colour as her's – daffodil gold.

Luckily for Annie's constitution, the following year Deirdre began to have serious doubts about the age difference between herself and her husband-to-be and questioned how she would cope living with such a disapproving mother-in-law. Eventually she came to the conclusion that she was too young to be getting married in the first place. When she spoke up, Billy packed his bags and went to run a wine bar in Jersey, while Annie breathed a sigh of relief.

This was to be a year of heartache for the Rovers bar staff – unbeknown to Bet, Martin Downes, the son she'd given up for adoption as a baby nineteen years earlier, had arrived in Weatherfield with a mate, Steve Baker, and was searching for his birth mother. The pair wandered around the area looking for a barmaid called Elizabeth, only to arrive at the Rovers to be confronted by two possibilities: Betty and Bet. Once Martin had realised it was tarty Bet that was his mother (wearing a particularly low-cut and revealing dress that day), he left without identifying himself.

The following year Steve Baker was back in Weatherfield, but this time he was alone. He broke the news to Bet that Martin, a soldier, had been killed in a car crash. Devastated, the usually brassy barmaid fell to pieces and nearly took an overdose. She was talked out of it by gentle giant Eddie Yeats, who forced his way into her flat and listened while Bet poured her heart out about how she'd given birth to Martin when she was sixteen and hadn't been given any other option than to hand him over for adoption. What kind of life could she have offered him? A supportive Betty also came to the rescue, and told Bet they had more in common than she could possibly think – she confided in her that she'd also been forced to give up her own child.

Meanwhile, the future of Coronation Street hung dangerously in the balance when councillor Len confided in Rita that the London Development Company had top-secret plans to demolish the area and redevelop it, information that Rita then passed on to everyone in the Rovers. The LDC front man attempted to buy up the properties and Len celebrated when they wrote Rita a down-payment cheque of £1,000 for The Kabin, but she ripped it up, saying the shop was in her name and she wasn't selling. Len told Rita to choose between

↑ Eddie proves to be a caring confidante when Bet hits rock bottom.

↓ Sullen faces all round as Ken lays down the law to Kevin's gang.

'You've as much chance of keeping a secret round here as you have of keeping a tan.'

Bet

him and The Kabin – so she picked The Kabin. While Len attended a planning meeting an angry resident threw a brick through his window, but in the end the builder realised he couldn't vote against Rita's wishes and the redevelopment plan was thrown out by the committee. In the meantime, the locals were shocked when the anonymous brick thrower came forward and apologised – it was Emily Bishop.

Ken's touchy-feely approach towards the disaffected youth of Weatherfield was to prove a feeble failure in 1975, when three of his former pupils attempted to get their teenage kicks by terrorising the locals. He instructed the boys to go back to school but they just laughed in Ken's face and chose to smash in a window at the community centre instead, the shattering glass just missing Albert who was inside. Ken offered to pay for the window as long as the police weren't brought in, suggesting it was society that was to blame for the youths' behaviour.

Furious, Albert reported the incident himself and the lads broke Ken's windows, thinking he was the one that had shopped them. Then they tipped rubbish over his back yard and let down his car tyres so he couldn't get to work. The gang ringleader, Kevin Marsh, told his father that Ken had hit him, which resulted in Mr Marsh threatening to have Ken charged with assault, but he soon changed his mind when Ken showed him the destruction his son's gang had caused.

'You think you've found a man to lean on – half the time you wind up with a little lad who just wants mothering.'

Rita

TOP FIVE Wish you were here?

When the locals fancy a change of scenery their holidays rarely go according to plan...

Majorca, 1974

The Weatherfield women won a package deal to Majorca by entering a 'Spot The Ball' competition. Once there, Emily suffered with sunburn and mosquito bites and Hilda's hand-washing blew off the hotel balcony, leaving her knicker-less. Meanwhile, Rita pulled a handsome Spaniard (as did Mavis, much to everyone's surprise) and Bet missed the plane home.

Blackpool, 1985

It was brassy Bet who probably best described the joys of the seaside resort: 'You can't beat Blackpool. There in a couple of hours in a charabanc. Everybody's letting their hair down and you can cut the smell of shrimps and best bitter with a knife. It's paradise...' Along with Rita and Mavis, the barmaid let her hair down by picking up a group of holidaying sales reps – but Bet was left seething when Mavis nabbed the only one who wasn't married.

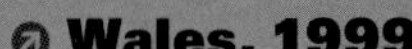

Wales, 1999

The Websters' and Platts' caravanning holiday was spoilt when they discovered the boisterous Battersby clan were staying at the same campsite. Toyah developed a crush on the site-owner's son, but he only had eyes for her mum, Janice, who considered leaving Les for him. Meanwhile, Les suffered an electric shock and Martin ended up saving his life.

Paris, 2006

While Kevin and Sally celebrated their wedding anniversary with champagne, romance and reminisces, loved-up teen Rosie was planning to run away with boyfriend Craig to start a new life in Berlin. Back at the hotel, her panicked parents discovered her goodbye note and hotfooted it to the train station. Luckily for them, Rosie had a last-minute change of heart and Craig absconded without her.

Malta, 2007

At the resort Steve and Street Cars' co-worker Eileen were forced to share a double bed, thanks to an accommodation shortage. But a drunken Steve was in for an even bigger shock when he pulled a sexy holidaymaker only to discover Shania was not all 'she' seemed. Mortified, Steve made Eileen promise his encounter with a drag queen would remain their little secret – but she soon blabbed!

OVERHEARD

Mavis and Rita enjoy beach life in Majorca, 1974

THE SUN BEATS DOWN ON MAVIS AND RITA. MAVIS IS LYING ON HER STOMACH AS RITA SQUIRTS SUN CREAM ONTO HER BACK.

RITA: (PEERING AT HER OWN ARMS) Look a' that. I just go pinker and flamin' pinker.

SHE SLIPS HER SHOULDER STRAPS DOWN FROM HER SHOULDERS.

MAVIS: (SLEEPILY) I suffer if I'm not careful. I always have. Me and me mother have got the same skin.

RITA: I bet that can be very uncomfy. (SHE SQUIRTS CREAM ON HERSELF) Look at that. Little sun blisters all along me rotten cleavage. (SHE SIGHS) Shall we go mad and have a champagne cocktail?

MAVIS: At four o'clock in the afternoon?

RITA: It doesn't feel like four o'clock. It's not the same four o'clock as what we have back home.

MAVIS: I don't want to even think about home.

THEY BOTH RELAX, EYES SHUT. RITA ROLLS ONTO HER TUMMY AND UNHOOKS THE TOP HALF OF HER BIKINI. SHE OPENS ONE EYE AND SEES A PAIR OF BARE MALE FEET STANDING BY HER TOWEL. SHE LOOKS UP TO TAKE IN A REASONABLY ATTRACTIVE SPANIARD IN HIS LATE THIRTIES, WEARING ONLY BATHING TRUNKS.

RITA: (MURMURS TO MAVIS) I think I've cracked it. 'Ere, hook me up. Either that or go for a long swim.

JAIME: (TO RITA) You enjoy pedallo?

RITA: Only with chips.

MAVIS: I think he's asking you to go for a ride.

RITA: (TESTILY) I know what he's asking me to go for!

SHE LOOKS AT HIM – HE'S NOT THAT BAD AND SHE'S BEGINNING TO FEEL A LITTLE BORED WITH MAVIS. SHE HOLDS OUT A HAND, HE GALLANTLY HELPS HER TO HER FEET.

Adios amigo. (TO MAVIS) And keep an eye on me flamin' handbag. (TO JAIME) Come on, sailor!

THEY RUN TOWARDS THE PEDALLOS. SIGHING, MAVIS FOLLOWS THEM WISTFULLY WITH HER EYES.

Mike Baldwin

Played by **Johnny Briggs**

The once ruthless, cigar-twirling, rag-trade boss died on the cobbles from a heart attack in the arms of his arch enemy Ken Barlow. He'd spent the previous months battling Alzheimer's, which saw Mike become ever more befuddled and a shadow of the flash cockney who'd breezed into Weatherfield and turned the burnt-out shell of the warehouse into a Baldwin's Casuals sweatshop.

The cocksure lothario famously bedded married young mum Deirdre Barlow. Other dalliances resulted in sons: Mark Redman (from his fling with florist Maggie Dunlop), and Adam Barlow (courtesy of his disastrous marriage to Ken's daughter, Susan), whose existence he didn't know of till years later. In 2005 his factory sidekick Danny Baldwin was gobsmacked to discover that Mike wasn't his doting uncle, as he had previously thought, but actually his dad.

In 2000 manipulative former machinist Linda Sykes revelled in her new status as the fourth Mrs Baldwin, but it was Mike's third wife, good-hearted Alma Sedgewick, who proved to be the love of his life. 'I'm not sure Mike could've ever settled down with one woman because he always had the roving eye. But I really enjoyed working with Amanda Barrie and when Alma died from cancer with Mike by her bedside it really hit a nerve with people. I remember I even had a hardened London cab driver who, when asked how much I owed him, said: "It's on me mate – me and the missus were in tears the other night. Keep up the good work!"'

In 1953 Battersea-born Johnny Briggs starred in the first British x-rated movie *Cosh Boy*, alongside Joan Collins. In 1960 he made his television debut in Granada drama *The Younger Generation* and has appeared in over fifty films, including three *Carry On*s. In 1974 he popped up fleetingly in *Corrie* as a truck driver, he then had a recurring role in motel soap *Crossroads* before being offered a more long-term return to Weatherfield.

'The producer, Bill Podmore, had noticed ratings for the *Street* weren't as high down south and wondered if putting a Londoner in the show would help. So, to cut a long story short, he brought me in for three months and it went up to number one in the ratings in the London area. The rest, as they say, is history...'

↑↑ The factory boss's affair with Deirdre becomes a storyline sensation.
↑ Cheery times with third wife Alma.
← Mike's heart-rending final moments.

Occupations: Factory owner and businessman.
On screen: 1976–2006
Defining moment: In 1983 Mike has a tumultuous affair with married ex-girlfriend Deirdre Barlow and kicks off a bitter lifelong feud with her irked husband Ken.

'Your trouble is yer soft. You see life through rose-coloured specs. Or you bury yer head in the sand altogether if there's summut you don't want to see.'

Albert to Ken

Kevin and his mates then hid from his father's wrath by sneaking into the back of the warehouse storeroom. The youths spent the night hiding out there and in the morning they fled, leaving a cigarette smouldering in an armchair. Gradually the fire began to spread, and when warehouse worker Edna Gee opened the door, hoping no one would notice her sneaking off for a crafty cigarette, she was immediately engulfed in flames. The alarm was raised and the staff evacuated the smoke-filled warehouse, which was full of flammable goods.

As the fireman battled unsuccessfully to control the destruction, supervisor Ivy Tilsley (*see page 90*) frantically searched the vicinity for best friend Edna Gee, who was nowhere to be seen. When the fire was finally extinguished, all that was left of the building was a gutted shell, and it was left to an inconsolable Ivy to break the news to Fred that his wife had met such a terrible end. The following year, the warehouse was refurbished and was back in business when cockney wideboy Mike Baldwin (*see opposite*) roared into Weatherfield and opened his second Baldwin's Casuals denim factory there.

When volatile lovers Deirdre and Ray suddenly announced they were getting married, there were more than a few raised eyebrows, particularly from Len and Jerry who thought their mate Ray was out of his mind. For a start, Ray was Deirdre's boss at the yard, and quite a bit older than her, and only a matter of months had passed since Deirdre had been about to marry Billy. Plus, the ballsy secretary was about as far as you could get from the submissive, stay-at-home type that usually caught the eye of ladies' man, Ray.

Tragedy as the warehouse goes up in flames.

Ivy Brennan

Played by **Lynne Perrie**

Unable to stand another moment with her philandering one-legged husband Don, the staunchly Catholic battle-axe took her leave of Weatherfield in 1994 to join a uncompromising religious commune. She had a stroke and died peacefully while there, but even from beyond the grave 'Poison Ivy' still managed to meddle with those she'd left behind. In 1996 both her best mate Vera Duckworth and granddaughter Sarah Louise Platt became convinced they'd seen Ivy's ghost haunting the street, but it was the unearthing of her diary ten years later that was to cause the most trouble, when an already unstable David discovered Ivy's rage at former daughter-in-law Gail for wanting to abort him.

Factory worker Ivy Tilsley first appeared on *Coronation Street* in 1971, but it was eight years later that she took up residence at Number 5 with her adored son Brian and her affable first husband, Bert. She became a character viewers loved to hate and was notorious as Mike Baldwin's militant shop steward and for her savage rows with Gail. Four years after Bert died of a stroke, she married widowed cabbie Don Brennan, but after Brian's murder in 1989 and grouchy Don's affair with a barmaid, Ivy became increasingly bitter and solitary.

Lynne Perrie had worked briefly as a bus conductor and in a sock factory before she started singing in clubs and went on to become a regular support act for The Beatles. Her breakthrough acting role was as Mrs Casper in Ken Loach's award winning film, *Kes*, which brought her to the attention of Granada's casting directors.

Known as 'Little Miss Dynamite' due to her vibrant personality, over the years Lynne battled with addiction and mental-health problems, and then a heart attack in 2000 left her unable to perform. The faded star later died following a stroke in March 2006 at the age of seventy-four.

Helen Worth remembers, 'For her to come into the *Street* was her life's ambition and it was very sad the way it all ended. But while she was here Lynne was a larger-than-life person in every way. She had such energy about her and she kind of swept you along with it – I was a lot younger but sometimes you just couldn't quite keep up with her!'

The Tilsleys are chipper as they move into Number 5.

Her second marriage to Don isn't a happy union.

Ivy has another clash with former daughter-in-law Gail.

Occupations: Factory supervisor and Bettabuy shelf-stacker.
On screen: 1971–1972, 1974, 1975, 1976–1994
Defining moment: In 1991 Ivy sees Martin's planned adoption of Nick as an insult to the memory of her beloved Brian, so she informs social services that Gail and Martin are unfit parents.

➔ Eyebrows are raised when Ray and Deirdre announce their engagement.

'He's a pint and baccy merchant for all his airs and fancy talk. He's a lout, a loudmouth and a trouble-maker. I bet he watches telly in his stocking feet, picking his nose at same time...'

Blanche on Ray

Never one to hold back on her opinions, Deirdre's mum Blanche called her daughter a fool and made it quite clear she didn't think Ray was any better. As far as Rovers cleaner Hilda was concerned, there could only be one possible explanation for the couple's haste to get wed – Deirdre was pregnant. Actually, she wasn't, just young, loved-up and impetuous.

It wasn't the most romantic of wedding days, by any stretch of the imagination. Deirdre was married in her work suit at the local registry office and there was a half-hearted gathering at the Rovers afterwards. The couple missed the train for their honeymoon in London and ended up whiling away their wedding night at Blanche's. The next day the Langtons gave up on the idea of London altogether and enjoyed a lovey-dovey newlywed picnic in a Weatherfield park instead.

Meanwhile, Mavis (*see page 70*) wasn't having much luck in her bid to find a suitor. For a start she bought two gross of misshapen tights from a sweet-talking but dodgy door-to-door salesmen called Les Buckley (each pair had one leg shorter than the other), then she joined a dating agency under a false name, only to be paired on a restaurant blind date with a stunned Ken!

After a mysterious phone call, Len sprang into action and began to spring-clean Number 9 in preparation for an unnamed houseguest. The local gossips were chomping at the bit to find out the identity of his visitor, none more so than Hilda (who'd been paid

TOP FIVE Eddie Yeats' scams

The bin man with a heart of gold was a natural when it came to fleecing his neighbours...

1975 Spotting a money-making opportunity, Eddie and Stan bought a guard dog called Fury and branched out into the security business. Fury patrolled Len's yard but a thief broke in, stealing hundreds of pounds' worth of copper piping – and the dog!

1977 Eddie sold uppity Rovers landlady Annie a carpet with her initials monogrammed on it in gold. She was horrified to discover it was an off-cut snatched from the Alhambra Weatherfield Bingo Hall, which was being refurbished.

1979 He bagged a weekend job on an ice-cream van and used it as a cover to sell beer illegally on Sundays. He was making a tidy sum from the queue of thirsty dads until the police caught on and breathalysed him.

1979 Eddie peddled one of Hilda's atrocious modern-art paintings to Annie for 20 guineas, claiming it to be by an up-and-coming young artist. When Mrs Walker discovered it was by her own cleaning lady she was furious and vowed to get her revenge.

1982 Hilda had her heart set on a new three-piece suite but was turned down by the hire-purchase company as a bad credit risk. So when Eddie was paid a fiver to dispose of an old sofa, he sold it on to the Ogdens at a profit, calling it a 'modern antique'.

to dust off his spare bedroom) and Deirdre, who'd agreed to wash his sheets. Even Annie's subtle interrogation skills couldn't get a secretive Len to spill the beans. Then, just as Hilda had finished her cleaning duties and slammed the door of Number 9 behind her, a familiar face sauntered around the corner into Coronation Street, suitcase in hand. After three years in Newcastle, Elsie was back in Weatherfield, where she belonged.

Over a cup of tea Elsie opened her heart to Len and explained she and Alan were having a trial separation, although it was unlikely they'd ever be reconciled. Later, when she made her comeback in the Rovers with old friend Len, jaws dropped. Elsie was the last person they were expecting to be bedding down at Number 9, and before you could say 'handbags at dawn' she was once again caught up in a battle of wills with her old foe Ena, who immediately made Elsie feel at home by telling her, with a twinkle in her eye, that she was showing her age. As Elsie commented ruefully to Len, it was as if she'd never been away.

'I've always said that woman were a Jezebel. And this is proof of it. I mean, why else would anybody want a pink bath?'

Hilda on Elsie

The rover returns: Elsie pours out her woes to Len.

'You know it's extraordinary. They seem to act like blotting paper to each other. Soaking up each other's woes.'

Annie on Len and Elsie

Soon Elsie moved back into Number 11 and became manageress of lingerie shop Sylvia's Separates, earning herself £40 a week. She took on chirpy Gail Potter (*see page 110*) as her assistant and they formed a close mother-daughter-style bond, so much so that Elsie invited Gail to move in as her lodger. Elsie felt settled being back in Coronation Street, and she soon reverted back to her old surname of 'Tanner' and decided not to return to Newcastle to give married life with Alan another go.

As Hilda Odgen knew only too well, all was not right in the world if her sloth-like other half Stan was off his beer. So when Stanley turned down a pint in the Rovers, opting for a cup of tea and a quiet night in at Number 13 instead, Hilda feared the worst. Despite the fact that he swore he was ill, Hilda insisted he went out to work, but later that day he fainted and collapsed while cleaning windows at the top of his ladder. After a stay in hospital, Stan was diagnosed with a middle-ear condition, which meant his sense of balance was all over the place and therefore window cleaning was out of the question. He worried that someone would pinch his round while he recovered, so Hilda decided to take it on for him. Armed with a bucket, a shammy and a helping hand from Eddie, warbling window cleaner Hilda went down a storm with the locals and more than doubled Stan's usual takings!

Mavis became Weatherfield's answer to Catherine Cookson when she secretly penned a steamy bodice-ripper, *Song Of A Scarlett Summer*, drawing her inspiration from the goings on in the Street and using the same initials as the residents for her characters. Len became Lionel Forrest and Stan was transformed into the very dashing Santos Olivier. Much to her own amusement, Rita was renamed Rosalind Lane, not that Mavis had given her Kabin colleague permission to read her opus. While the unlikely author was making the elevenses, Rita had taken the manuscript from Mavis's handbag and read it out loud to amused customer Deirdre. 'Rosalind glided onto the shadowy balcony and into the waiting arms of Lionel. Her white throat gleamed in the moonlight as she raised her face to his, she tossed back her chestnut curls and unable to control his passion Lionel bent his strong mouth to her waiting rosebud lips. Time stood still as his eager hands...' Rita fell silent and then chortled as she read about Lionel's wandering hands. Needless to say, the possibly libellous novel was rejected by publishers.

In 1976, fed up with forever being down on her luck, Hilda began entering competitions in a bid to improve her quality of life and won a trolley dash around a local delicatessen. She was very excited at the news, but first the Ogdens had to work out what exactly a delicatessen was...

The couple practised for their dash in the corner shop, but thanks to Hilda removing all the wrappers from the tins she'd bought, Stan found himself eating dog food for his tea that evening. On the day of the actual event, Stan's dodgy back gave way so a gung-ho Deirdre stepped into the breach and, alongside a breakneck Hilda, managed to grab £107-worth of products. To Hilda's delight the deli owner agreed to swap her posh grub winnings for £75 – which she then used to pay off an outstanding TV rental bill. However, she did keep one special item from the deli dash, and that night the Ogdens settled down to a supper of caviar and chips.

Stan's luck definitely wasn't in during the May Day Bank Holiday street party, organised by Ken, which included Morris dancers, a barrel organ, and a Punch and Judy show. Stan had also invited an old army chum to entertain the gathered throng – a liquor-loving escapologist named Wally. Having scrounged a lift to Weatherfield with a brewery rep, Wally was already more than merry by the time

Hilda scores over a hundred pounds' worth of delicacies during her trolley dash.

he arrived, yet still managed to perform successfully. When he challenged anyone to have a go for a fiver bet, Stan stepped up to the mark, convinced he knew the tricks of Wally's trade. Unfortunately for Stan, though, he'd piled on the pounds since he'd last tried the illusion and because of his girth was now unable to free himself. Stan spent the rest of the day trussed up in Wally's padlocked chains while the locals attempted to find the elusive escapologist who had disappeared with the key. Eventually they discovered him sozzled in the ladies at the Rovers!

For Deirdre 1977 was a year of mixed emotions, starting on an upbeat note with the birth of her daughter, Tracy. She'd been in and out of hospital with false alarms and it was only when she was discharged and home alone (having forced husband Ray to attend the community centre dance) that Deirdre at last went into labour and had to call an ambulance herself.

Deirdre Barlow

Played by **Anne Kirkbride**

As nosy neighbour Vera Duckworth once observed: 'She could fill a Sunday paper on her own. There's a lot goes on behind them glasses you don't know about.' While there's no doubt Deirdre has tried to be a good mother, wife and daughter, it's also true she's made some seriously bad decisions and her attempts to follow her heart have frequently ended in gossip-worthy scandal. None more so than in 1998, when the innocent, bespectacled 'Weatherfield One' was imprisoned for fraud after being scammed by bogus-pilot boyfriend, Jon Lindsay. Then there were her marriages to older builder Ray, cheating Ken, Moroccan toy-boy Samir, and her famed affair with cockney lothario Mike Baldwin, all of which ensured Deirdre Hunt-Langton-Barlow-Rachid-Barlow remained the talk of the town.

'I originally came to Granada for a completely different interview, it was a bit part for a spin-off they were thinking of doing about the bin men characters, which never got off the ground. While I was there I got told to nip down the corridor to the *Coronation Street* office because they were looking for someone to just do three lines in a pub. I didn't even have to read for it. I had a good Northern accent so I was hired.'

The young Oldham-born actress had been spotted by the show's casting directors while in an ITV *Saturday Night Theatre* play, *Another Sunday and Sweet FA,* penned by former *Street* scriptwriter, Jack Rosenthal.

'My very first scene was in a pub called The Vine with Alan Howard. I was the dolly bird he was chatting up and my sole purpose of being there was to annoy Elsie. Then I had a brief visit to the actual street when Elsie was away and Billy Walker organised a party at Number 11, as Deirdre was one of the girls invited. I had a brilliantly funny speech, written by Harry Kershaw, where she was drunk and talked about what she wanted most in the world was a wardrobe – because she lived in rented rooms and all her clothes were just hanging over chairs. Then she falls asleep on the bed and Elsie comes back the next day to find this girl coming down the stairs and gets the wrong idea. I was brought back more permanently when Sandra Gough [who played Irma Barlow]

50 CORONATION ST. ICON

left unexpectedly and they were stuck for storylines.'

Throughout all the upheavals in Deirdre's life there have been several constants: her husband Ken (after separating in 1990 and divorcing in 1992 they remarried in 2005, when her ex, Ray, died at the reception); her murderous handful of a daughter, Tracy; and her acid-tongued mother, Blanche Hunt. It may not have been the most idyllic of family set-ups, but they were all she had.

'I am privileged, really privileged to spend so much time working with Bill [Roache]. That man has taught me so much about life and we're soul mates, we really are. And we've both loved working with all our Tracys. Dawn [Acton] was in it for the longest from the age of nine, so I really saw her grow up and she became our little girl.'

In 2010 emotions ran high for both Anne and Deirdre after the sudden death of much-loved veteran actress Maggie Jones, who played waspish Blanche.

'Maggie and I became great friends straight away and continued to be so until the day she died. We'd just had Maggie's memorial when we started filming the death of Blanche, and on the day I did Blanche's eulogy I ended up having to do nine takes and I was drained by the end of it. That night when I got home I just dropped my bag in the hallway, sat in the chair with my coat on and cried for an hour. It had all been so emotional, but it did give Maggie and Blanche a great send off.'

The actress also remembers a much happier time when she met her future husband, David Beckett, on the show in 1990. He came in to play her love-interest, joiner Dave Barton, and provided Deirdre with a manly shoulder to cry on following Ken's affair with his secretary, Wendy Crozier.

'He's the best thing that has ever happened to me; so with Bill as my partner on-screen and Dave as my husband off-screen, I've been very lucky with my men and I've got *Coronation Street* to thank for that. People often ask me if I'll ever leave, but this is my life, it's really hard work, but what else would I do? *Coronation Street* is the only thing I'm good at!'

'Fag ash Lil with a glass of Merlot in her hand? Why d'you think I got into drugs in the first place? To get away from you with your glasses and your necklines and your moaning and your coughing and everything stinking of fags!'

Tracy to Deirdre

- The Langtons make themselves at home.
- Tracy with her parents in happier times.
- Loved-up with toy boy Samir.
- Tracy's murder trial drives Deirdre to drink.
- Blanche reminds her daughter and son-in-law who's boss.
- Deirdre feels a fool after falling for Lewis's crooked charms.

Occupations: Former secretary, corner shop assistant, council worker and bookies' assistant.
On screen: 1972, 1973–
Defining moment: In 1998 her boyfriend Jon Lindsay commits credit-card fraud in her name; she is jailed but is later released when his ex-wife testifies against him.

'James Bond? Now that's a role suited to me many talents.'

Ray

Born in the early hours of 24 January, Tracy Langton weighed 8lb 4oz and while Blanche cooed over her first grandchild, she could only give Ray the evil eye for failing to be there when Deirdre had needed him. But more importantly, after weeks of panicking about the birth, as she cradled her little one in her arms new mum Deirdre was happy at last. By the time Tracy won the *Weatherfield Gazette*'s Beautiful Baby Competition, the young mum couldn't have loved her daughter more. (Not that Deirdre had any idea then of the trauma that cute pink bundle was to cause her in later life.)

But Deirdre's happiness was shortlived. While the rest of the Street were raising their glasses at a party celebrating Annie's fortieth year at the Rovers, Deirdre was followed home from a keep-fit class and indecently assaulted underneath the viaduct. Back at Number 5 after the attack, Deirdre was distressed and in a state of shock, but despite Emily's pleas she refused to call the police. Undeterred, Emily took helpless husband Ray to one side and begged him to make Deirdre reconsider, insisting this man needed to be put away. However, upon reading the local newspaper Deirdre and Ray discovered the man had already been arrested after he'd been reported by another woman he'd attacked that night.

In the weeks that followed Deirdre remained haunted by her ordeal and sank into a depression, often not leaving the house for

days on end. She refused point blank when a worried Ray suggested she see a doctor and shrank away from him whenever he tried to be intimate with her. She disappeared completely a month later and Ray feared the worst when he heard she'd last been seen heading for the canal by Sylvia's Separates' assistant Suzie Birchall. But there was no sign of her there and Ray and Emily decided it was time to call the police.

Meanwhile, a sobbing Deirdre was standing motionless on the side of a motorway bridge staring at the traffic and was only snapped out of her trance-like state by a lorry driver asking for directions. Pulling herself together, she headed home to a relieved Ray and confessed she had contemplated suicide. She agreed to see a psychiatrist but their marriage never really recovered.

After years of dilly-dallying Len and Rita finally tied the knot in April 1977 at St Mary's Church – Len having proposed formally just as Rita was leaving Weatherfield for a job as a cabaret singer at a Tenerife nightspot. She turned him down at first, but changed her mind in the departure lounge and the plane left without her. It was a mushy moment that thrilled romance-novel-loving Mavis no end (who was Rita's bridesmaid).

- Newborn Tracy wins the *Weatherfield Gazette*'s Beautiful Baby competition.
- A teary Deirdre sinks into depression after being indecently assaulted.
- The Faircloughs celebrate their nuptials.

1970s Births

Tracy Lynette (Deirdre and Ray Langton) 24 January 1977

Rule Britannia! The Rovers regulars celebrate the Queen's Silver Jubilee in patriotic style.

For Ken the year was about taking fatherhood seriously, and when his son Peter arrived from his grandparents' home in Glasgow during the summer holidays for quality time with his estranged father, Ken decided that a hiking adventure in the Peak District would be the ideal opportunity for father–son bonding. However, things didn't go quite according to plan when Ken fell and twisted his ankle. Fortunately, Peter turned out to be a quick-thinking, outdoorsy type and managed to summon the mountain rescue service, so they were airlifted to the nearest hospital.

'You can't rehearse majesty, Mr Tatlock. It's either something you've got or you haven't.'
Annie

Back on the Street plans for the Queen's silver jubilee celebrations were underway and the Rovers regulars decided on a parade float with the theme of 'Britain Through The Ages'. Despite Emily being earmarked for the role, Annie went ahead and ordered herself a Queen Elizabeth I costume – hoping to repeat the success of her last fancy-dress appearance. Bet teased a drooling Fred that she was going as Lady Godiva, but on the day she was instead suitably patriotic as Britannia. Eddie went back to basics as a caveman, Ena was resplendent as Queen Victoria and Ken – rather incongruously, considering his recent hiking debacle – was mountaineer Sir Edmund Hillary. Unfortunately for all of them Stan had flattened the batteries of the brewery lorry by leaving the lights on all night, so the regal simper was soon wiped off Annie's face when she had to hitch up her crinoline and clamber off her throne to walk in the carnival procession instead.

Vera Duckworth

Played by **Elizabeth Dawn**

She was Coronation Street's original neighbour from hell with her foghorn voice and stone-cladded pretensions, yet gossiping factory worker Vera Duckworth went on to become one of Weatherfield's best-loved residents. Whether she was raging at Mike Baldwin over the contents of her pay packet or tricking long-suffering husband Jack into believing she'd served up his beloved pigeons in a pie, there was never a dull moment when Vera was at full throttle.

In 2008 the couple were due to move to her dream destination of Blackpool, but she never made it and died peacefully while asleep in her armchair at Number 9. When a bereft Jack discovered her body, the nation reached as one for their tissues.

Before joining the cast Liz Dawn had slogged away in a toothpaste-tube factory by day and sold wigs at night to make ends meet. After winning a talent contest at a holiday camp near Scarborough, she embarked on a career as a club singer, which lead to minor television roles in the likes of *Z Cars* and *Crown Court*.

'I found the *Street* much easier than standing on a stage trying to entertain three or four hundred people, because when I started playing Vera the only person I had to please was the director. I wasn't bothered about the acting as such, I never set out to be an actress – I just needed to earn some decent money. I had three kids under school age and another son, so it was a big thing to get into that programme.

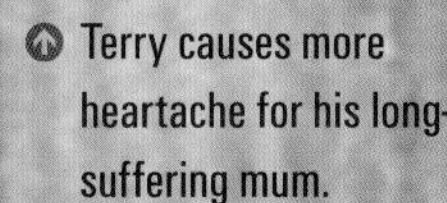

Terry causes more heartache for his long-suffering mum.

Vera prepares to donate her kidney to grandson Paul.

Having a laugh with Tyrone and Molly.

'Luckily, Jack and Vera became so popular we got offered extra jobs at weekends opening shops and turning on Christmas lights. In fact, I think the only thing I didn't open were a toilet – and if the money had been right I'd have done that as well,' chuckles Liz, who was forced to quit the show after thirty-four years because of the effects of emphysema.

'It's funny, because since I left I feel as if I am on an extended holiday. Everywhere I go people are so lovely and say, "How are you?" and smile. I just think I'm so lucky to have people smile at me on a daily basis, and I've only got Vera to thank for that.'

Occupations: Baldwin's Casuals machinist, Rovers landlady and Roy's Rolls fryer-upper.
On screen: 1974, 1976–2008
Defining moment: Signing with a dating agency in 1983 to catch cheating hubby Jack, then surprising him on their date disguised in a red wig.

1977

It was in the middle of a blazing row that the Odgens learnt they'd won a luxury second honeymoon, when a Mr Pritchard from the company that made the new 'young moderns' beverage, 'Loving Cup', turned up on their doorstep. The prize was a night in the bridal suite of a five-star hotel, plus a whopping £25 spending money. Their freebie was all down to Hilda's winning competition slogan that outlined the recipe for a happy marriage: 'Be a mistress as well as a wife, and your husband will still be your boyfriend.' With Hilda in a pristine new frock and Stan bristling in his Sunday best, the Oggies were chauffeur-driven to the hotel, where they sipped vintage champagne as Hilda fondled the fancy cushions and marvelled at the very idea of matching bedside lamps. Hilda was in her element – and when a sozzled, snoring Stan fell asleep before she'd put her seductive nylon negligée (borrowed from Rita) to good use, she didn't mind. She'd felt like royalty and it didn't get much better than that. However, it was back down to earth with a bump when the Ogdens arrived at home at Number 13 the next day.

OVERHEARD

Competition winners Hilda and Stan enjoy a second honeymoon, 1977.

A FIVE-STAR HOTEL SUITE. 6.30PM. HILDA IS DOING HER MAKE-UP AT THE DRESSING TABLE. STAN IS MAKING HIMSELF ANOTHER WHISKY FROM THE MINI BAR. THERE IS A KNOCK AT THE DOOR – IT IS ROOM SERVICE.

TONI: Champagne sir. With the compliments of the management. Aren't you the lucky ones?

HE MOVES INTO THE ROOM.

STAN: You couldn't get me a pint instead, could you mate? I could kill a pint.

TONI: You can't be drinking beer tonight, sir. Can he madam? I bet madam's tastes don't run to beer tonight, do they madam?

HILDA: (IN HER BEST VOICE) They very rarely do actually. I hope it's properly chilled.

TONI: Saw to it myself, madam. It's colder than a dead foot, if you pardon the expression. (HE POPS THE CORK OUT) Ooh, always frightens me to death does that.

HILDA: Makes your nose go all funny just to look at it doesn't it?

TONI: (HANDING THEM GLASSES) Madam. Sir. And may all your troubles be little ones.

HILDA: It's a bit late for that.

STAN: Would you like a glass, mate? You're very welcome.

TONI: No thank you, sir. I'd be skipping about like a baby fawn all night if I did.

TONI LEAVES THE ROOM.

HILDA: Hey it's going to me head already. Still, that's the idea, isn't it? You know I can't believe it. A fabulous hotel, champagne, dinner for two, probably prawn cocktails and all that. It's a dream come true. (SHE PAUSES) Do you really think I look smashing?

STAN: Yeah, I said.

HILDA: Give us a kiss.

STAN: Eh?

HILDA: You heard. Come on you big lump. This is us second honeymoon. Not us first. Though I do remember you weren't all that backward in coming forward then.

THEY KISS.

STAN: What's that lipstick taste of?

HILDA: (WITH RELISH) Woman, Stanley. Woman.

When mild-mannered wages clerk Ernest clocked in for another run-of-the-mill shift at the factory on the 11 January 1978, he had no idea that within hours he'd be staring down the barrel of a sawn-off shotgun and fighting for his life. Having seen boss Mike leave the factory and head for the pub, two young thugs burst in and confronted Ernest as he sorted out that week's wage packets in his office. Ernest was a gentle person, but he was also a man strong on principle, and so he decided that by keeping a cool head and by appealing to the thugs' better nature he might be able to foil their robbery attempt. His plan might have worked had Mike not returned unexpectedly and accidentally knocked the arm of the man holding the gun – which went off and hit Ernest at point-blank range. The robbers scarpered and a shell-shocked Mike knelt down next to his bleeding employee and called the emergency services.

⊕⊕ There's heartbreak for Emily when Ernest is murdered during a factory wages raid.

Emily was oblivious to all this as she happily browsed through holiday brochures with corner shopkeeper Renee Roberts, setting her heart on a cultural trip to Greece with Ernest later in the year. She fainted when she first heard about the raid, then she rushed to the Weatherfield Infirmary to be by her husband's side. But after hours of surgery Emily was given the crushing news that Ernest had died on the operating table. Guilt-ridden, Mike revealed that Ernest had been shot because he wouldn't hand over the wages and insisted his loyal employee had died a hero.

'Killed. That's the word, Ken. That's what's happened to Ernest. He's been killed. And now he's been buried. And he's lying in that silly box in that cold hole and I want him back, I want him back!'

Emily

Meanwhile, when Ena complained about being sleep-deprived, the generous residents had a whip round and raised £40 for the pensioner to buy a new bed. But proud Ena declared she didn't accept charity and returned their cash. It was Emily who came up with the cunning plan of diverting Ena, while someone else broke into her flat and replaced the bed. So while Albert invited Ena out for a drink, Ray and Eddie set up her new divan. Later in the Rovers, a grim-faced Ena announced her bed – which contained all her life savings – had been stolen. The shocked regulars were lost for words, but then Ena started to cackle, admitted she was winding them up and thanked everyone for their good will.

With Deirdre still shaken by her attack, the Langton's relationship began to deteriorate. The bespectacled mum was not impressed when Ray forgot their third anniversary either, probably because his mind was on other matters – namely his burgeoning affair with waitress Janice Stubbs. Len and Emily found out about Ray's extra-curricular activities and warned him to stop, but he wouldn't listen. Eventually, Deirdre began to suspect Ray was seeing someone behind her back and was proved right when she quizzed Emily on the matter. When she confronted Ray he insisted the affair was over and in the past.

During the weeks that followed, Deirdre pondered the future of her marriage, before making up her mind that a new beginning was what they needed, maybe in Australia or New Zealand. Blanche hit the roof when she found out the reason for the move and headed straight round to the builder's yard to give her son-in-law a piece of her mind. She even slapped him round the face for good measure.

Thankfully, at their Rovers farewell party a few weeks later Deirdre had developed cold feet and realised she was about to make a terrible mistake. She admitted to a relieved Blanche that she could never trust Ray again and that his affair had brought back the horrible empty feelings she'd experienced after being assaulted under the viaduct. When she told him their marriage was over he begged for a second chance, but Deirdre refused and a chastened Ray left Weatherfield for a new life in Holland.

Back at the factory, Mike's hatred of parting with his cash landed him in hot water when he refused to buy cleaner Hilda a much-needed new broom. Fuming, Hilda went on strike until she was given a replacement. Instead of giving in, Mike sacked her. Union rep Ivy demanded Hilda be reinstated immediately, but Mike, stubborn as ever, refused. The factory women voted to strike alongside Hilda, which left Mike to man the sewing machines all by himself. When the picket line descended into a full-scale riot – which saw the factory's van smashed and the police called – Mike finally relented and gave Hilda her job back – and a new broom!

Ivy leads the charge as the factory workers strike against Hilda's sacking.

Picture perfect: an appreciation of Hilda Ogden's infamous 'muriel' and her iconic flying ducks

Even now, twenty-three years after it disappeared, Hilda's mural remains one of the most enduring images of *Coronation Street* – and thanks to her mispronunciation it will forever be affectionately known as 'the muriel'.

There were actually two murals. The first appeared in July 1976 when Hilda decided she wanted to redecorate Number 13. A reluctant Stan was given a tenner and the task of tracking down some fancy wallpaper she'd seen in a magazine. However, half the wallpaper he bought was faded and unusable.

New lodger Eddie found the mountain mural as a replacement and papered it over the whole back wall. Which mountain range it depicted was never established – Stan thought it was the Canadian Rockies while Hilda believed it to be the Alps. Whatever the landform, Hilda was thrilled to bits and couldn't wait to show it off to the likes of Annie and Bet.

Annie felt giddy on seeing the range for the first time and sighed, 'Would you mind if I sat facing the other way until I'm acclimatised?' While Bet quipped, 'What do you do if there's an avalanche?'

While there never was an avalanche, there was a landslide of soot a year later when Suzie and Gail tried to clean Elsie's chimney with the novel method of dropping a brick down it. Except they got the wrong chimney and Hilda, Stan and her mural ended up covered in ashes. 'Me mountains look like a slagheap and me snowy tops are like a coalman's hat,' Hilda wailed.

Fortunately, it cleaned up, but her muriel wasn't so lucky when Stan's bath overflowed and ruined the precious picture. In her desperate efforts to repair it, Hilda tore it and was inconsolable – until Stan bought another mural of a cliffside seascape. Hilda loved it, and at about this time the three plaster ducks flew in, with the middle duck always looking to plummet into the sea.

When Hilda moved to the country in 1987, taking her ducks with her, she sold the house to previous lodgers, the Websters, who papered over the iconic wall. They rediscovered it in 2002 when, after stripping the walls, the decorator offered to restore it, but he was quickly turned down. However, Kevin briefly became moist-eyed and the couple indulged in a rare moment of nostalgia. He sighed: 'She was a good'un was Hilda. That mural, it brings back a lot of memories...'

'I've come in here more times than I care to remember. Cold. Wet. Bone tired. Not a penny in me purse. And seeing them ducks and that muriel... well they've kept me hand away from the gas tap. And that's a fact.'

Jack Duckworth

Played by **William Tarmey**

Veteran *Street* producer Bill Podmore paid this tribute to William Tarmey in his memoirs: 'As Jack Duckworth, hen-pecked hubby, would-be Romeo and loser in life, Bill found his fame and fortune. It couldn't have happened to a nicer man.'

Indeed, the former construction worker-turned-club singer had started out as a Rovers extra before being promoted to the role of Jack, the brow-beaten husband of brash factory worker Vera Duckworth. His first appearance in the *Street* was at Gail and Brian Tilsley's wedding in 1979.

But regardless of Jack's enduring appeal, Bill still doesn't consider himself to be an actor: 'I've worked with some wonderful actors on this show but I'm still just a singer who got very lucky. Liz [Dawn, who played Vera] and I were a right pair because neither of us were the best when it came to learning our lines, so we had fun – put it that way. I had lines on everything – on the cornflake box, in the newspaper, even in the bottom of the flippin' sink if I was stood by it.'

Bill more than proved his acting stripes in 2008 when Jack was left heartbroken after his 'little swamp-duck' Vera passed away unexpectedly in her armchair. 'They were very upsetting scenes to do, and if I watch them now I still shed a tear, because I know I was saying goodbye to a dear friend.'

The Duckworths' marriage was tempestuous, and the former Jack the Lad's cheating ways ensured comedic fireworks when Vera found out. In 1982 all hell broke loose when Jack bedded Bet Lynch, and in 2004 he used his cunning to help the Rovers women's bowling team win a match by dressing in drag as Ida Fagg. He was so convincing that Vera feared Jack and Ida were having an affair.

'People always assumed Liz and I were married in real life as well, even now. A lady asked me the other day: "How's your Vera?" And I said: "Still dead."'

In 2009 Jack moved to suburbia with his new lady friend, Connie Rathbone, and the following year Bill announced his full-time retirement as Weatherfield's most dedicated pigeon fancier. 'I'll be sorry to say goodbye, but I'm pleased that when I leave I'm leaving it in the hands of some very good kids – there's some smashing talent on the show and I'll be honoured to pass on the torch.'

Finger-wagging Vera bends Jack's ear.

Terry and Vera are unimpressed by work-shy Jack.

Cross-dressing as lady-bowler, Ida Fagg.

Occupation: Rovers cellarman-turned-landlord.
On screen: 1979, 1981–2010
Defining moment: In 1995 he inherits £30,000 and buys the Rovers Return – but three years later the skint Duckies are forced to sell up.

'A public house isn't just somewhere that serves beer. It's a focal point of the community in which we live.'

Annie

By the way that Annie and Bet reacted when the Rovers was chosen to appear on the cover of *Over The Bar*, the new Newton and Ridley in-house magazine, you'd have thought they'd been asked to grace the front pages of *Vogue*. On the day of the shoot, dressed up to the nines, the pair pouted and preened for the camera while a disinterested Betty made little effort and continued to serve ale. When the photographer Norman Hill popped back with the proofs a few days later, Bet and Annie were overjoyed with the results and began counting down the days until the magazine's publication. However, when a copy did finally arrive, much to Annie and Bet's fury it was Betty and slobby customer Eddie who were smiling back at them from the front cover!

Deirdre searches for baby Tracy under the load of the overturned lorry.

In 1979 near disaster quite literally hit the Rovers when the driver of a passing lorry had a heart attack at the wheel, and his heavy goods' vehicle sped out of control and ploughed into the crowded pub. Mike and Len were badly injured and Alf was discovered lying unconscious under a pile of rubble. But perhaps it was Deirdre who suffered the most on that fateful day; she'd left baby Tracy outside the Rovers in her pram while she quickly nipped inside to have a word with Annie. While they were in the back of the pub they'd heard the smash and Deirdre dashed out to find the lorry impaled into the building exactly where she'd left Tracy in her pram.

When the lorry driver was pronounced dead Deirdre became hysterical, screaming out Tracy's name, and aided by Betty and Ken she attempted to search for her baby under the wreckage. But there was no sign of her daughter in the debris. Emily bundled a shocked Deirdre back to Number 3 where the traumatised mother convinced herself Tracy was dead. When Emily turned her back for a moment, Deirdre also disappeared.

However, unbeknown to anyone, Tracy had been snatched by Sally Norton, an unstable girl Deirdre had befriended in the maternity hospital who was still dealing with the fact she'd been forced to give up her own fatherless baby for adoption. As the police located Sally in the park playing mum with baby Tracy, Deirdre was found suicidal on the canal bank and would only step away from the edge when she realised she was being the told the truth and that Tracy really had been found unharmed.

Rita was not a happy woman when hubby Len informed her, just as she was in the middle of packing, that he was too busy at the yard to go on their caravanning holiday in Morecambe. When he condescendingly explained to her that work came before a holiday, Rita felt like flinging her suitcase right at him, such was her fury. So later in the Rovers, when Bet moaned she had nothing planned for her week off, Rita invited her barmaid pal instead.

At the caravan site a saucy Bet picked up two men and invited them round for a cup of tea. The next day the men took Bet and Rita out fishing, and that night they all cooked their catch on the caravan stove. After dinner the men realised they'd lost the keys to their caravans and Rita allowed them to stay the night – so long as they slept in the spare bunks.

'I'm what they used to call in them old Hollywood films, a dangerous woman. Barbara Stanwyck could've done a picture about me.'

Bet

Meanwhile, a guilty Len had decided to pay his wife a surprise visit and burst into the caravan just as Bet and Rita were cooking their new friends' breakfast, causing red faces and hasty explanations all around. In the end, Len remained unconvinced all was as it seemed and gruffly sent the men packing.

Unimpressed by the amateurish designs of her Christmas cards, Hilda decided to take up painting. She even managed to sell one of her pieces of modern art (created by randomly splattering paint at a canvas) for 20 guineas when Eddie conned Annie, claiming it to be by an unknown primitive artist. Overjoyed Hilda split the cash with art-dealer Eddie and later in the Rovers she pretended to be impressed by Annie's thought-provoking new wall hanging. Her boss, surprised at Hilda's good taste, loftily admitted that 'art transcends all barriers'. Later, when Annie, stoney-faced, read a message scrawled on the back: 'Stan – am at bingo. Your dinner's in the oven!', she was not amused.

Gail Potter's mantelpiece was groaning with greetings cards in April – a combination of 'Happy Easter', '21 Today' and perhaps most significantly, 'Congratulations On Your Engagement', because hunky Brian Tilsley had asked her to marry him. It wasn't the most romantic of proposals, but his heart had been in the right place. While the young mechanic was repairing a car Gail had asked him if he wanted to finish with her because she knew his disapproving mother Ivy was making his life a misery. Out of

⬆ Bet's on the pull while holidaying with Rita in Morecambe.

➡ The first of many wedding days for unlucky-in-love Gail.

'Mrs Ogden has just walked into the living room grinning like an idiot and muttering, 'Ignorance is bliss' – if that were the case, of course, she'd be the happiest woman in the world.'

Annie on Hilda

the blue Brian responded by asking if she fancied getting engaged instead. Gail smiled, shrugged her shoulders nonchalantly and muttered, 'Alright then.'

While Ivy refused to attend their engagement drinks in the Rovers, Gail's flirty mum Audrey (*see page 118*) arrived in town and couldn't wait to get the party started, kicking it off with a high-octane conga down the street. Later, widowed cellar-man Fred Gee tried his luck with a tiddly Audrey, but she was more interested in ridiculing his bald patch. The next day, re-thinking his image in order to improve his luck with the ladies, Fred reappeared behind the bar in an ill-fitting toupe, much to the amusement of the regulars.

In November the pretty young things were married at St Boniface's Church with Mike walking the bride down the aisle and her best friend Suzie as her bridesmaid. As the vicar declared them man and wife Ivy began to sob – whether they were tears of joy or tears of despair because she didn't think Gail was good enough for 'Her Brian', no one will ever know – but whatever the reason, Ivy wanted to keep the couple firmly under her thumb. So she allowed them to move in with her and husband Bert at Number 5 while the newlyweds saved a deposit for a home of their own.

The approaching new decade was to bring more joy for Gail and Brian when, at the same time the following year, Gail would be pregnant with their first child, Nicky. But tragedy would also be on the cards for the increasingly volatile young couple...

1970s Marriages

Elsie Tanner and Alan Howard	22 July 1970
Emily Nugent and Ernest Bishop	3 April 1972
Janet Reid and Ken Barlow	29 October 1973
Maggie Clegg and Ron Cooke	10 July 1974
Deirdre Hunt and Ray Langton	7 July 1975
Rita Littlewood and Len Fairclough	20 April 1977
Renee Bradshaw and Alf Roberts	20 March 1978
Gail Potter and Brian Tilsley	28 November 1979

Gail McIntyre

Played by **Helen Worth**

Gail probably thought things couldn't get much worse after third husband Richard Hillman attempted to gas her whole family before drowning them in the canal. But being banged up on a murder charge for killing her pill-popping fourth husband, Joe McIntyre, must come a close second. Then there was her first love, boozer Brian, who cheated on her before he was stabbed to death outside a nightclub. Not forgetting husband number two, Martin Platt, who also played away – but, uniquely when it comes to Gail's spouses, he managed to escape with his life. In short, the former greasy spoon co-owner hasn't had the best of luck when it comes to her gentlemen friends.

'The men in her life all seemed okay when they met her and then they just went wrong – whether that was Gail's fault I don't know! What I do know is it always makes a much better story if Gail isn't happy...'

The black widow's most recent man trouble came in the form of debt-ridden former kitchen fitter Joe McIntyre, who accidentally drowned in Lake Windermere while trying to fake his own death as part of an insurance scam, leaving poor Gail as the police's prime suspect.

'People seem to love seeing Gail go through these hellish situations. She makes them feel their lives aren't that bad. We filmed in a real prison this year and they were all shouting out "Free Gail! Free Gail!" when they saw me, so they were obviously fans of the show. On the other hand there were some scenes Jack [P. Shepherd, who plays David] and I did at the Lakes which we just thought were hysterical. I'm not sure if they were meant to be, but we decided to play the black comedy of it all, because sometimes in life you find yourself in the most horrendous situations and to get through it and survive you have to find the humour.'

'Oh, she loves a drama, that Gail. Practically encourages it. Never happy unless she's got someone else's hands round her throat.'

Blanche

At least the only person Joe managed to kill was himself, unlike smiling assassin Richard Hillman, who at first had seemed perfectly charming but proved to be a murderous psychopath. Over an eighteen-month period the twists and turns of 'Hillmania' took the country by storm and became one of the *Street*'s most gripping and unpredictable plot lines.

- Carefree times with Elsie and Suzie at Number 11.
- Glum-faced with first husband Brian.
- It's a boy! Proud parents Gail and Martin parade baby David.
- Shocked Gail is a tower of strength for pregnant teen Sarah Louise.
- The happy Hillmans hold hands on their wedding day.
- Joe's plan to fake his death leaves Gail gobsmacked.

'The storyline grew from very humble beginnings but ended up being truly remarkable. I don't know if you know but there's a subplot there as well – because I'm not sure that he wasn't brought in to kill me off… but it didn't happen, thankfully.'

Gail Potter's first scene was with Tricia Hopkins (the role Helen had originally auditioned for), whose family had taken over the corner shop. The teenagers were on a bench when builders Ray Langton and Jerry Booth passed by and, knowing Tricia fancied Ray, giggling Gail took the opportunity to playfully flutter her eyelashes at them. Soon she was lodging at Number 11 with her flirty new best mate Suzie Birchall, under the watchful eye of their surrogate mum, Elsie Tanner. Gail lost her virginity to married man Roy Thornley in the stockroom of fashion boutique Sylvia's Separates, where she worked.

'Whenever anyone new arrives you do think back to your own first day because it's such a horrendously daunting experience. I remember I sat out on a windowsill for my first three months because I didn't have the nerve to go in and sit with everyone else in the green room.'

By the time the Wakefield-born actress was twelve years old she had already begun reading children's stories on Granada TV's *Scene At 6.30* and had spent nine months in London's West End as a Von Trapp youngster in *The Sound Of Music*. After graduating from drama school she spent a year with the BBC Radio repertory company and also has six episodes of *Doctor Who* under her belt.

Despite being the show's sixth-longest-serving cast member, Helen reveals it took her an unexpectedly long time to feel truly anchored on *Coronation Street*.

'It will surprise you how late if I was to actually tell you the truth. I think it was when my new family started when Tina [O'Brien, who played Sarah] and Jack came in that I felt properly grounded. I think the first time I felt grown up was Sarah's teenage pregnancy storyline, when I had a family around me. I don't feel that I was doing anything particular before that, then you have these two wonderful young actors come in and you suddenly realise exciting things are happening around you. I have certainly done very well with my children and with my mum – Sue Nicholls came in around ten years after me and that's just been glorious fun from the day she arrived.'

Current occupation: Medical centre receptionist.
On screen: 1974–
Defining moment: In 2001 she falls for financial advisor Richard Hillman after meeting him at Alma's funeral – a decision she lives to regret.

1980s

In 1980 the *Street* celebrated its 2000th episode with the cast still counting four of the original pioneers – William Roache, Pat Phoenix, Doris Speed and Jack Howarth – amongst their number. However, by the end of the decade, either through ill health or old age, only William Roache remained, and he'd been part of one of the biggest storyline sensations ever – the infamous 'will she, won't she' love triangle between a torn Deirdre, her husband Ken and lover Mike Baldwin. Over a two-month period in 1983 the nation waited with baited breath for the young mum to choose between the polar-opposite men in her life. The three actors were to receive a rousing standing ovation later when they were named joint recipients of the *TV Times* Personality Of The Year award.

Johnny Briggs remembers: 'The pubs would close for half an hour when that storyline reached its peak because they used to say no one comes in anymore during *Coronation Street*. They even flashed the result up on the scoreboard at Old Trafford when Manchester United were playing Arsenal: 'Ken and Deirdre reunited! Ken 1 – Mike 0!' and the crowd roared. It was just incredible...'

Christmas Day 1987 saw the exit of yet another legend as Hilda Ogden waved goodbye to Weatherfield. The departure of Jean Alexander was no secret, but the producers had planted several red herrings in the previous months, including a marriage proposal and a vicious attack. Eventually she took up a housekeeper position in Derbyshire and her tear-jerking exit was watched by a whopping 26 million viewers.

Despite the loss of many iconic residents throughout the Eighties, the decade also saw the *Street* looking to the future. In 1982 the go-ahead was given to build a new set on the back lot at Granada Television, much to the relief of the cast who'd dubbed the previous plasterboard exterior set – which was further from the studio and rattled in the wind – as 'the street where the sun never shines'.

Doris Speed proudly laid the foundation stone for the new set and original designer Denis Parkin started work to create the full-size street; this time constructed with authentic, reclaimed Salford brick and roofing slates. With the paint barely dry, it was finished in the nick of time for the arrival of the Queen and the Duke of Edinburgh, who'd been invited to give the new-look street the once-over. With the set decked out in red, white and blue bunting, the royal party made its way down the cobbles as the cast stood in costume outside their houses and took in Weatherfield's grandest visitors to date.

'I was wearing Charles and Diana earrings, which I'd had designed specially, and Prince Philip pointed at them and said: 'I think I recognise those two...' says Julie Goodyear. 'I remember Doris, who was standing next to me outside the Rovers, raising her eyebrows in the Queen's direction and saying very loudly: 'Doesn't her make-up look dreadful!' I just wanted the ground to swallow me up because the Queen must've heard her. But that was typical Doris – she knew what she was doing, I would put money on it!'

As the decade drew to a close an extra Friday episode was added from October 1989. The same year saw the arrival of the lively McDonald clan and the set was further updated, with the old factory and community centre demolished to make way for new business premises – including the relocated Kabin and three modern townhouses with their own pocket-sized gardens. A back lawn instead of a yard? Coronation Street was definitely coming up in the world.

- Larking around to celebrate the show's 2000th episode.
- The Queen gives *Corrie* the royal seal of approval.
- The ever-growing cast gather in the Rovers to toast another decade.

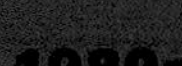

The Roberts were on the up in 1980, with Alf making plans to sell the corner shop and move to Grange-Over-Sands to run a village post office. The couple were full of plans for their new start, and in order to enjoy the country life to the full, Renee decided to learn to drive and enlisted poor Alf as her instructor. As she got to grips with the gear stick, Alf finally secured a buyer for the shop. To celebrate, the pair went on a country drive for a taste of what their new life had in store and treated themselves to a cheesy ploughman's lunch in a quiet village pub.

However, the couple's happiness was short-lived – their return journey ended in tragedy. Renee stalled the car at a set of traffic lights and as Alf hopped out to take the wheel from his wife, a lorry smashed head-on into the car

The Roberts' country drive ends in disaster when Renee is killed by a truck.

Ena swaps her trademark scowl for a rare smile.

and Renee, who later died on the operating table from a ruptured spleen and liver, leaving shell-shocked Alf a widower. After his wife's funeral, Alf decided to withdraw from the sale of the shop and stayed put on the street, where he had the support of his friends and neighbours to help him through his grief.

Renee wasn't the only departure to change the lives of the Weatherfield residents that year. After decades of finger-pointing, stout-swigging and caustic put-downs, battleaxe Ena bid what turned out to be her final farewell to Coronation Street. Having been forced to move out of her flat while the council revamped the community centre, Ena finally put her myriad issues with Elsie to one side when she became a lodger at Chez Tanner. The pair discovered they actually enjoyed each other's company and Ena even invited her old enemy to take Martha's long-vacated stool in the Rovers snug. Eventually, sick of being messed about by the delays to the refurbishments, Ena decided to pack up her hairnet and stay indefinitely with her cousin in Lytham St Annes. The sea air obviously suited Ena and she never returned to the cobbles.

Unlikely lovebirds Ken and Deirdre weren't the only couple to begin dating this year; Emily finally put the ghost of Ernest to rest and accepted the advances of a new man. Pet-shop owner and widower Arnold Swain wooed Emily and the pair wed in September at Weatherfield Registry Office, before honeymooning on the Isle of Wight. But Emily's happy ending wasn't to be, and she discovered Swain was no more a widower than Albert was a ballet dancer. Bigamist Arnold admitted he had walked out on his first wife Margaret – who was still very much alive and living in Bournemouth – to a horrified Emily, who spent a miserable Christmas alone after swallowing her pride and contacting the police about Arnold's double life.

Ken and Deirdre make a date for romance.

Emily discovers one wife isn't enough for bigamist Arnold.

Meanwhile, old soldier Albert had refused to accompany his friend Monty Shawcross to the London Remembrance Day Parade, but was heartbroken when he was informed Monty had collapsed and died before the ceremony. Albert made amends in the only way he knew and sold his precious medal for £22 in order to purchase

When Flying Horse landlord Tony Hayes challenged Rovers cellarman Fred Gee to a barber-shop quartet sing-off, the first thing Fred had to do was put together a barber-shop quartet, sharpish. Alf, Bert and Eddie all agreed to join (mainly due to the promise of free beer), but they began to panic when Fred set the date of the competition for the following week. When they rehearsed 'Sweet Adelaide' in the pub Annie winced at their lack of harmony, while an unimpressed Ena suggested they try again, but without Fred, who was clearly out of tune. They did and it sounded a lot better, but then the question arose as to who would take Fred's place at such short notice. The regulars pointed out there was nothing in the rules suggesting the competitors had to be men – cue Renee in a false moustache joining the line-up. Despite the dulcet tones of their new addition, the Flying Horse team were out of the Rovers league and a deflated Fred conceded defeat.

a wreath. All alone at the Manchester Cenotaph at the appropriate time, Albert paid his own emotional one-man tribute to his fallen comrades – and, of course, to Monty.

A solitary figure: Albert pays his respects.

Round at Number 13, Hilda was cooking the tea when a formal-looking letter arrived for Stan from a solicitor. Lodger Eddie excitedly told her to open it, but Hilda faked nonchalance and left it on the sideboard until Eddie was out from under her feet – then she frantically attempted to steam it open. Stan arrived home and caught her red-handed and together the pair nervously read the letter's contents. It turned out that a Mrs Dora Entwistle of 2 Chapel Yard, Weatherfield, had named Stan as a beneficiary in her will and Stan would have to show his face at the solicitor's office to find out the exact details of her bequest.

Bemused, Stan reckoned she was probably a satisfied customer and the next day he went to see the solicitor, while an over-excited Hilda waited expectantly at home, convincing herself the surprise inheritance was going to be a life-changing sum. Actually, Mrs Entwistle had left Stan a cheque for £100 and a china dog ornament to thank him for always being so cheerful on his rounds. Not enough to pay off their debts, sighed Hilda, but enough to treat themselves to a few extra ales in the Rovers, which they promptly did, swanning in as if they'd had a huge windfall.

Audrey Roberts

Played by Sue Nicholls

When flirty Audrey Potter first appeared in Weatherfield, much to her daughter Gail's embarrassment she started a conga down the cobbles. It was immediately clear that this good-time girl would be anyone's for a couple of gin and tonics.

In fact, Audrey summed up her situation quite succinctly a few years later, explaining: 'It's not easy being a gad-about, you know. Late nights, tight dresses, high heels. You're always fighting your body. But what's a girl to do? You don't get gold bracelets sitting at home pickling onions, do you?'

More recently it has been Audrey who's been forced to fork out for the comfort of strangers. Despite being older and wiser, the lonely hairdresser fell hook, line and sinker for suave male escort, Lewis Archer. But while she planned to sell both her salon and her semi to fund their new life together in Greece, an increasingly shady Lewis had other ideas...

'My first appearance was walking in the door of Elsie Tanner's house, where Gail was living at the time, on the day of her engagement party to Brian, and going: "Hello love! At least you could look pleased to see me..." My hair was long and blonde and Audrey was a tarty, flirty piece back then. I think "easy" may possibly have been the best word to describe her. You gleaned she'd been around the block a bit, otherwise she wouldn't have deserted her children as she did.

'I love that in later years she's become more family orientated and wants them around her, I think that's really nice. Meanwhile, I've been very lucky this year because I've had this fantastic dramatic storyline with Lewis, played by Nigel Havers, which I have enjoyed immensely. It's been wonderful to have something to throw myself into that's about Audrey as a person and not about Audrey as a grandmother.'

50 CORONATION ST. ICON

Another storyline that saw Audrey in the thick of it was the Richard Hillman

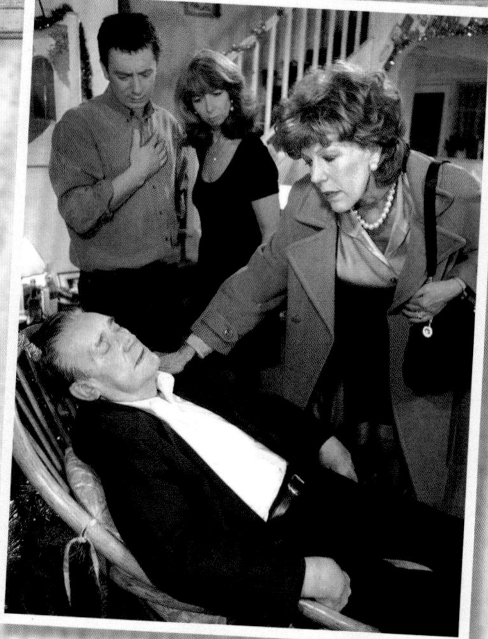

saga, which won Sue Best Dramatic Performance and Hero Of The Year at the 2003 British Soap Awards. When added to her gong in 2000 for Best Comedy Performance, it makes for an impressive tally of accolades.

'Getting Best Dramatic Performance was especially lovely because, much as I've enjoyed all the comedy Audrey has had, it was brilliant to do some really good drama. I put my heart and soul into it and for a character who was only ever supposed to be in *Coronation Street* for two episodes, it's not bad, eh?'

Over the years Audrey has had many gentleman admirers – she called off her engagement to George Hepworth when he made a pass at Gail, she twice turned down marriage proposals from booming butcher Fred Elliott, and then she found herself bored in unremarkable relationships with taxidermy enthusiast Keith Appleyard and builder Bill Webster. The only man to make an honest woman of flighty Audrey was Alf Roberts, and despite her husband's tight-fistedness being a constant irritant, she truly loved him and was devastated when he died of a heart attack at her grandson Nick's birthday party on New Year's Eve in 1998.

'Audrey Potter's had more fancy men than Elsie Tanner – and she set a flamin' record!'

Ivy

'They were quite an interesting coupling and I would've loved to have been a fly on the wall in the storyline meetings to see why they chose to put those characters together. But they do say opposites attract and I suppose Audrey's been very lucky – she's always had her fair share of suitors, although they've usually been Rita's rejects. Even Alf only came to Audrey after Rita had turned him down.'

By the age of seventeen Sue had won a place at the Royal Academy Of Dramatic Art, and in 1964 she joined *Crossroads*, spending four years as waitress Marilyn Gates – she also had a hit song, 'Where Will You Be?', which reached number 17 in the charts in 1968. She starred in sitcom *Up The Elephant And Round The Castle* (also featuring Brian Capron, who later played Richard Hillman), *The Rise And Fall Of Reginald Perrin*, and as Miss Popov in the cult Eighties children's series *Rentaghost*. She became a permanent addition to the *Coronation Street* cast in 1985 and has been perming the manes of Weatherfield's pensioners and providing Gail with a shoulder to cry on ever since.

'I can remember when I was younger even thinking I'd like to be a hairdresser, so I've loved working in my salon over the years with my girls Candice, Natasha and Maria. The only scenes I don't like doing are in the Rovers – for some reason the lighting in the Rovers always makes me look exceptionally like I am ninety-two and that I haven't slept for the last decade!'

Audrey and Gail enjoy some mother-daughter bonding.
It's payday for sulky crimper Candice.
Her Alfie passes away on New Year's Eve.
He's behind you! Hillman sets his sights on Audrey.
Loved-up Audrey plans a future with shady escort Lewis.

Current occupation: Hairdresser and salon owner.
On screen: 1979, 1980, 1981, 1982, 1984, 1985–
Defining moment: She's the only one who's suspicious of son-in-law Richard Hillman, so in 2002 he convinces Audrey she's going senile and tries to kill her by burning down her house.

Ken and Deirdre are all smiles on their wedding day.

An amused Bet asked Stan whether the money was for being cheerful all those years or for something more intimate. She went on to explain that Dora was to Chapel Yard what Elsie was to Coronation Street. Unamused, Hilda scowled snootily at this comment before admitting sheepishly that neither of them had a bank account so they couldn't cash the cheque – luckily Annie was on hand and offered to do the honours.

In 1981 Charles and Diana's wedding played second fiddle to the union of Street royalty when Ken finally got his girl and married Deirdre. In fact, the wedding very nearly didn't happen at all, as the year started with Deirdre being swept off her feet by smarmy Dutch businessman Dirk Van Der Stek. However, Deirdre's hopes for a clog-wearing life in Amsterdam for herself and Tracy came to nothing when the relationship fizzled out.

Ken's second hurdle came as flashy Mike began to woo Deirdre. But the rag-trade magnate's promise of a life of posh cars and foreign holidays didn't impress homely Deirdre and she began to realise there was only one man worthy of her affections – safe, reliable Ken. The couple opted for a short engagement after Ken proposed

Elsie showed no sign of allowing her increasing years to get in the way of her man-eating tendencies. After taking a shine to slot-machine manufacturer Wally Randle, who she'd met in the café, Elsie took him in as a lodger, fully expecting him to make a move on her. But when Wally revealed he wasn't interested in Elsie's feminine charms, only her box room, she had her heart broken – admitting that she'd fallen in love with him. Feeling old, Elsie took to the gin. After Wally moved out, Elsie hit the town with Bet and drunkenly seduced sleazy Bill Fielding. Her shameful one-night-stand turned into a nightmare when Bill's wife broke into Elsie's and tore up her clothes in an act of revenge. Too mortified to tell the police, she was unable to make a claim on her insurance and learnt a very valuable lesson at the cost of her collection of polyester blouses...

'You're like false teeth and toffee. Yer can't let go.'

Stan to Hilda

on holiday in Scotland and in July they married at Weatherfield's All Saints Church, with a surprise telegram from Deirdre's ex, Ray, giving them his blessing.

After honeymooning in Corfu the couple settled down to married life with Tracy at Number 1, keeping Uncle Albert on as their grumbling lodger. He was difficult to please as ever, and when Ken bought himself a Volkswagen Beetle, Albert refused to set foot in it, calling it a 'Jerry car'. Hoping to make their family official, Ken sought Ray's approval for him to change Tracy's surname to Barlow, but Ray refused permission, thwarting an otherwise blissful year for the Barlows.

Rather less jubilant was Emily. Her recovery from the shock of discovering she had married a bigamist was hindered when she returned home one day to discover Arnold sitting bold as brass in her living room. Terrified, Emily endured a hostage situation with manic Arnold trying to talk her into entering into an overdose suicide pact with him so they could be together in heaven. Emily craftily pointed out to Arnold that God would disapprove of his plan, and while Arnold went to find a bible to prove her wrong, she let herself out the front door and fled to safety.

The police swooped on delusional Arnold and he was carted off to the local lunatic asylum, where he spent a final few months before his death. Emily holidayed in Malta with best friend Mavis to recover from the ordeal, but on her return was stunned to be informed that Arnold had left her £2,000 in his will. Not happy

1980s Births

Nicholas Paul (Gail & Brian Tilsley)	31 December 1980
Mark (Maggie Redman & Mike Baldwin)	9 May 1981
Paul (Andrea Clayton & Terry Duckworth)	19 Feb 1986
Sarah Louise (Gail & Brian Tilsley)	3 February 1987

keeping his money, do-gooder Emily gave a gift of a trampoline to the community centre and spent the rest on endowing a bed at Weatherfield Infirmary in the name of her other late husband, Ernest. However, when Arnold's penniless wife Margaret called unexpectedly, Emily felt terrible for the widowed woman and gave her £2,000 from her own savings.

'I've seen gongs in boarding houses less brass-faced than her.'

Vera on Bet

Young love wasn't all it was cracked up to be for Brian and Gail when Gail found out about her husband's affair with flirty garage customer Glenda Fox. But having been propositioned and tempted herself by Brian's mate Colin, Gail made up her mind to forgive him. Despite the fact their marriage had just been through a decidedly rocky patch, the couple went ahead and entered a 'Mr and Mrs' competition which was being organised by Bet at the Rovers.

While Bet hunted for willing participants, landlady Annie mused that many of the Street's marriages wouldn't survive such public scrutiny, and it was no surprise when Bert and Ivy and the Faircloughs turned down Bet's offer to take part. Hilda told Bet she couldn't rely on Stan to get her name right, never mind him knowing anything more personal about her likes and dislikes. But eventually she gave in to Bet's persuasive techniques, as did Bert and Ivy Tilsley.

Gobby factory worker Vera Duckworth (*see page 101*) also signed up with her husband Jack (*see page 106*), who seemed unbothered by the fact Vera had recently cheated on him. During the competition Ivy was mortified by Bert's answers about their sex life, and a shocked Vera lost the quiz for the Duckworths by swearing Jack had never been unfaithful to her, only for Jack to reveal that he had. The Ogdens failed to get any questions right, despite spending the whole day swotting up on each other. While all the other couples rowed, Brian and Gail were declared the winners and given a much-needed bottle of champagne.

In December, fresh from a break at the seaside, Annie was fizzing with ideas for how to keep business brisk, and this time she hit on the introduction of a Cocktail Happy Hour. Staff members Fred and Hilda weren't overly convinced by the idea but Bet was game and agreed it was worth a try. When they ran the cocktail concept by loyal customer Stan, he surprised them all with his enthusiasm – but it soon became clear this was because pints would also be ten pence cheaper under the new scheme.

Bet plays gooseberry with the rowing Duckworths.

Kevin Webster

Played by **Michael Le Vell**

When Alf Roberts' car broke down in Bolton, a likeable young hitchhiker who was handy with a spanner repaired it on the spot. As a thank you, the grateful grocer treated the teen to a pint at the Rovers, and thereby Kevin Webster set foot on Coronation Street for the very first time.

A struggling actor working as a plasterer between jobs, it was a happy coincidence that Michael Le Vell (who'd briefly appeared in the show two years earlier as paperboy Neil Grimshaw) found himself being lined up to play Kevin.

'I was sat there about to go in and audition for a series called *Scully* when Judi Hayfield, a casting director, spotted me and asked if she was seeing me the next day for *Coronation Street*. I told her she wasn't so she phoned my agent and twenty-four hours later I was back auditioning to play Kevin Webster. That encounter effectively changed my life. *Coronation Street* was the biggest show in town and suddenly I was in it. I could hardly believe my good fortune.'

Twenty-seven years later, dad-of-two Kevin is still at his happiest when greased up under a bonnet, although these days he has graduated from being Brian Tilsley's youthful lackey to world-weary garage boss. He's been married three times – an ill-fated union to pregnant factory machinist Alison Wakefield (who later committed suicide after the death of their baby) and twice to his first love, Sally Seddon, whom he cheated on in 2009 with shop assistant Molly Dobbs, the wife of his business-partner buddy, Tyrone.

'There are old pictures of the cast all over the studios, and my overriding thought when I see them is that I can't believe I had that long mullet hair and that horrible moustache. The only reason I grew it in the first place was so I could get served in pubs and I soon got sick of it. I asked the producers several times if I could shave it off and but they refused point blank. In 1990 when I got a script saying "Steph Barnes lures Kevin upstairs and shaves off his moustache" I nearly jumped for joy. No one was more glad to see the back of that 'tache than me!'

The loss of their baby destroyed Kevin's relationship with Alison.

Playing away from home with Molly.

Kevin comforts Sally as she prepares for cancer treatment.

Current occupation: Mechanic and garage owner.
On screen: 1983–
Defining moment: Kevin wins girlfriend Sally's heart when he heroically saves Bet from the blazing Rovers in 1986.

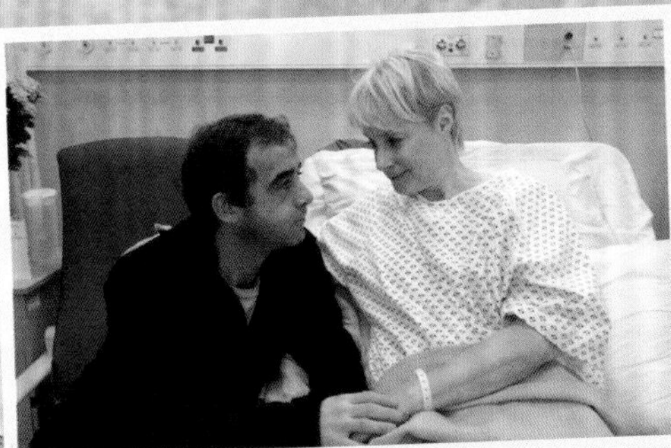

50 CORONATION ST. ICON

↑ Len and Rita have their hands full with foster daughter Sharon.

↓ Flirty Sharon soon sets her sights on Brian.

Instead of going home that evening, Stan stayed in the pub to get his money's worth – so Hilda ate his tea as well as her own. However, Annie's plan backfired when the regulars discovered that another pub, the Laughing Donkey, also had a happy hour that started immediately after the Rovers and they all abandoned their local for more cheap drink elsewhere.

Rita and Len's decision to start fostering in 1982 brought wild, outspoken seventeen-year-old Sharon Gaskell to the Street. From the word go Sharon attempted to bring some teenage anarchism to the cobbles by throwing herself the mother of all birthday parties, which had all the neighbours' net curtains twitching. The shindig was brought to a standstill by the return of Len from the pub, just in time to catch Sharon sneaking her boyfriend Steve upstairs. So it was with some relief that the Faircloughs waved goodbye to Sharon when she was eventually relocated to a permanent foster home.

Sharon didn't stay away for long, though, and two months later she returned, complaining she hated her new foster parents. Social Services allowed Sharon to move back in with the Faircloughs, and with her feet back under the table again, the tempestuous teen started to stir up trouble. Mechanic Brian, who had been working away in the Far East and had newly returned to the Street, caught Sharon's eye and she wangled herself a

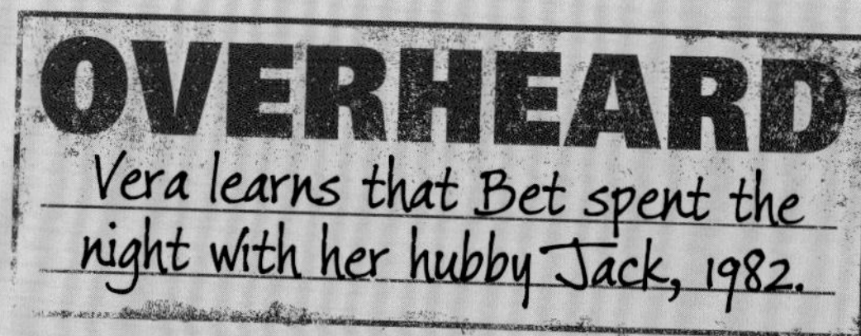

THE ROVERS. ANNIE AND FRED ARE SERVING. MAVIS AND ELSIE PROP UP THE BAR. VERA ENTERS AND HEADS STRAIGHT FOR BET, WHO IS CLEARING TABLES.

VERA: (ANGRY) Who was I with last night?

BET: (AS IF PROVIDING AN ALIBI) You was with me, love. And I don't care who says different.

VERA: Yeah, we've got that sorted out, now who were you with last night?

BET: (PLAYING DUMB) Well, if you was with me, love, I must have been with you, right?

VERA: No, it doesn't always follow and you know it doesn't. So who were you with last night?

BET: This is beginning to sound like a very old joke, Vera.

VERA: Yeah, that's probably what it is, an' all. I suppose you've been stood there thinking I'm the joke.

BET: (INNOCENT) I've not been thinking nothing, love.

VERA: You hard-faced cow!

BET: (DROPPING THE ACT) Oh, don't start calling me names, Vera.

VERA: I will call you. And I'll call you to your face an' all. D'you know, you've no more morals, you, than a cat's behind!

BET: Well, that is a laugh. Now listen who's talking.

ANNIE: I have listened to quite enough and I will listen to no more. Mrs Duckworth, the door is behind you where you came in.

VERA: Well, don't you worry, Mrs Walker. I don't even want talk to her. I don't want to communicate with her. (TO BET) No, you'll hear from my solicitors, love, don't you worry.

VERA HEADS FOR THE DOOR.

ELSIE: (ASIDE, TO MAVIS) And they say television's killed live entertainment.

BET: I don't know why you married him, Vera, he's not even got hairy shoulders.

VERA WALKS BACK TOWARDS BET AND SHAKES A FIST IN HER FACE.

VERA: Now, listen here, you, I'm gonna warn you...

BET: You are a flaming hypocrite, Vera.

ANNIE: Fred! Fred, kindly escort Mrs Duckworth off the premises.

VERA: Me? Me? I'm a hypocrite?

BET: It's sauce for the goose, Vera. That's why you don't like it, love.

FRED TAKES HOLD OF VERA AND LEADS HER TO THE DOOR. BUT VERA'S NOT FINISHED WITH BET YET.

VERA: (LIVID) Get back to the gutter, you, where you crawled from. Yeah, go on. You think this is a laugh, don't you? Well, you'll be laughing on the other side of your face!

FRED: Come on, cool it, Vera, let's have you...

VERA: (HITS FRED WITH HER HANDBAG) Get off me!

role babysitting young Nicky. Convinced that Brian reciprocated her crush, Sharon bought him a zodiac star sign keyring for his birthday and attempted to seduce him one night. To his shame, a drunken Brian kissed Sharon back – a move he later regretted when Sharon broke news of their 'affair' to Gail.

The situation saw Gail turning on both Sharon and blindly loyal Rita and it was only when Brian put Sharon straight – telling her that she was young and stupid – that the smitten babysitter got the message and backed off. Before Christmas, a bored Sharon realised that Weatherfield wasn't the home she'd hoped for and skulked off to Sheffield, taking a job as a kennel-maid there.

When 'Slim Jim', aka Eddie, began conversing with 'Stardust Lil', alias Marion Willis, on his new CB radio he never thought they'd ever actually meet – so Eddie waxed lyrical about his successful business and his luxury apartment. This proved to be problem when Marion suggested a date, so he borrowed the keys for Mike's flat from housekeeper Hilda and entertained Marion there. By the second time the CB pals were due to meet up, Mike had found out about Eddie's scam, but he did allow him to use his home one last time in order to tell Marion the truth. However, Marion surprised Eddie by saying she didn't think they were right for each other, admitting she was intimidated by his swanky lifestyle. Relieved, Eddie told her the truth about his humble abode and his lowly bin-man status and took Marion to the Rovers to meet his landlady, Hilda. With his working-class status well and truly proved, Eddie suddenly became more attractive to a relieved Marion and their romance was back on. Eddie and Marion later found out she was pregnant, got married and moved to Bury.

Rovers barmaid Betty had a rough old year, starting with the reappearance of her beloved son, Gordon. Back to show his mother his new fiancée, Caroline, Gordon's plans to get hitched thrilled Betty. Less pleasing, however, was the revelation that Gordon's wedding plans didn't involve her, and Betty later discovered that Gordon and Caroline had already had their big day without inviting the mother of the groom to join them. Depressed, Betty's year deteriorated further when she became the victim of a violent mugging at the hands of Raymond Atwood, a rogue from the local Youth Club and ended up in hospital with a broken arm.

The attack was reported in the newspapers and by chance the article was seen by a wartime lover of Betty's, Ted Farrell. Hoping to catch up with his former sweetheart, Ted tracked Betty down to her hospital bed and the pair reminisced that the last time they'd seen each other was in 1947 at London Road Station, Manchester. What Ted didn't realise was that after he left Betty at the station she'd found out that she was pregnant with their son. With no way of contacting Ted, Betty had no option but to give birth to Gordon as an illegitimate baby. Knowing that Ted had since married and raised a family of his own, an emotional Betty decided against telling her one-time love the truth about Gordon and the pair parted company once again.

'Once Betty Turpin's took a stand, King Dick couldn't shift her.'

Jack

Terrible Teens

A round-up of Weatherfield's most troublesome tearaways...

Lucille Hewitt

The original Street teen's roll-call of misdemeanors included skipping exams to follow her pop-star idol Brett Falcon to London, and running away to Gretna Green to marry Gordon Clegg – but the couple got cold feet when they missed the train.

Sharon Gaskell

The Faircloughs' tomboy foster daughter introduced herself by informing Len: 'Just to put you in the picture. Me dad's in the nick, me mam's in a world of her own, I don't get on very well with me three brothers, so they've farmed me out. And you have won the jackpot!' She'd only been in Weatherfield a matter of days before she threw a booze-filled party that very nearly ended in a riot.

Rosie Webster

Former school bully Rosie was banned from seeing her fellow-goth boyfriend Craig after her mum Sally found out they'd slept together. As a result she attempted to elope to Berlin with him. But the manipulative minx's moment of glory was her illicit affair with her English teacher, John Stape, which saw her held hostage in his dead granny's attic for five weeks.

Steve McDonald

From the moment he set foot on the cobbles, car-radio thief Steve amused himself by mischief-making. Highlights included smashing Alf's shop window with a football and nearly destroying the premises completely during a joyride on an out-of-control JCB.

David Platt

His reign of teen terror included sending his mum Gail sinister greetings cards from her dead husband Richard Hillman and hiding drugs in a doll belonging to his niece, Bethany, causing her to overdose. After finding out that his mum had helped his girlfriend, Tina, to have a termination, David pushed Gail down the stairs and left her for dead.

Curly Watts

Played by **Kevin Kennedy**

So-called because of his straight hair, Curly (or 'Norman', as his landlady Mrs Bishop preferred to call him) was Coronation Street's intellectual stargazer. While his career may have progressed healthily from working on the bins alongside Eddie Yeats and Chalkie Whitely to the dizzy heights of supermarket management, his attempts to woo the opposite sex could only be described as hapless, verging on doomed.

'I think the viewers could relate to this average guy and his search for a girlfriend and a chance to better himself. Everyone was willing him on to find happiness, but hard as he tried, he just seemed to lurch from one disaster to another.'

After the relief of losing his virginity to factory worker Shirley Armitage, Curly began dating shelf-stacker Kimberley Taylor, but her determination to save herself for her marriage was too much for Curly and she broke off their engagement when he became over amorous. Meanwhile, red wine was to blame for two unlikely liaisons – first there was his mortified housemate Angie Freeman, then came scatterbrained Maureen Naylor, after she had walked out on her fiancé, Curly's Bettabuy boss Reg Holdsworth.

However, luck seemed to be on Curly's side when he fell head over heels for check-out girl and wannabe model Raquel Wolstenhulme. They got engaged, only for Raquel to break it off at their engagement party, revealing she was really in love with Des Barnes. Eventually Raquel realised Curly was the more reliable option and organised a short-notice wedding, but she then ditched him a year later when she quit Weatherfield for Kuala Lumpur. Perhaps the first woman to truly reciprocate Curly's love was his second wife, police officer Emma Taylor, with whom he had a son, Ben (who was delivered by Norris Cole). The Watts family left the Street in 2003 when Emma took a promotion in Newcastle.

Someone else who understood Curly completely was his egomaniac supermarket partner-in-crime, Reg Holdsworth. Kevin recalls that 'Reg was the classic fat bloke who thinks he's the conquerer of the world and Curly was his daft mate who believes everything he says. Ken [Morley] and I had a ball working together, we really did. I'm not saying they were in the same class as Laurel and Hardy by any stretch of the imagination, but they were definitely in that vein.'

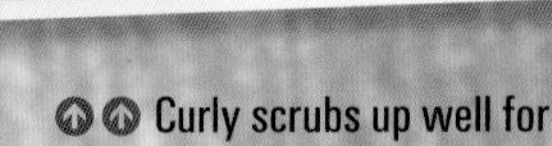

Curly scrubs up well for a night out.

With two of the women in his life – Angie and Raquel.

Proud parents Emma and Curly with baby Ben.

Occupations: Bin man turned supermarket manager.
On screen: 1983–2003
Defining moment: Winning his beloved Raquel from rival Des Barnes and swiftly marrying her in 1995.

Over at The Kabin, with each passing day Mavis grew increasingly frustrated with her life. Her year started off with few highlights and as she headed towards her forty-fifth birthday she began to think she was going to be left on the shelf forever. Her only hobbies seemed to be knitting a cardigan for Princess Diana's unborn baby at night, or tending to her budgie Harriet – or Harry, as he was called until Mavis noticed her much-loved bird had laid an egg and instigated a hasty name change. (The egg roused Mavis's maternal instincts and she even converted her bra into an incubation cubicle.)

Hoping to take matters into her own hands, Mavis joined a literary class at the local college and met the exotic, cultured Victor Pendlebury. When Mavis attempted to show Victor off at a Christmas party, she found herself humiliated when instead of taking her for a spin around the dancefloor, he asked Emily to dance with him. Furious, Mavis stormed out of the party, vowing to devote her time to needlecraft and domesticated birds once more.

'My mother said I was to save meself. And I saved meself until the danger was completely passed.'

Mavis

In September 1983 the Duckworths moved from their home in Inkerman Street and into Number 9 and became fully-fledged residents of the Street. However, before they officially moved in Jack had used Number 9 to stash some furniture, thereby avoiding storage charges, which resulted in it almost being taken away when the removal men arrived to move the furniture of the previous owner, Chalkie Whitely.

As before, the Duckworth's marital problems continued to cause ructions that could be heard across the whole of Greater Manchester. Following Jack's brief attempt at flirtation with Bet the previous year, the caddish layabout embarked on a new philandering scheme and enrolled in a video dating agency. Donning a dodgy white suit, Jack filmed a clip posing as 'Vince St Clair', a medallion-wearing American who claimed to be in showbusiness. Jack's luck ran out though when Bet, enrolled at the same agency, saw his video and plotted revenge for his treatment of her the year before.

So Bet encouraged Vera to join the agency and have some fun of her own, but the factory worker was mortified to discover her husband was also on the agency's books posing as a cheesy ladies' man. Not one to take being made a fool of lying down, Vera arranged a meeting with 'Vince' and arrived at the Rovers in her own disguise – as feisty red-haired widow 'Carole Munroe'. When Jack swaggered in thinking he was on to a good thing, he found himself at the receiving end of Vera's wrath and was humiliated in front of a crowded pub.

⬆ Mavis comes over all maternal when Harriet lays.
⬇ Vera transforms herself into Jack's date 'Carole Munroe'.

The goings-on that got everyone gossiping that year was Deirdre's affair with Mike. Bored with married life, an insecure Deirdre began to date the smooth-talking factory owner in secret and felt alive again for the first time in ages. While Mike made her feel special, valued and desired, Ken seemed uninterested in Deirdre's needs and took her for granted. By the time Emily overheard Mike on the phone to Deirdre and put two and two together, the pair were hooked and Mike even pressed Deirdre to leave Ken and marry him instead.

After a couple of months Deirdre's guilt was too much and she confessed everything to a stunned Ken. In one of the most explosive confrontations the Street had ever seen, Ken came face to face with his rival when Mike called round and Ken refused to let him in. The pair came to blows on the doorstep of Number 1, a tearful Deirdre watching helplessly as the two men in her life fought for her affections. Back inside, a pumped-up Ken vented his fury on Deirdre, both physically and verbally, telling his sobbing adulterous wife a few home truths in the process.

After their tempers had cooled, Deirdre and Ken sat down to try and salvage their marriage and eventually the Barlows were reconciled. But the incident sparked off a bitter feud between Mike and Ken that was to torment the pair for the next twenty years...

- ⬆ Passions run high for Mike and Deirdre.
- ⬇ Deirdre begs Mike not to come round.
- ➡ A furious Ken lashes out when love rival Mike puts in an appearance.

OVERHEARD

Ken rows with Deirdre about her affair with Mike, 1983.

THE KITCHEN AT NUMBER 1. THE ATMOSPHERE IS TENSE. KEN IS COMING TO TERMS WITH DEIRDRE'S REVELATION THE NIGHT BEFORE.

DEIRDRE IS DOING THE WASHING UP.

KEN: Now tell me. Just when did this nasty little affair get underway?

DEIRDRE: Oh. It has to be nasty, does it?

KEN: (SNAPPING) Of course it has to be nasty and don't try to pretend that it isn't.

DEIRDRE: Well, maybe it is. I don't know whether it is or it isn't.

KEN: Just how long has it been going on?

DEIRDRE: Not long, since about Christmas.

KEN: Oh, I see. The season of goodwill to all men. Especially Mike Baldwin.

DEIRDRE: Look, do you really want to know about this? Or are you just going to sneer and make nasty remarks, because if that's all you're...

KEN: No, I want to hear about it.

DEIRDRE: Well, like I say, it started about Christmas. You and me were rowing. I just needed someone to turn to and he was there. And he talks to me and he listens too.

KEN: Oh, I see. You're seriously claiming I don't talk to you now, are you?

DEIRDRE: Well you don't, Ken. You talk at me. It's like a missionary talking to the natives. Oh, very nice and polite but a million miles above their heads. And if the natives want to have a little jabber you'll nod and smile, but you're not really taking any notice of what they're saying. Do you know what you do, Ken? (HER VOICE CRACKING) You tolerate me. I wanted to be close to you and it's just like you're a hundred miles away.

KEN: You know what you're doing, don't you? You're just picking up any excuse you can think of to justify yourself...

DEIRDRE: I'm not trying to justify it – I'm trying to explain it!

KEN: (APPALLED) How could you do it, Deirdre? I mean, my God, it's less than two years since we got married.

DEIRDRE: (BITTER) Well it doesn't feel like it. Shall I tell you what it feels like to me? It's like I'm part of the wallpaper or a piece of furniture that's been around for ever. I mean, you hardly ever look at me, Ken. If I grew another head it'd be a week before you noticed. Honestly, the way you act it's like we've been married for 20 years.

KEN: (HE PAUSES FOR A MOMENT) Yes, well, maybe that's how I am. If Val was still alive I would've been married for twenty years. It's a fact of life. For most of my adult life I have been married.

DEIRDRE: (SOBBING) But not to me, though! Dammit, Ken. Not to me!

SHE STORMS OFF.

Fred Gee attempted to woo the local ladies with his latest purchase – Annie's old banger, restored to life by Brian. The amorous pot man asked Bet out for a Bank Holiday drive, but was put-out when Bet agreed on the condition that Betty came along as a chaperone, with Bet commenting she wouldn't trust Fred's hand to stay on the driving wheel any further than she could throw a grand piano. Naturally, Fred hadn't expected a chaperone, but he felt he could hardly withdraw his invitation. The drive ended in calamity when the car rolled down a hill and into a lake – with Bet and Betty still inside! Fred showed his gallant side by giving Bet a piggy back to the banks of the lake, but made a right mess of things when he deposited his date directly onto a cow-pat. Needless to say, Bet and Fred's romance didn't get off the ground after this soggy fiasco.

1983

In December poor old Rita was served a double dose of misery when her husband Len was killed in a motorway smash. Having been working away from home on a contract, Len fell asleep at the wheel of his car, resulting in a tragic crash. The newsagent crooner was informed of her husband's death while singing in the Rovers at a special party to celebrate the Ogdens' fortieth wedding anniversary. In shock, Rita was led home from the pub and given comfort by Sharon on a brief visit, who helped her make the funeral arrangements.

When things looked like they couldn't get any worse, Rita made a discovery that broke her heart. Confused as to why Len had been driving on the wrong road, she was given a clue in the form of a mystery phone number. Calling the number, Rita's world crashed down around her once more with the news that Len had been leading a double life and he'd been visiting his secret mistress, Mrs Proctor. Wanting answers, Rita enlisted Alf to drive her to Bolton to visit her late husband's lover, only to have the door slammed in her face. Newly widowed and bitter at the revelations, Rita spent a bleak festive period trying to piece her life back together.

Meanwhile, Mike fancied himself as a bit of a Peter Stringfellow-style magnate when he decided to widen his business interests

Fred: 'Bit too much mouth for my liking, but I can think of plenty worse.'

Betty: 'That's very moving is that, Fred. I'm sure he would've been deeply touched.'

On recently departed Len

and convert the disused warehouse on Rosamund Street into a discotheque. Council members Alf and Len agreed to support his venture, but Emily and his love rival Ken were not quite so enthusiastic and started a residents' petition against the development. However, they couldn't persuade Hilda to sign as Mike had already promised her the highly prized position of cloakroom attendant at the new venture.

The grand opening of the Graffiti Club was in September, although it was an invitation-only event, so when the factory girls turned up at the club and were refused entry, gobby Vera started insulting customers and had to be dragged away by the bouncers. To get his own back, Ken – who was now working at the *Weatherfield Recorder* – wrote a damning piece about the unsuitability of the club, but his furious boss insisted he wrote another, more flattering, article as Mike was spending a fortune advertising with the paper. Ken sulkily did as he was told, sarcastically praising Mike's public-spirited nature and describing him as 'the debonaire dynamo of denim'.

1984 was overshadowed by three big departures from the cobbles. First of all Billy returned from Derbyshire, where Annie was staying with her daughter Joan, to reveal to the stunned regulars that Rovers figure-head had decided to retire as landlady and that, for the time being, he would be continuing as the sole licensee.

Billy informs Betty and Bet that he's their new boss.

'When a Tanner does summut that looks normal, keep your eyes peeled for a rat with clogs on.'
Hilda

Next, after twenty-four years on and off as the scarlet woman of Weatherfield, Elsie's tenure on the Street also came to an end. The return of old flame Bill Gregory – who'd once broken her heart by not telling her he was married – had sent the normally decisive Elsie into a spin. Now single, he asked her to marry him and give up the grimy backstreets to help run a bar in sunny Portugal. Surprisingly, it took Elsie some time to make up her mind, but in the end she realised that she had little left to stay in Manchester for. After she'd dropped her house keys in at the Barlows, she took a final walk down the Street before climbing into a taxi and driving out of Weatherfield for good. When the chatty cab driver asked her how long she was going for, Elsie gave an enigmatic smile and purred: 'Ah, now there's a question...'

At Number 13 another resident got a less happy ending. Poorly Stan had to be admitted to hospital in November after an exhausted Hilda collapsed from the strain of her cleaning jobs as well as looking after him. Just weeks later Hilda received the phone call she'd been dreading – as a consequence of an infection, Stan had passed away.

The neighbours rallied round a devastated and eerily silent Hilda, with Alf arranging the funeral and Billy laying on the food for

the wake at the Rovers. She was so numbed by her loss that at first Hilda was unable to cry. But that evening a parcel containing Stan's belongings was delivered from the hospital and in a hugely moving moment the widow finally allowed herself to weep, whilst cradling Stan's trademark spectacles.

Mavis became hot property that year with not one but two gentlemen in pursuit of her hand in marriage. Derek Wilton managed to finally convince the shop assistant that he was a worthy man, and over dinner in an Italian restaurant she accepted his marriage proposal. Resigned to becoming Mrs Wilton, Mavis was understandably stunned when old flame Victor arrived back on the scene, desperate to lure her away from Derek. After much soul-searching Mavis sent foppish Victor packing and agreed that Derek was the one for her. But when it came to the wedding day Mavis had cold feet and stood Derek up at the altar. Her guilt at having jilted Derek soon turned to anger, however, when she learned that she wasn't the only one with pre-wedding jitters and Derek hadn't turned up for the ceremony either!

A final farewell: Elsie trades Weatherfield for the Algarve.
Absentee son Trevor joins Hilda for Stan's funeral.
Pointing the finger: Victor and Derek vie for Mavis's affection.

'She's you in a tweed skirt. Neither of you would be able to decide what time it was in a roomful of clocks.'

Derek's mother on Mavis

When the Rovers Return took on the Flying Horse in the Pub Olympics, Percy was spitting feathers that Alf was chosen over him as head of the organising committee. Instead, sour-faced Percy had to settle for the deputy position and spent most of the day trying to get Alf's megaphone off him, desperate to bark out orders on it himself. In the egg-and-spoon race Bet entered with an egg stuck to a spoon with chewing gum, but she still managed to come last. Meanwhile, Vera was first across the finish line, but she was later disqualified when it became clear she'd deliberately knocked the egg off the spoon of the woman in front of her. With Vera disqualified, a smugly triumphant Hilda was declared the winner. There was also victory for Brian and Gail, who romped home in the three-legged race, and ballsy Betty, who won the welly-throwing contest.

Dour ex-army man Percy Sugden, who lodged with Emily Bishop, had a year marred with catastrophe and misunderstanding. The pensioner was devastated in August to discover his beloved budgie Randy was missing and embarked on a mission to find his feathered friend. Offering a £10 reward, Jack saw an opportunity to make a quick buck by buying a look-a-like bird for £2 and trying to make £8 in profit from his elderly neighbour. However, Jack's plan backfired; while he was finding a Randy doppelganger, the real budgie returned, leaving Percy furious when Jack attempted to scam him. The following month Percy faced further trouble when he tried to do the neighbourly thing following a robbery at the corner shop. Setting up a neighbourhood-watch scheme, Percy found himself on the wrong side of the law when he was mistaken for a peeping Tom and was frogmarched down to the police station.

'You could meet Alf riding on a horse in the middle of the Sahara desert and still know he's a grocer.'
Audrey

Alf finally makes an honest woman of Audrey.

1980s Marriages

Eunice Nuttall and Fred Gee	13 May 1981
Deirdre Langton and Ken Barlow	27 July 1981
Marion Willis and Eddie Yeats	31 October 1983
Elaine Prior and Bill Webster	9 January 1985
Audrey Potter and Alf Roberts	23 December 1985
Susan Barlow and Mike Baldwin	14 May 1986
Sally Seddon and Kevin Webster	8 October 1986
Bet Lynch and Alec Gilroy	9 September 1987
Gail Tilsley and Brian Tilsley	24 February 1988
Ivy Tilsley and Don Brennan	13 June 1988
Mavis Riley and Derek Wilton	9 November 1988

The next year romance swept the Street as a pair of unlikely couples caused the rumour mill to go into overdrive. Widower Alf finally got over the death of Renee by throwing himself into dating Rita. The relationship didn't work out, however, and she turned down his proposal, leaving the corner-shop owner a single man again – but not for long. Gail's flirty mother Audrey swooped in to take Rita's place and won Alf's heart, surprising both Gail and the wider community – with Ivy muttering that someone of Audrey's morals was an unsuitable wife for a respected local councillor. But, defying the critics, Audrey and Alf made things official when they married on 23 December 1985.

Another surprise coupling came in the form of Mike and the much younger Susan. Needless to say, Ken was less than impressed by his newly returned daughter getting romantic with his sworn enemy, but he was powerless to stop their relationship. As Mike invited a smitten Susan to a New Year's Eve party down in London, Ken could only sit back and cringe as Deirdre's former lover once again made life at the Barlows' a misery.

Sally Webster

Played by **Sally Dynevor**

Destiny crossed Sally Seddon's path when Kevin Webster drove past her in his van, sped through a puddle and sprayed muddy water all over her shiny white PVC boots. Kevin took the disgruntled blonde home to dry off, wangled a date, and within a year they'd married and moved into Number 13 with landlady Hilda Odgen. Like her fictional namesake, actress Sally Dynevor reckons her life on *Coronation Street* may also have been written in the stars.

'When I was a little girl Pat Phoenix came to give a speech at the town hall in Oldham and I remember standing outside the gate looking at her. I'd never seen anybody from the telly before so to actually see her in the flesh was so exciting. I must've only been ten or eleven and I shouted, "I want to be an actress!" at her at the top of my voice. She came over to me and said, "Well, if you want to be an actress you have to put it before anything else. Forget boyfriends." She explained how dedicated you had to be and I garbled "I will be, I will be!" Then she sped away in this big car and I remember thinking, "Wow, she's so glamorous".

'I did listen to what she said and I went to drama school in London where everyone kept going, "Oh, you'll end up in *Coronation Street* because you've got that accent." So it was always a bit of a joke there that I'd end up on the *Street* and, of course, I did!'

In more recent years the factory machinist has developed delusions of grandeur, but back in the mid-Eighties Sally was definitely from the wrong side of the tracks and very nearly ended up as a punk.

'On my very first day I went into make-up and one of the girls, called Cathy, said "I know, why don't we make her up as a punk?" At that point Mary in *EastEnders* was a punk and I said, "Yeah, great idea." So I had really black eye make-up, really purple cheeks and awful brown lipstick. I looked very scary and when Michael [Le Vell] walked into make-up he was shocked and said, "Kevin would never go out with a girl who looked like that." Thank God he did, really, so I washed it off and put on normal make-up or else Sally might've been written out quite early on looking like that.

50 CORONATION ST. ICON

'How does it feel to be so dried up and sour at your age? I didn't have to rip Kevin out of your arms. He was bored stiff.'

Natalie to Sally

'I'd first met Mike when we were at the Oldham Theatre Workshop together when we were both thirteen, so to be playing his wife for the last twenty-five years has been really strange as well as wonderful because we knew each other as kids.'

It was Kevin who kicked off the couple's sequence of affairs by bedding vampish Natalie Horrocks and, of course, he's been the most recent Webster to stray from the marital bed. But over the years, while married and after her divorce, Sally's notched up her own conquests, including hunky mechanic Chris Collins, violent factory boss Greg Kelly, and even Kevin's best mate, Martin Platt. She nearly married nice-guy stallholder Danny Hargreaves, but he dumped her after discovering her one-night stand with Kevin, who she remarried the following year. Sally went on to cheat again in 2005 with her garage-owner boss Ian Davenport, and three years later she developed a crush on English tutor John Stape – but he only had eyes for her strumpet eldest daughter, Rosie.

'Sally and Kevin have been through the mill but there is genuine love there. I just don't want to be having another affair. I'm getting too old for all of that and Sally's got her hands full with the girls now. Jean Alexander [who played Hilda Ogden] was a wonderful role model for me and I'd like to I think I am for my girls – Helen [Flanagan] and Brooke [Vincent]. I hope I've been a very good friend to them both as well as an on-screen mum.'

In 2010 the actress revealed she had been diagnosed with breast cancer in real life, just as her character battled the disease on screen. 'The breast cancer storyline will now stay with me forever. It has been life changing because if I hadn't been doing the storyline I might not have found the lump in my breast. It sounds bizarre, but before I was diagnosed I was so excited about doing that story because it was the most important story I'd ever been given. Now I'm just ever so thankful for it.'

As for the future, Sally would still like to be playing her alter ego when she gets her bus pass and beyond. She laughs, 'I can see her as a cross between Hilda and Mavis – she'll be a bit bossy and prim, looking down her nose at everyone and not altogether happy with anything!'

She can't resist Kevin's cheeky-faced charms.
The young lovers under the watchful eye of Hilda.
Her relationship with Greg becomes abusive.
Sally falls for nice guy market trader Danny.
The proud mum with her girls: Sophie and Rosie.

Current occupation: Underworld machinist.
On screen: 1986–
Defining moment: In 2004 Sally becomes a pushy showbiz mum and tells Rosie: 'This is just first-night nerves. Dame Judi Dench used to vomit before every performance – she used to keep a bucket in't wings.'

From barmaid to licensee: Bet goes up in the world.

In the same year, Bet made history when she became Newton and Ridley's first unmarried landlady to take over the top job at the Rovers Return. Within a matter of minutes of her name being over the door, she swiftly made changes to the boozer – installing Jack as her pot man and sacking pretty barmaid Gloria Todd, insisting she didn't have enough experience for the job, which led an angry Gloria to accuse Bet of not liking having competition behind the bar. Eventually the adversaries called a truce and became firm friends.

After close inspection of the dregs of her morning elevenses, Hilda insisted on putting her psychic talents to good use and read the tea leaves of the Rovers employees. She gleaned that barmaid Betty was going to come into silver, landlady Bet was about to hear from a long-lost relative, and Wilf Starkey, who briefly helped out behind the bar, was soon to travel to the East. With Hilda endlessly wittering on about the power of her 'gift', a mischievous Bet decided to give the supposedly psychic scrubber's predictions a helping hand. So she set Hilda up by giving Betty a silver necklace, Wilf pretended to have been invited all the way to East Manchester, and Bet arranged for an old friend to pretend to be her estranged 'Cousin Arthur'. Hilda was over the moon at these developments, until Betty revealed they'd all been having her on. However, the smile was wiped off Bet's face when her real Uncle Ted – a tramp – turned up unexpectedly at the Rovers.

'Well, it's a rough old pub and it needs a rough old bird to keep charge of it.'

Mike to Bet

Crimes of Fashion

When it comes to mutton dressed as lamb, the residents have had their fair share of bad clothes days...

Lucille Hewitt

Cilla Battersby-Brown

Roy Cropper

Kelly Crabtree

Raquel Watts

Bet Lynch

Liz McDonald

Towards the end of the year Bet took a break from life in the pub to enjoy a holiday with Rita and Mavis in sunny Blackpool. The trip was a disaster, though, with Bet rebelling against Mavis's desire to go on day trips, preferring to trawl the bars for men. In the end all three were chatted up by a trio of sales reps, but the excitement turned to disappointment for Bet when her admirer guiltily admitted to being a married family man. Only Mavis had any success, with widower Norris Birchall – much to Rita and Bet's annoyance.

Down-to-earth Connie Clayton barely had time to move into Number 11 before she was involved in a full-scale street brawl with Vera. It had all begun over a tacky outfit Vera had designed for herself to wear to a dance with Jack. Its frills – which obliging dressmaker Connie had slaved over on her sewing machine – looked awful, and Vera was not best pleased with the results. While Connie agreed the style may not have suited Vera, she also pointed out she was merely following Vera's design requests and that the dress fitted properly and therefore was worth the £45 fee. But Vera refused to pay and a feud developed between the families. Caught in the crossfire were young lovers, tearaway Terry Duckworth and Connie's daughter Andrea, whose relationship was ruined by the hostilities.

⬆ Andrea, Connie and Sue Clayton settle in at Number 11.
⬇ Love's young dream: Kevin and Sally are joined at the hip.
➡ As the Rovers goes up in smoke Kevin attempts to rescue Bet.

At the Rovers, the residents of Coronation Street attempted to prove their intelligence when the boozer entered a team into a local 'Brainiest Pub' contest. Their arch-rivals proved to be the White Swan pub, run by snobby landlady Stella Rigby. In the final heat, the Rovers and the White Swan were neck and neck until poor Percy let the team down by failing to answer a question about football correctly. The team lost by one point and were left to commiserate back at the Rovers with a warm pint, while Bet had to suffer Stella lording their win over her.

In June the following year the Rovers Return was devastated by a blazing fire. Sparked by Jack's shoddy skills as an amateur electrician, the inferno took hold in the dead of night while Bet was getting her beauty sleep in the staff quarters upstairs. Luckily, young lovebirds Kevin Webster (*see page 123*) and Sally Seddon (*see page 138*) were on their way home from a pop concert when they spotted smoke billowing from the pub's windows and managed to raise the alarm. If Sally wasn't sure about Kevin

yet, the sight of her moustached macho man heroically climbing a ladder to save Bet from burning to death cemented his place in her heart, and they married four months later.

Bet had woken up and tried to escape but the fumes forced her back and she collapsed unconscious. Kevin smashed Bet's window and climbed in as the fire engine arrived, then the firemen took over and carried Bet to safety. Kevin was proclaimed a hero, Bet was admitted to hospital and a few days later she moved in with Betty in order to recuperate. When she visited her beloved pub, now a gutted ruin, she broke down and cried.

Percy: 'Did you know I was a twitcher?' Bet: 'I had me suspicions.'

On Percy's hobbies

Romance had first blossomed for Kevin and Sally when he'd accidentally sprayed her with muddy puddle sludge while driving past in his van. Despite such an inauspicious start, the young couple were smitten, although their nearest and dearest weren't quite so easily charmed. For a start, Kevin's landlady Hilda didn't think 'common' Sally was good enough for her nice-boy lodger, and when the couple announced their engagement to the Seddon clan, it was made clear to a heartbroken Sally that if she married the mechanic they'd have nothing more to do with her. As a result the skint couple had a bog-standard registry office wedding, but the residents chipped in to make sure the day still felt special; Sally's mate Lois helped the bride find her dream peach-coloured dress, Emily made the wedding cake and Hilda ensured they had some privacy on their wedding night by bedding down at the Rovers so the young lovers could have Number 13 all to themselves.

When she was informed that the brewery had decided to knock down the building, all the colour drained from Bet's face. After all, the Rovers was her life. The residents thought they'd supped their final pint at the bar as well, until a last-minute reprieve saw the boozer getting a renovation job rather than being bulldozed.

Pregnant Gail proved that the apple doesn't fall far from the tree when she confided in mum Audrey that she was unsure about the paternity of her unborn baby. Unhappily hitched to Brian, Gail had been having a sizzling affair with his smoother cousin, Ian, visiting from Australia. Meanwhile, Brian, oblivious to Gail's deception, had been busily making plans for the family to emigrate to Australia.

Unable to work out which of her lovers had got her pregnant, Gail told Brian she was considering an abortion,

Brian's cousin Ian puts the smile back on Gail's face.

The Tilsleys' marriage deteriorates when Gail admits her affair.

'I'm sick of being a drudge, which is what this marriage has made me. No one can live their life, year in year out, for other people.'

Gail

causing an angry reaction from the mechanic. When Brian refused to let her get rid of 'his' child, she was forced to admit everything. Appalled, Brian walked out on Gail and their son Nicky and started to sow his wild oats across Manchester, filing for a divorce in 1986 which was granted on 19 January 1987. After the birth of Sarah Louise, Ian took some blood tests that ruled him out as the father of the baby. Initially a stubborn Brian still refused to forgive his wife, but they reconciled and remarried the following year for the sake of the children.

Randy pensioner Phyllis Pearce's relentless pursuit of Percy (*see page 156*) took a new twist in 1987 when she realised his bowling rival Sam Tindall had won a fortune on the pools in the 1950s. Turning her attention to Sam, Phyllis intended to use Percy to make Sam jealous. Typically, things didn't go to plan, so rather than the ploy making Sam green with envy, he assumed Phyllis was a loose woman and dumped his potential new lady friend. Phyllis didn't accept the blame lay on her doorstep and instead accused an outraged Percy of driving Sam away.

Haven't we seen you somewhere before?

For some familiar faces their most famous incarnations weren't their first appearances in Weatherfield...

Bill Waddington (Percy Sudgen)
1967 A pipe-smoking man who struck up a conversation with Emily in a café.
1974 Jack – a customer who ended up drunk in the Rovers.
1978 Eric Summers – an old friend of Rita's who considered lending Len money.
1980 George Turner – best man at Emily's wedding to bigamist Arnold.

Sarah Lancashire (Raquel Watts)
1987 Wendy Farmer – a nurse who responded to Jack's advert for a lodger at Number 9.

Beverley Callard (Liz McDonald)
1984 June Dewhurst – a friend of Brian and Gail Tilsley.

Malcolm Hebden (Norris Cole)
1974–1975 Carlos – Bet's Spanish neighbour who proposed to Mavis in order to get a work permit.

Brian Capron (Richard Hillman)
1981–1982, 1986 Donald Worthington – the social worker who helped Rita foster Sharon and then Jenny.

Suranne Jones (Karen McDonald)
1997 Mandy Phillips – a one-night stand for ladies-man mechanic Chris Collins.

Maggie Jones (Blanche Hunt)
1967 Maggie Monks – a shoplifter at the police station with Annie.

Steve Huison (Eddie Windass)
1997 Michael Pearce – a businessman who looked around Jim's Café with a view to buying it.
2003 Andy Morgan – the thug who held Katy hostage and shot her dad Tommy.

Jill Summers (Phyllis Pearce)
1972 Bessie Proctor – Hlda's fellow cleaner at the Capricorn Club.

Geoff Hinsliff (Don Brennan)
1963 Vincent – very nearly Jerry Booth's best man until fiancée Myra persuaded him to step down in favour of Dennis Tanner.
1977 Eric Bailey – a criminal who robbed the corner shop

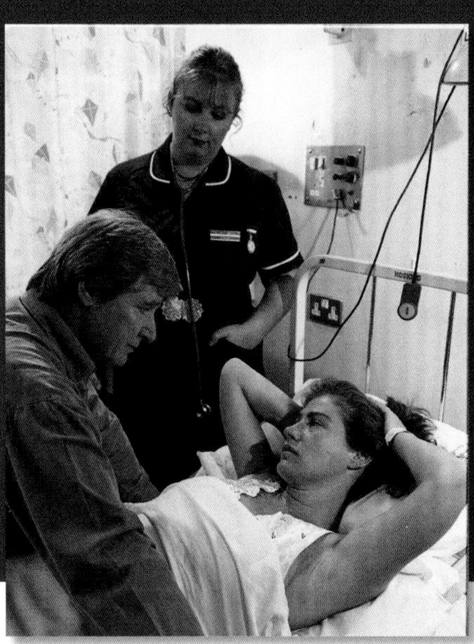

Sue Cleaver (Eileen Grimshaw)
1994 Sister Treece – the nurse who looked after Denise Osbourne when she miscarried.

Alison King (Carla Connor)
2004 Mrs Fanshaw – the housewife who ended up bedding Jason after he'd plumbed in her radiator.

Causing panic for everyone, Sarah Louise Tilsley was born prematurely and spent her first weeks fighting for her life in an incubator in the baby-care unit at Weatherfield Hospital. Convinced she wasn't his, Brian stayed away for months, and even though the blood tests eventually revealed he was Sarah Louise's real father, he still stubbornly spurned Gail's pleas and refused to have anything to do with the wide-eyed little tot. However, fearful of losing his son Nicky in the divorce, Brian attempted to take him with him to Ireland. When Nicky made it clear he didn't want to go, Brian returned to find Gail had informed the police who were out looking for them. Thankfully, Brian then finally held Sarah Louise in his arms and was besotted by her, so the couple reconciled for the sake of their children and remarried the following year.

On Christmas Day 1987 the streets of Weatherfield became a quieter place when raucous Rovers cleaner Hilda decided to leave the area for a new life in the countryside. After being violently assaulted by burglars at the home of another employer, Dr Lowther, Hilda grew too scared to be in her home alone. Depressed and lonely, the once gregarious character became a shadow of her former self.

So, when Dr Lowther asked her to join him at his new practice in the Derbyshire hills, Hilda realised it was time to say an emotional farewell to the street she'd called home for over two decades and Number 13 was swiftly sold to her former lodgers, Kevin and Sally Webster. It was the end of an era. In a packed Rovers, Hilda celebrated her final toast with a typically ear-piercing, but all the same heart-rending, rendition of 'Wish Me Luck As You Wave Me Goodbye'. As a parting gift the pub regulars chipped in to purchase Hilda a fitting gift – a brand new set of heated rollers!

Bet's lifelong search to find a man who would stick around for longer than breakfast came to an apparent end when she embarked on a sparky relationship with money-grabbing Alec Gilroy (*see page 150*). The sometime theatrical agent, sometime Graffiti Club boss, was Bet's perfect match –

▼ The Rovers regulars give Hilda a send-off to remember.

► After an unpredictable courtship, Bet and Alec tie the knot in style.

'He's been brought up in the same school of life as what I have. The tough one. Makes us birds of a feather. So maybe it's a marriage made in heaven.'

Bet

they each had their own interests at heart and could give as good as they got. Not only did Bet snare Alec, but she landed control of the Rovers too, which was being offered for sale by Newton and Ridley. When Alec bought the pub and gave Bet the licence as a wedding gift it seemed that Bet was getting the fairytale ending she had always desired.

It wasn't all smooth sailing up the aisle, though. Alec soon became suspicious of Bet when he realised her relationship history was more chequered than a gingham tablecloth, while Bet fretted that settling down wasn't going to suit her. In the end the pair wed in a big church affair at St Mary's, with the couple bickering right up until the moment they were pronounced man and wife.

Alec Gilroy

Played by **Roy Barraclough**

They say opposites attract – and they didn't come more poles apart than skinflint schemer Alec Gilroy and gregarious landlady Bet Lynch. The bickering couple had been backstreet-boozer rivals when Alec had managed the nearby Graffiti Club and the pair were still rubbing each other up the wrong way as they stood at the altar on their wedding day in 1987.

'The public loved to hate Alec because he was such a devious so-and-so and was up to every scam in the book. The viewers loved all that roguery, I think. Of course, when he got together with Bet he was really up against it because she had the measure of his craftiness. I think both Julie [Goodyear] and I were a bit horrified when we were told Bet and Alec were getting married. We both said: "Oh, come on, nobody's going to believe that!" But their relationship worked incredibly well and it ended up being the most fabulous partnership – they were so funny together.

'Bet and Alec were only ever seen in bed together once and it was a total disaster to film as the pair of us were in hysterics. Julie was wicked to me, because under the covers she had on a pair of novelty knickers which when you pressed the crotch played "The Only Way Is Up" by Yazz. We couldn't get through it for laughing and had to do about eight takes – the producer even threatened us with the sack.'

Miserly Alec made his first appearance in 1972 as a compere at the New Victoria Working Men's Club, then reappeared three years later as crooner Rita Littlewood's agent, before settling in for a longer stint from 1986 onwards. In 1998, with his marriage to Bet long gone by the wayside, he quit Weatherfield for good to go into business with his granddaughter, Vicky McDonald, running a restaurant in Brighton.

But Alec wasn't Lancashire-born Roy's first crack at *Street* stardom – he'd already popped up in four guest roles in the Sixties which included a day-trip tour guide and a smarmy salesman desperate to flog Hilda Ogden a new marital bed: 'All I remember is bouncing up and down on a mattress with Jean Alexander – now, if that isn't a claim to fame, I don't know what is...'

↑ Bantering with Bet in the back-room of the Rovers.

← Toasting the future with granddaughter Vicky.

↙ His Rovers partnership with the Duckies ended in animosity.

Occupations: Compere, theatrical agent, club manager, Rovers landlord and travel agent.
On screen: 1972, 1975, 1986–1992, 1995, 1996–1998
Defining moment: In 1987 he lends Bet the cash to buy the Rovers, but she can't afford to pay him back and goes to Spain. Realising how much he misses her, Alec flies to Spain and proposes to her.

Mike begs Susan to consider having his child.

Elsewhere, the Barlow–Baldwin rivalry continued to spiral out of control, with the controversial marriage of Susan and Mike breaking down completely. Having found herself pregnant, career-minded Susan reacted badly when Mike suggested she give up her job in order to raise their baby. Susan arranged an abortion and told Mike that she was not ready to have their child. After Mike accused Susan of being a child murderer, the couple finally split for good, with smug Ken breaking the news to his son-in-law and rival. Susan moved to Newcastle to start a new life, omitting to tell Mike that she didn't go through with the termination and was still carrying his baby – a fact that didn't come to light until years later.

In the spring, Bet returned from her Moroccan holiday with some jaw-dropping news for husband Alec – she'd been to see a doctor and he'd confirmed it: Bet was pregnant. While Alec wasn't sure he wanted a child, Bet admitted she didn't understand how she could become pregnant so easily at her time of life. The Gilroys were both uneasy at the prospect of parenthood so late in life, while Betty was overjoyed at the news. She started feeding Bet extra hotpots and took great pleasure in winding Alec up, calling him 'Daddy' at every opportunity.

'I must say, Emily, I don't know how you manage to work with the odious little man without having to leave at regular intervals to throw up.'

Ken on Mike

OVERHEARD

Alec comforts Bet after her miscarriage, 1988

THE ROVERS' BACK ROOM. BET IS LYING ON THE SOFA COVERED BY A BLANKET. ALEC POKES HIS HEAD AROUND THE DOOR.

ALEC: Are you asleep?

BET: (QUIETLY) No.

ALEC ENTERS AND CLOSES THE DOOR. HE KNEELS BESIDE BET.

ALEC: You should be in bed, you know.

BET: I've told you, I don't want to go to bed.

ALEC: Yes, but you should be resting. I mean, you've got to go careful.

BET: And it's too late for going careful.

ALEC: (GENTLY) Aye. D'you know, I didn't realise… I didn't think it'd hit me as hard as it has. I mean, when you said you were expecting, I can't pretend I was overjoyed. Not at first. But it grew on me...

BET: (TAKING ALEC'S HAND) I know.

ALEC: And now…

ALEC STOPS HIMSELF FROM GETTING TOO EMOTIONAL.

Take no notice of me, love. As long as you're all right, that's what really matters.

BET: (TOUCHED) Oh, I'm right enough, love.

ALEC: Well then...

ALEC KISSES BET ON THE HEAD. SHE SITS UP.

BET: Anyway, you'd have looked a right Herbert pushing a pram.

ALEC: Aye, you're right I suppose, now you mention it.

BET: We'd have spoiled it rotten, you know. They always do, old parents.

ALEC: Eh, not so much of your old!

BET: Well, we're old for bringing kids up. Anyway, what sort of life would it've had round 'ere? Growing up in a backstreet pub.

BET STRUGGLES TO FIGHT BACK HER TEARS.

I wanted it, you know. I wanted it right from the first minute I knew I'd caught.

NOW THE TEARS FLOW MORE FREELY. ALEC HOLDS HER. Still, don't always get what you want, do you? So that's that.

ALEC: I got what I wanted when I got you. And shall I tell you summut else?

BET: (THROUGH HER SOBS) What?

ALEC: I wouldn't swap places with any man in England. Not for a gold clock.

BET: (GRATEFUL) You are a little love. (GETTING A GRIP) Right then.

BET STANDS AND WIPES THE TEARS AWAY. ALEC PUTS HIS ARMS AROUND HER.

ALEC: Now then, I'll tell you what. I'll bring you a hot drink up when you get in bed.

BET: I'm not going to bed.

ALEC: Eh?

BET: (ALL BRAVADO) We've got a pub to open in five minutes. That's what we do, me and you, kid. We run a pub. Let's get on with it, eh?

Sadly, just as the Gilroys started to get their heads around their potential patter of tiny feet, after experiencing a sharp pain in her side Bet was taken to hospital and lost the baby. Back home and alone with Alec, Bet broke down, sobbing that she'd wanted the baby so much. Surprised by how badly their loss had hit both of them, the tragedy brought the often warring Gilroys closer together.

After years of dithering indecision, Mavis finally made up her mind about Derek and accepted his second proposal of marriage. But with a track record as unsuccessful as theirs, plans for a second attempt at a wedding in 1988 proved to be a source of amusement

Both Mavis and Derek turn up to get hitched this time.

Deirdre finds herself in hot water after visiting Brian Roscoe.

'You have a lot in common with Marilyn Monroe – you're not aware of the power of your own sexuality, Mavis.'

Derek

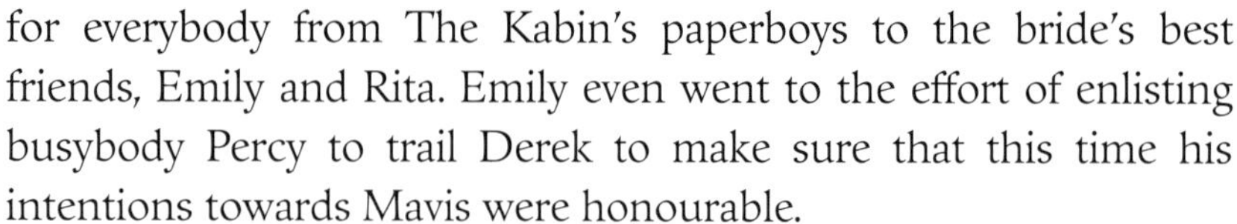

for everybody from The Kabin's paperboys to the bride's best friends, Emily and Rita. Emily even went to the effort of enlisting busybody Percy to trail Derek to make sure that this time his intentions towards Mavis were honourable.

Concerned that their friend was going to be disappointed once more, Mavis's mates sat her down and gave her a serious talking to about trusting Derek not to jilt her again. Mavis assured her friends that both the bride and groom would turn up for the ceremony this time. True to her word, there were no cold feet for the couple and their November wedding went ahead without a glitch. A Paris honeymoon sealed the deal and the Wiltons embarked on a new life together in the flat above The Kabin.

At Number 1, Deirdre had successfully stood for election as a Weatherfield councillor, but her well-meaning response to a cry for help sparked a disastrous chain of events. Moved by the plight of Brian Roscoe, who was dealing with re-housing issues, Deirdre found herself getting personally involved. Feeling sorry for Brian, she brought gifts to the down-on-his-luck family man's flat in the hope of cheering up his children's Christmas.

Wayward Terry's return to Weatherfield brought its usual tidal wave of trouble with it. Unhappy that his former henchmen Kevin and geeky Curly Watts (now dating machinist Shirley Armitage) were under the thumbs of their respective other halves, Terry embarked on a campaign to return them to their single days. Unsuccessful, Terry was equally rubbish at earning an honest crust as Mike's driver. When he 'borrowed' Mike's Jag to impress his latest crush, Kathy, on a night out, he ended up in hot water. Kathy's unimpressed husband spray-painted the words 'Stay away from my wife' along the side of the motor, sending Mike into a red rage. With no job, no girl and no money, Terry admitted there was nothing left in Weatherfield for him and headed off into the sunset once more.

What Deirdre found was a bitter and resentful Brian, distraught because his wife had left him and taken the kids with her. Well-meaning Deirdre ended up being threatened by Brian, who blamed her for the council's failings. Although she managed to escape by throwing his television set at him, she wound up getting a mighty ticking off from her bosses and daughter Tracy suffered nightmares thinking about her mum's ordeal. Deirdre herself later admitted to Bet that she had feared that she was going to be raped and that the whole nightmare had shaken her more than she had admitted to anyone.

'If you're not being talked about in this pub, love, you're not worth serving.'

Betty

For the first (but certainly not the last) time, in 1989 Gail found herself with the grim task of burying her husband. Brian's untimely death at the hands of knife-wielding muggers in a back alley outside a nightclub came just hours after Gail had told her boozy husband that she wanted to end their relationship.

The previous months had seen Brian and Gail growing further apart as the lothario mechanic began to spend his nights away from their marital bed, opting for a bar stool in one of Weatherfield's many public houses instead. Brian's final bender came after Gail informed him of her intention to divorce him. During an attempt to protect a woman from being bothered by a pair of thugs, Brian himself paid the ultimate price and was stabbed for his chivalry.

However, his death did nothing to heal relations between Gail and Brian's mother Ivy, who had married cab driver Don Brennan a year earlier after her first husband died from a heart attack following a nervous breakdown. The staunch Catholic knew of Gail's desire for

Alma Halliwell

Played by **Amanda Barrie**

With her mane of back-combed hair, primary-coloured trouser suits and a fondness for upturned collars, warm-hearted Alma Halliwell divided her time on the Street between acting as a friendly shoulder to cry on for the likes of Hayley Cropper, and being put through the emotional wringer by the bed-hopping antics of her ageing lothario husband, Mike Baldwin. In her very first appearance, in 1981, the harassed greasy-spoon proprietor was struggling to run Jim's Café single-handedly, so she offered to reinstate recently sacked Elsie Tanner, but in so doing demoted her from manageress to general skivvy.

'On my first day I filmed a scene laying down the law to Pat Phoenix and of course I was trying to concentrate but all I could think was: 'Oh my God, I'm acting with Elsie Tanner!' Everyone forgets that in her early days Alma was always being bossy, shouting at everybody and leaving Gail to do all the work in the café while she went out to have her hair done. Then she joined more permanently and became very kind and caring. But I used to love working with Helen Worth on that set, even though dear Brian Mills, the director, was always obsessed with doing close ups to make it look like a real café. You'd find yourself over a pan full of frying eggs and bacon until it was quite literally spitting fat in your face before he'd shout cut,' remembers Amanda. The actress was already a familiar face when she joined *Corrie*, thanks to a lifetime on the West End stage and the title role in the 1964 big-screen comedy classic, *Carry On Cleo*.

In 2001, after a heartbreaking battle with cervical cancer, Alma passed away with sorrowful ex-husband Mike and best pal Audrey Roberts at her bedside, and there wasn't a dry eye in the house.

'For me, being part of *Coronation Street* was the most immense privilege. But my least happy experience was when Alma worked at Firman's Freezers and Freshco – filming there meant the bottom half of your legs froze off because you were just standing in front of giant industrial freezers all day. The Freshco siege episodes were even more of a nightmare because we had to spend all of our time sitting on the floor being held hostage – by the end of it our poor bums were just numbed with cold.'

- Gail and Alma swap fry-up tips.
- She soon falls for Mike's chat-up lines.
- Deranged Don tries to kill her as revenge on Mike.

Occupations: Café owner and assistant supermarket manager.
On screen: 1981, 1982, 1988, 1989–2001
Defining moment: When Mike ditches her for wealthier Jackie Ingram, Alma takes up with his arch rival, Ken. But she confesses she's still in love with Mike and finally marries him in 1992.

Phyllis and Percy: a Love Story

A tale of pensioner passion, unrequited love and a budgie called Randy...

Joining those legends of love Romeo and Juliet or Taylor and Burton, is the tale of Phyllis Pearce and Percy Sugden, as played to peeved perfection by Jill Summers and Bill Waddington. Phyllis was a blue-rinsed battleaxe with a heart of gold and a (much-impersonated) voice like granite. Percy was a jobsworth flat-cap man with a regimental blazer and a sense of humour bypass.

Percy's arrival in Coronation Street in 1983 as the community centre caretaker set Phyllis a-flutter, and on a day trip to Southport the following year she even hid his shoes and socks while he was paddling in the sea so that they would miss the coach and could spend longer together.

Percy later became a lollipop man and as such he stole Phyllis's heart by saving her from a road traffic accident. After this gallant and courageous act, Phyllis desperately sought his attentions. Even though Percy remained resistant to her charms, Phyllis wasn't easily put off. In 1993 she won a 'Man In Your Life' magazine competition in which she had described her dream suitor. It was, of course, Percy, who, after much persuasion from landlady Emily, agreed to accompany his gravel-voiced admirer to the dinner she'd won.

'Phyllis: Are you going to kiss me under this mistletoe?'
Percy: 'I wouldn't kiss you under an anaesthetic!'

After their 'date', Phyllis floated on cloud nine and later penned a love sonnet, 'Ode to Percy', which won her first prize in the brewery poetry competition and included the immortal lines: 'When God made Percy he was smiling. He took lusty arms and took two sturdy legs and he stuck them on the body of my darling...'

Despite his constant rebuffs, there were hints that Percy was fonder of Phyllis than he let on. When she was ill, he nursed her and fell asleep by her side – much to her delight.

In 1996 Maud Grimes read Phyllis's teacup and told her that the man of her dreams was waiting for her. This prompted Phyllis to ask for Percy's hand in marriage – unfortunately he thought it was a wind-up and stormed off. Later that year Phyllis moved into the Mayfield Court retirement complex, but hopefully that wasn't the end of the story because a year later, Percy also moved there.

another divorce and blamed her daughter-in-law for driving Brian into the downward spiral of backstreet boozing that was to cost him his life. To make matters worse, Gail wasted no time in replacing Brian when she moved in toyboy lover Martin Platt as a lodger eight months after Brian's death. Outraged Ivy found unlikely support from Gail's own mother, Audrey, who was equally upset by Gail's merry-widow routine. But with Martin taking young Nicky and Sarah under his wing, the mothers in arms were eventually forced to realise that Gail's new man was here to stay.

Round at Number 1, Ken evened the infidelity scores when he embarked on an affair with mousey council secretary Wendy Crozier. Their relationship began as a purely professional one, with Wendy supplying insider information from the council for Ken to print in his newspaper, the *Weatherfield Recorder*. But the scoops caused ructions for the Barlows when councillor Deirdre found herself being blamed for the leaks. Ken finally admitted to Deirdre that his mole was Wendy, and in order to protect herself, Deirdre dropped Wendy in it, losing the secretary her job.

Secretary Wendy Crozier becomes another notch on Ken's bedpost.

The McDonald twins take a JCB for a joyride.

She may have put a stop to Ken's council exclusives, but Deirdre unwittingly pushed her husband and Wendy closer together when a guilty Ken offered Wendy a job at the *Recorder*. Soon the two were sharing more than just journalistic tip-offs and ended up in bed together. When the truth came out, Deirdre put up little effort to save their marriage, sending Ken back into Wendy's arms by throwing him out and ending the Barlow marriage for the time being.

As the decade came to a close, new blood arrived on the Street in the form of the McDonald family. With Alf and Audrey moving to leafy Grasmere Drive, the new owners of their old home, Number 11, were ex-army man Jim (*see page 162*) and barmaid Liz (*see page 160*), accompanied by their teenage sons, Andy and Steve (*see page 166*), who caused mayhem for the residents. Not least Alf, who found his brand new display window smashed to smithereens when Steve took a joy ride on a JCB truck through the front of the shop.

Reg Holdsworth

Played by Ken Morley

'Madman or genius, Betty? I just don't know – and I work with him every day,' sighed trainee manager Curly Watts, as he pondered the maniacal mind of his unpredictable mentor, supermarket boss Reg Holdsworth. With his trademark comedy specs, raging libido and an over-inflated opinion of himself, Reg ruled the aisles of Bettabuy – and later Firman's Freezers – like a despotic dog on heat. It wasn't long into Curly's apprenticeship that Reg was discovered having it away with store detective Renee Dodds in the stockroom, which his sidekick then used to blackmail him and ensure recently sacked shelf-stacker Vera Duckworth was given her job back.

'Reg was an archetypal berk and was instantly recognised by all the people who'd ever worked for a little twerp like him, and because of that he became very popular. I think self-love was one of his main foibles and some really funny plots began to develop as the management frequently tried to seduce the workforce.'

Convinced of his irresistibility, Reg lecherously attempted to work his way through the Street's middle-aged matrons, although both Rita Fairclough and Bet Gilroy were to dampen his ardour by rebuffing him. In 1993 he was stunned to discover his first love, scatterbrained Maureen Naylor, had begun working at the store and the giddy pair soon picked up where they'd left off. They finally tied the knot in 1994 and bought the corner shop, much to the disapproval of Maureen's grim-faced wheelchair-bound mother, Maud, who'd never been a fan of her daughter's overbearing beau. Maud was proved right when randy Reg moved in with fellow Firman's employee, Yvonne Bannister, who worked at the Lowestoft branch, leaving Maureen heartbroken.

Managers Reg and Curly bicker at Firman's Freezers.

Old flames are rekindled for Reg and Maureen.

'The storyline everyone remembers is when Reg tried to seduce the lovely Maureen, played by Sherrie Hewson, on his ridiculous leaking waterbed. Actually, when we filmed it the props guys hadn't heated the waterbed properly and it was like jumping onto a freezer. Knowing the scene would be seen in all the offices on the closed-circuit TV system they have at Granada, I wreaked a dreadful revenge on them – as I turned to camera I dropped the towel, revealing myself in complete nakedness… you could hear the screams from the other side of Manchester!'

Occupations: Supermarket manager and corner-shop owner.
On screen: 1989–1995
Defining moment: In a bid for eternal youth in 1995, Reg buys a toupee to wear at work – when Maud dares him to put it on in the Rovers, he's a laughing stock.

1989

Understandably, Ivy wasn't overly chuffed when her taxi-driver husband Don, a reformed gambler, acquired a greyhound called Lucky from a customer who couldn't afford to pay his fare. Rabidly frothing at the mouth would probably be a good way to describe Ivy's feelings on the subject. But the dopey dog didn't seem to have the winning streak so Don gave up on her. Meanwhile, Ivy had become quite attached to the hulking hound and decided to take over her training, aided and abetted by co-trainer Audrey. But the first time Ivy and Audrey raced Lucky the reason for her sluggishness on the track soon became apparent – Lucky was pregnant. Delighted, Don sold the dog and the pups for a whopping £800, enabling him to pay back a thrilled Ivy for bailing him out of his gambling debt earlier in the year.

At Number 7 Rita gave a home to papergirl Jenny Bradley, but no one could have foreseen the sack-load of trouble she was about to deliver into the newsagent's life. Jenny's mum had been killed in a road traffic accident and she kept running away from her children's home, prompting the big-hearted Rita to foster her. However, keeping the feisty teen in check proved hard work and Rita tracked down her long-lost dad.

Alan Bradley seemed charming and chivalrous but the reunion with his daughter was a far from happy one, as she still harboured resentment for him abandoning her when she was eight years old.

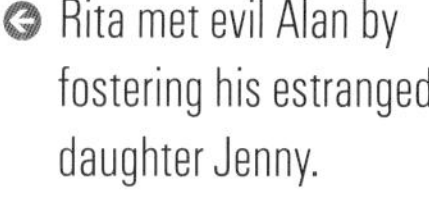

Rita met evil Alan by fostering his estranged daughter Jenny.

Liz McDonald

Played by **Beverley Callard**

Having been assaulted by her volatile husband Jim, mourned her daughter Katie (who was born prematurely), and been held hostage by the henchman of her gangster lover Fraser Henderson, Liz McDonald has been through the mill over the years. But for Beverley Callard there have been plenty of laughs along the way, as lycra-loving Liz has transformed herself from browbeaten army wife to ballsy grande dame of the Rovers Return.

'Sometimes Simon Gregson and I have great difficulty looking at each other without laughing and we have to play scenes where we avoid eye contact. He's got the most twinkly eyes and will make me laugh on purpose. Julie Goodyear was another one who constantly made me howl. I remember once doing a scene in the Rovers with Julie, Bill Tarmey and Roy Barraclough – I was actually laughing so much I was on all fours behind the bar and cried my make-up off.

'Then there's the other side of that which is fantastic for me because Liz can go from high comedy to high drama, and I love doing both. I remember a new director once said to me: "I really want Liz to cry in this. Do you need a tear stick or can you cry real tears?" And Charlie [Lawson, who played Jim] just turned around and said: "Can she cry? She can fill a flippin' bucket!"'

With her short skirts, plunging necklines and mane of red-headed frizz, Liz first set foot on the cobbles when she accompanied hubby Jim on a viewing of Number 11 in the hope of buying it from Alf Roberts. The mother of tearaway teen twins, Andy and Steve, she was taken on as a Rovers barmaid, but her relationship with Jim deteriorated and they divorced in 1997 after he assaulted her when she confessed to an affair.

A year later she nursed him when he was temporarily paralysed in a fall, but had an affair with his physiotherapist. When Jim was imprisoned for the manslaughter of bad-boy Jez Quigley the McDonalds remarried behind bars, although after Jim's sentence was extended Liz refused to wait for him and the union was dissolved.

'The thing with Jim and Liz is they'll love each other forever. They'd row physically and passionately and then the way they made up would also be very physical and passionate. When I first read for the part with Charlie we

'Skirt no bigger than a belt, too much eyeliner and roots as dark as her soul.'

Blanche on Liz

both knew the chemistry was there straight away, it was just an instinctive thing. We met Simon and Nick [Cochrane, alias Andy McDonald] for the first time when we were auditioning them. We'd done readings with hundreds of boys by that point and they were down to the last twelve. Then the producers decided we should all jot down on a piece of paper who we wanted for Andy and Steve and what was quite spooky was everyone that was there had, without exception, written down both Nick and Simon's names.'

After years of working as a barmaid – and a short period in the bakery dodging the ribald advances of owner Diggory Compton – Liz finally became Rovers landlady in 2006 when Steve bought the boozer. In 2007 she married slothful musician and employee Vernon Tomlin, who forgave her affair with Derek the Drayman. But the following year she called it a day with Vernon and embarked upon a relationship with Steve's best mate Lloyd Mullaney, before falling for the charms of rough-diamond building contractor and overprotective dad, Owen Armstrong.

'Male viewers like Liz for the miniskirts but women love Liz because she has that ability to bounce back. Both she and Steve have this self-destruct button about their relationships because they get bored easily. Vernon would've probably loved her for the rest of her life, but for Liz he just wasn't quite exciting enough. She loves that element of danger she had with Jim and, who knows, maybe Owen will be the one to give it to her again...'

Having first appeared in *Corrie* for a three-episode stint in 1984 as June Dewhurst, a good friend of Brian and Gail Tilsley, Beverley admits she'd now happily play Liz for the rest of her days.

'Sometimes I look across at Betty Driver and I'm in awe of her completely. I would love to see myself in the show when I'm her age, but hopefully Liz's miniskirts will have got a bit longer by then. Maybe one day I'll suddenly switch into Emily Bishop's costumes – at least then I'd be warm. I always seem to get massive storylines when I'm standing there, frozen to death, in a backless lycra minidress in the middle of winter!'

- The McDonald clan make Number 11 their home.
- Liz gives Jim a piece of her mind.
- Gangster's moll Liz with bad boy Fraser Henderson.
- Vernon sports a bloodied nose thanks to Jim's fist.
- Michelle's ears burn as Liz and Steve discuss her.
- Love is in the air: sparks fly between Liz and Owen.

Current occupation: Rovers landlady.
On screen: 1989–1998, 2000–2001, 2003, 2004–
Defining moment: In 1993 she has enough of Jim's jealousy and throws him out when he falsely accuses her of cheating – and goes on to enjoy a fling with lithe young buck Colin Barnes.

Jim McDonald

Played by **Charles Lawson**

When it comes to punching people, fiery former squaddie Jim McDonald seems unable to stop himself. From the moment he arrived in Weatherfield he'd found it hard to adapt to civilian life and tended to think with his fists rather than engage his brain.

When his wife Liz confessed to an affair on the car ride home from an army reunion, Jim lashed out with a thump and abandoned her at the side of the road.

The couple married and divorced twice thanks to Jim's boozed-up temper, but he had a taste of his own medicine when Steve pushed him off a scaffold during a row, leaving him temporarily paralysed. He saw red again when, adding insult to injury, Liz started an affair with his physiotherapist.

In 2000 Jim was convicted of manslaughter after a frenzied attack on drug dealer Jez Quigley, who then died of a ruptured spleen. He was eventually released just prior to Liz's wedding to musician Vernon Tomlin. Teetotal Jim appeared to be reformed, but his jealous temper flared on the day of the wedding and he gave the poor groom a battering before Steve told him to get lost.

'There are very few "proper men" in the Street, and I don't mean that in a flippant way, but Jim was a real man, warts and all, and I think that's why he was popular with blokes. He was a man's man who made terrible mistakes but fundamentally he was an honest human being who just lost the plot sometimes.'

When Jim wasn't getting involved in fisticuffs he kept himself busy telling everyone to 'catch yerself on' and ending his every other utterance with 'so it is, Elizabeth'. 'My scripts were initially written in a Mancunian dialect which was just daft, so instead of saying "Good morning" I'd say, "What about you" to make him sound more authentically Northern Irish, and I suppose it became a bit of a catchphrase for him.

'Looking back I have very fond memories of my time on *Coronation Street*. It's no secret at all that I used to enjoy my drink, but I never got into any trouble. I had a couple of warnings about smelling of booze in the morning, but otherwise I had an absolute ball!'

Jim and Liz pucker up.
A scrap with Steve lands Jim in hospital.
The former squaddie adapts to life in a wheelchair.

50 CORONATION ST. ICON

Occupations: Ex-army sergeant, mechanic, builder's labourer and security guard.
On screen: 1989–2000, 2003, 2005, 2007–2008, 2009
Defining moment: When Steve is hospitalised by Jez Quigley in 2000, Jim is overenthusiastic with his revenge and ends up killing him.

Rita is used and abused by sinister Alan.

'We've all had our nightmares. We're all the walkin' wounded. It's just that some of us get more wounded than others...'

Rita

But with Rita's help he slowly won her affections and in the process began to win over Rita as well. They soon became a couple, but Alan had a sinister side; not only did he have a vicious temper, which saw him beat up Terry, but he was also unfaithful and conniving.

Alan had an affair with barmaid Gloria, and when Rita found out, he decided that it was Gloria he wanted to be with. When she rejected him, Alan managed to convince a shattered Rita that he'd made a mistake and had really chosen her over Gloria. Just as Rita trusted in him again, he was made redundant and he told a heartbroken Rita he was leaving and taking a job in Dubai.

However, when he returned three months later, he pursued Rita with a passion and announced he wanted to marry her. Although flattered, Rita was reluctant to commit and instead he moved in. He tried to spring a surprise wedding on her by luring her to a registry office, but the surprise for Alan was that she said no. Although furious, he stayed with her and was soon tugging at her purse strings, pretending he'd been offered a partnership in a burglar-alarm-fitting firm but instead used her £6000 on a fancy new car. He sweet-talked his way out of her fury, before starting an affair with a comely client called Carole. This time he did leave Rita for the other woman, but he soon returned when Carole refused to lend him any money.

1980s Deaths

Renee Roberts (lorry collision)	30 July 1980
Len Fairclough (car crash)	7 December 1983
Bert Tilsley (heart attack)	16 January 1984
Albert Tatlock (heart attack)	14 May 1984
Stan Ogden (died in his sleep)	21 November 1984
Joan Lowther (heart attack)	23 November 1987
Brian Tilsley (stabbed)	15 February 1989
Alan Bradley (run over by tram)	8 December 1989

Alan takes the hands-on approach with receptionist Dawn.
A muddled Rita thinks she's still the club-singer of yesteryear.
Alan attempts to bundle Rita into his car.
Her nightmare is over when Alan is killed by a tram.

By now Alan was after one thing and one thing alone: cash – and lots of it. He found the deeds to Number 7 and, passing himself off as the late Len Fairclough, managed to remortgage Rita's house for £15,000. Next, he set up the Weatherfield Securities shop and employed sassy Dawn Prescott as his receptionist. He later tried to rape Dawn, and in the meantime Carole had warned Rita that Alan was using her for cash. Rita confronted him on the night of Jenny's 18th birthday, but a smug Alan remained calm and confident, telling her he would soon have enough money to pay her back so she could keep her tatty little house. However, Alan lost it when Rita informed him that she'd alerted the building society and he was about to go under. He wasn't going without a fight – he exploded with rage, hitting Rita and then trying to suffocate her with a cushion. Fortunately, Jenny disturbed them and he was arrested.

After spending time in prison, Alan returned to the Street, full of hatred for a terrified Rita and hellbent on punishing her. When she disappeared, the residents suspected he'd killed her, and the police even searched a building site for her body. Then Alec got a call from a Blackpool hotel manager asking about a client of his who'd turned up asking if she could sing in his bar, and he realised it was Rita.

Alec and Bet rushed to Blackpool to find Rita happily belting out a cabaret song as if nothing had happened. And to her mind it hadn't – in her anguish and fear Rita had retreated to the safer world of yesteryear and was talking to dead hubby Len as if he was still alive, and how he might like his kippers for breakfast.

On finding out where she was, a furious Alan followed them to the seaside, determined to make her pay for all the misery he believed she'd put him through. He grabbed Rita in the street and bundled her into his car, but before he could drive off, she escaped. It was a thrilling, chilling chase as a panic-stricken Rita darted across the promenade with the grim-faced Alan in hot pursuit. She narrowly avoided being hit by a tram but, in what is probably the most memorable of Street deaths, Alan ran straight into its path and was instantly killed. As Rita turned to see him die, her memory returned and she collapsed, sobbing hysterically into Bet's arms.

Thankfully, the upcoming Nineties would prove to be a happier time for Rita, when she was to find true, reciprocated love once again. The new decade would also usher in the arrival of angel-faced babe-in-arms David Platt and see the tearjerking end of an era at the Rovers…

Steve McDonald

Played by **Simon Gregson**

When Steve McDonald arrived in Weatherfield he was a cocksure teenage tearaway whose mischief-making antics included joyriding a JCB straight through Alf Roberts' shop window.

'Steve was definitely a naughty boy in the beginning, whereas I was just a shy sixteen-year-old lad who was learning on the job. I hadn't been to drama school and the only thing I'd done before I joined *Corrie* was a paper round.'

No one was more surprised than Simon when he was offered the chance to be part of the Street's volatile new McDonald clan. With no acting experience behind him, he found himself auditioning as Granada's casting directors trawled Manchester's secondary schools looking for two young lads to play twins. 'I only took the job because I wanted an Escort Mexico,' he says, with a grin.

'From the start the McDonald twins took off and it was like being in a boy band. Nick [Cochrane, who played Andy] and I would go to places and there would be girls screaming their heads off with our names on their t-shirts. I remember we'd been in the show less than a year when we went to a club and by the time I'd walked through the place my shirt had been ripped off. I just couldn't get my head around it and I admit I lost the plot for a few years. It's funny watching the kids that come in now because all the attention seems to be like water off a duck's back for them. They handle it much better than I did. Thankfully, these days the press leave me alone and now all anyone wants to talk to me about is what Becky's like!'

When it comes to romance, Steve's failed relationships could give Ken Barlow a run for his money. He managed to get a ring on the finger of Becky Granger at their second attempt, but there have been two previous Mrs McDonalds – Alec Gilroy's heiress granddaughter, Vicky Arden, and factory machinist Karen Phillips, whom first time around he married for a bet. His other love interests have included hairdresser Fiona Middleton (who also had an affair with his dad, Jim), gangster's moll Ronnie Clayton, barmaid Michelle Connor, and of course Tracy Barlow, who became pregnant with daughter Amy after their one-night stand.

'The viewers seem to love it when I'm rowing with strong feisty women – and so do I. Whether it's Steve and Becky or Steve and Karen, I think people like the fact they give each other crap all the time but deep down they love the bones of each other. There's a thing I decided a long time ago, which is to try and play those scenes as much tongue in cheek as possible. I love being able to do that comedy and if the crew are laughing then you know you're doing something right.'

But Simon hasn't always felt so self-assured in front of the camera. 'When I was younger I had absolutely no confidence at all. At the point I had to do my first screen kiss, with an actress called Tania Rodrigues [who played Steve's first girlfriend Joanne Khan], I remember saying to the producer that I had reservations about it. He asked me what the problem was, and I was like, "I'm just a normal fifteen-year-old lad who is now meant to be snogging this twenty-five-year-old woman on TV. That's my problem."

'I don't think it ever sunk in to people there at that point that I was just some normal kid off the street with no acting training or experience. How I got away with it is beyond me, but now there's nothing that fazes me. At one point they kept writing in the script "Steve comes out of the bedroom in just his boxer shorts", because they'd been doing those kind of shots with Jason or Ciaran, who've been down the gym loads, whereas I've just got this big beer belly. So I thought, "Well, I'll just stick it out even more" and I started pretending to pull fluff out of my belly button. Or I'd sit there scratching my backside and it soon got written differently. I was like, you'll give up before I do. I don't embarrass that easily anymore...'

So, what does Simon think when he looks back at clips of his fresh-faced younger self arriving on the cobbles? 'I think – what on earth was going on with my hair? I look like something out of a Duran Duran video!'

'Steve wasn't even innocent in the womb.'

Andy

- Baby-faced brothers Steve and Andy.
- Vicky becomes the first Mrs Steve McDonald.
- On a prison visit he begs Fiona for a second chance.
- Street Cars' supremos Vikram and Steve man the switch.
- There's no love lost between Liz and Karen.
- Steve dumped Michelle in favour of Becky.

Curent occupation: Rovers Return proprietor and co-owner of Street Cars.
On screen: 1989–
Defining moment: Finally being forced to act like a responsible adult when he gets custody of daughter Amy in 2007.

1990s

Not since the 'Free Nelson Mandela' crusade had an injustice so captured the imagination of the British public as the imprisonment of Deirdre Rachid. The intention of the 'Free The Weatherfield One' campaign was to liberate the innocent travel agent after she had been found guilty on several counts of fraud, leaving her languishing in jail with only cellmate Jackie Dobbs (alias Margi Clarke) for company, while her scheming conman lover Jon Lindsay remained a free man.

Even the then Prime Minister, Tony Blair – with his tongue firmly in his cheek – spoke in the House of Commons about this gross miscarriage of justice and wondered if he or the Home Secretary should intervene on Deirdre's behalf. This led the *Daily Mail* to comment: 'The dividing line between *Coronation Street* fiction and real-life fact has now not so much blurred as completely disappeared up the nation's aerials.'

As the *Daily Mail* continued to despair, the *Mirror* and the *Sun* gleefully played along, issuing 'Free The Weatherfield One' t-shirts and car stickers. Meanwhile, Anne Kirkbride was bemused to find herself in the midst of the show's most high-profile storyline to date. 'I still have trouble getting my head around how big it got. It was mad. I remember my mother-in-law rang me up and said, "Put the telly on, you're on the *News at Ten* – you've been mentioned by Tony Blair!" It all became incredibly surreal and I did just want to say: "Look, it's not real, surely there are more important causes to be campaigning for?"'

The *Street*'s producers had always planned for Deirdre to be released after three weeks in the slammer, but when she was finally freed several newspapers suggested it was the public outcry on their front pages that had led to the decision.

- The release of 'The Weatherfield One' makes front-page news.
- A line-up to remember: the regulars commemorate another milestone.
- Future Prime Minister Tony Blair meets Weatherfield's finest.

The decade also saw the programme flourish, with a fourth weekly episode added in 1996 and the outdoor set expanded. The derelict Graffiti Club on Rosamund Street was reopened as a medical centre and a new thoroughfare was created, Victoria Street, which became home to premises including Elliott & Son butcher's shop and Roy's Rolls.

In July 1997 the brash Battersby clan arrived and the residents looked on with horror at their new neighbours from hell. The brainchild of producer Brian Park (swiftly dubbed the 'axe man' after culling Derek Wilton on his first day in the job), the boisterous brood had been created to give the street a wake-up call. But off-screen as well as on it took until the end of the year for the public to warm to them – meanwhile the *Radio Times* went as far as to demand their removal.

'When we arrived there were just pages of comments from people on Ceefax saying how much they hated us,' explains Vicky Entwistle. 'But I liked that, because there's nothing worse than coming into a massive institution like *Coronation Street* with a whimper. You want to arrive with an impact, and by 'eck we got one.'

By December the increasingly entertaining new family had begun to win over their doubters. Even so, their festive antics resulted in a record number of complaints to the Granada duty office when Les Battersby brought a live turkey home with the intention of slaughtering it for their Christmas dinner. However, in the event, he only killed it by accident, mowing it down in his car. The bird, who was named Theresa, was actually a model.

In 1990 Weatherfield life was rocked to its very foundations when smarmy brewery boss Nigel Ridley announced he intended to gut the Rovers and turn it into an American theme pub called Yankees – complete with Stetson-wearing bar staff and diner-style bar stools. The young upstart offered Deirdre, who was still separated from Ken, a tasty £30,000 for Number 1 in order to knock through and extend the new-look pub. At first Deirdre wasn't convinced, but when Ridley upped the offer by another £5,000 she gave in to temptation, seeing the sale of the house as a way for her to start her life over again, away from Coronation Street. Meanwhile, the general consensus in the Street was that Deirdre was stabbing everyone in the back by selling out to the brewery.

Seeing pound-signs in his eyes, landlord Alec could barely contain his excitement at the idea of Yankees, but Bet was furious. When Alec realised just how upset Bet was underneath her bravado, he agreed to turn down the brewery's offer for a refit. However, it wasn't that simple, and Nigel made it clear if the Gilroys didn't come on board they'd be transferred to the Quarryman's Rest, a clapped-out and haunted old pub in Weatherfield's roughest neighbourhood. Desperate, Bet begged Deirdre not to sell and even Emily attempted to change her friend's mind, without any success. Deirdre snapped back: 'If you think it's a crime me selling my house to the brewery, well I'll tell you this. I've got Tracy to think about. It's her future, not just my own.'

By Nigel's next visit (armed with a tape measure and the brightly coloured plans for the new-look Yankees), Bet had finally reached the end of her tether and unceremoniously threw him out. Bolting the door behind him, she made a momentous decision – the Gilroys were going on strike. Despite the staff having officially downed tools, the Rovers regulars did still manage to get their hands on a freshly pulled pint by clambering over the back wall to get served.

'Where I went wrong was going into the licensed trade in the first place. Tropical fish – that was my other idea.'

Alec

▲ Bet and Alec are torn by the brewery's demands.

▼ Mike and Des mount the gate in a bid for a pint.

Unfortunately Christmas wasn't a season to be jolly for the Duckworths – instead a terrified Jack and Vera spent most of the festivities cowering upstairs in their bedroom while Boomer, the scary dog Jack had bought Vera for Christmas, held them captive and ate their turkey dinner! The angry pooch had chased the bickering couple up the stairs when, having arrived home from a festive tipple at the Rovers, they'd discovered him making a start on their turkey. It was only as Vera's cries for help were heard by passing lodger Curly that the couple were saved from Boomer's wrath. With the dog now sleeping soundly on a full stomach, Vera picked up some roast turkey remnants from the floor and suggested they make the best of it. Jack refused point blank to eat a dog's sloppy seconds and told Vera to fry them some chips instead. Vera was appalled, exclaiming: 'Jack, I'm not a religious woman, but even I know you don't get the chip pan out on Christmas Day!'

Soon the story became news and *The Gazette* interviewed the Gilroys – they even appeared on Radio Weatherfield. By the time their battle became a national news story, the brewery had decided enough was enough and served the Gilroys with notice that they were repossessing the pub. But just as the brewery's henchmen were banging on the door to take control of the premises, the much-loved boozer was saved at the very last minute by old Mr Newton, who had come out of retirement to stop the refurbishment. The former brewery boss poured scorn on Nigel's plans and insisted the Rovers would always stay a working man's pub and that was his final word on the subject. While the locals celebrated with a warm pint, Deirdre sat at home alone, wondering if she'd ever be able to face her neighbours again.

Meanwhile, Rita uprooted The Kabin from Rosamund Street into Coronation Street itself – as part of the new redeveloped side of the street where the old factory and community centre had been. And feeling unsafe in her home at Number 7, thanks to her Alan Bradley ordeal, she moved into the flat above the new shop.

In December that year two major events took place, the results of which are still having repercussions on the Street today – the births of stroppy Rosie Webster and devil-child David Platt. Little did the residents back then have any idea that Sally and Gail's little bundles of joy were going to cause so much drama so many years later.

While first-time parents-to-be Sally and Kevin celebrated their pregnancy news, mum-of-two Gail wasn't quite so chuffed about her situation and was unsure about the strength of her burgeoning relationship with toy-boy Martin Platt. Her first thought was to opt for a secret abortion – a fact teenage David (*see page 226*) found out in 2006 when he discovered the diary of his late grandmother, Ivy, who wasn't exactly over the moon at Gail's pregnancy. To be precise, Ivy was livid when she found out and ranted at Gail, ridiculing her morals and reminding her that Brian was barely cold in his grave. Gail's mum Audrey wasn't thrilled about the news either, but stuck up for her confused daughter the next time ranting Ivy laid into her.

Gail decided an abortion was the best way forward and it was only when Martin reassured her that he was committed and mature enough to be a father that she changed her mind. So Christmas brought the gift of life when Rosie Webster was born on Christmas Eve in the back of Don's cab, delivered by Liz. In hospital the next day a beaming Sally cuddled her newborn daughter and told the nurse they'd be naming her Rosie, as when she was born the taxi had been in Rosamund Street.

Angel-faced David Platt came into the world on Christmas Day, much to the joy of proud first-time dad Martin. Meanwhile, Gail and Sally were delighted they'd been assigned adjoining beds on the maternity ward and it was smiles all round as the besotted parents introduced their newborns to each other.

'That woman should be in perpetual black – like one of them old Greek women, little tufts of hair sprouting out of her chin and her head cast down. Picture of flamin' misery.'

Audrey on Ivy

The following year Vera said goodbye to one parent and gained another. At her mother Amy Burton's funeral, an eccentric elderly man, Joss Shackleton, introduced himself to a stunned Vera as the long-lost father she'd never known. Even more mind-blowing for Vera was when Joss let her in on a well-kept family secret – that he was the illegitimate grandson of none other than King Edward VII. This was music to Vera's ears because it meant she was now related to her idol, Her Majesty The Queen. Satisfied she truly had blue blood running through her veins, Vera admitted to a baffled Jack that she'd always 'felt royal'.

Jack wasn't quite so convinced about Joss's parentage and saw it as the perfect opportunity to wind up Vera. So when she wrote a letter to the Queen explaining their family bond and started putting on the kind of airs and graces even Annie would've balked at, Jack replied, pretending to be Her Royal Highness and wrote: 'Her Majesty is so sorry to hear of the death of your mother, and offers her condolences at this very sad time.' But when he saw how deeply moved Vera was with the letter, exclaiming it the proudest moment of her life, Jack couldn't bring himself to shatter his wife's illusions and let Vera believe in her royal connections for years to come.

Proud mums Gail and Sally show off their angelic offspring... David and Rosie.
Vera's heart belongs to Daddy.
The Queen's card makes Vera swell with pride.

1990s Births

Rosie (Sally & Kevin Webster)	24 December 1990
David (Gail Tilsley & Martin Platt)	25 December 1990
Katie (Liz & Jim McDonald)	1 January 1992
Tommy (Lisa & Terry Duckworth)	9 September 1992
Sophie (Sally & Kevin Webster)	4 November 1994
Daniel (Denise Osbourne & Ken Barlow)	4 January 1995
Brad (Tricia Armstrong & Terry Duckworth)	14 Feb 1997
Shannon (Zoe Tattersall & Liam Shepherd)	27 Aug 1997
Morgan (Fiona Middleton & Alan McKenna)	16 Feb 1998
William & Rebecca (Judy & Gary Mallett)	25 Dec 1998

Raquel Watts

Played by **Sarah Lancashire**

They were the wide-eyed twosome that everyone wanted a happy ending for, and when Raquel Wolstenhulme and Curly Watts did finally get hitched, more than twenty-two million viewers breathed a contented sigh of relief. However, their union proved to be bittersweet and soon Raquel admitted what she'd known all along – she loved Curly with all her heart, but she wasn't in love with him.

A bumper audience of twenty million tuned in for Raquel's tear-jerking farewell scenes as she left her husband of a year to start a new life as a beautician in Kuala Lumpur, Malaysia, and it looked like Raquel had gone for good. But three years later, viewers were nearly as gobsmacked as Curly when she returned for a very special two-hander episode which saw the former Rovers barmaid reveal to her estranged husband that he was a father and to ask for a divorce in order to marry her French wine-producer boyfriend.

'I never imagined I'd go back, I didn't think there was any reason for me go back, but when they came up with the two-hander idea it was just too good to turn down. And I felt privileged to be asked because it was the millennium episode, so it was an honour to help bring *Coronation Street* into the new century.

'It was all very cloak and dagger and I wasn't allowed to tell anyone about it, which was easier for me as I was away from the *Street*, but Kevin [Kennedy] was still very much in the fold, so it all had to be done very discreetly. We did our read through at the producer Jane McNaught's house, along with John Stevenson, the writer, and Brian Mills, the wonderful director who is sadly no longer with us. We didn't even film the episode in the *Coronation Street* studios because they didn't want anyone to find out what we were up to, so they dismantled Curly's set and took it into one of the studios in the main building at Granada instead. It was all terribly secretive and kind of exciting because of that.

'Raquel and Curly were similar characters; they were both innocents really. Honest, unthreatening and both slightly out of their depths. And while Raquel had this dizzy comic strand about her, there was a real tragic element to her as well. She seemed to be planted an inch off the ground, so when she fell, she fell with a thud.

'I said when I left the show that I'd been spoilt with storylines, and I still believe that, because there wasn't a day when I didn't want to go into work to play Raquel. And that's a joy, isn't it? Even if I had an episode where I only had two lines I probably had the best two lines in the show.'

Sarah's father, Geoffrey Lancashire, who died in 2004, was one of the show's original scriptwriters, working alongside creator Tony Warren. He wrote 73 classic episodes and that family connection made being on the *Street* even more special for Sarah.

'One thing that was really lovely was that because both my parents had worked at Granada there was always somebody who'd come over and go, "How's your dad?" or, "How's your mum?" which was really heart-warming. I always felt I was there in my own right, but at the same time I was hugely proud of my dad's work and he really enjoyed what I did and would always phone after a particularly good or poignant episode and tell me what he thought.

'I never expected to end up in the show, to be honest. Because I trained as a stage actress it wasn't even on my radar, but I feel blessed to have been part of it. It was a real privilege to serve what seemed almost like an apprenticeship with legends like Julie [Goodyear], Roy [Barraclough] and Betty Driver, who I adored. Raquel was like a little Bambi behind the bar in the Rovers and she floored them all so many times with her surreal take on things, but at the same time she was a great foil for Bet. I loved working with all the older cast members and I think that's actually what I miss most about the show, in that it was like a family and we passed the time of day together. These people do seep into your soul and you never forget them, ever.'

Meanwhile, when it comes to Raquel's infamous mis-matched mini skirts and pastel-shaded denim jackets, Sarah reveals that the clothes weren't as tacky as they looked. 'I'll tell you a secret. The extraordinary thing is that most of Raquel's clothes were from Marks & Spencer. So it just goes to show it's not what you wear, but how you wear it...'

'The amount of scent she wears, my nasal passages are in rags.'

Alec on Raquel

- Alec advises new barmaid Raquel on her pint-pulling technique.
- Bet and Raquel share the love.
- The sometime model enters 'Miss Bettabuy'.
- Nesting with Des: but he broke her heart.
- Raquel makes an unexpected millennium return.

Occupations: Rovers barmaid and aspiring model.
On screen: 1991–1996, 2000
Defining moment: Following a humiliating one-night stand with her ex, Des, she asks ever-eager Curly to marry her immediately in 1995.

When store manager Reg put Curly in charge of the Bettabuys float at the Weatherfield Carnival, his bespectacled deputy was left in no doubt that his egomaniac boss would expect to be the star attraction. When fashion student Angie came on board to design the float, a theme of 'The Horn Of Plenty' was agreed on and Reg couldn't wait to get into his toga and start lording it up as Bacchus, God of Wine. He wasn't quite so ebullient when he discovered his nubile vestal virgins were to be none other than middle-aged shelf-stackers Vera and Ivy. But it was all worth it when Bettabuys won the Herbert Crabtree Memorial Shield for best float. However, when Angie presented Reg with a design bill of £406 he refused to pay it, insisting the event was for charity. Instead he instructed Curly to give Angie a £10 Bettabuys voucher by way of a thank you. Furious Angie ripped up the voucher and it was up to Curly to step in, refusing to give the gleaming winner's shield back to Reg until he'd paid Angie in full.

Meanwhile, Mavis was desperate to know whether hubby Derek found her sexually attractive, and after reading about the aphrodisiac properties of parsnips she began inundating Derek with parsnip surprise casserole in the hope of some passion on the eiderdown. At first she was annoyed that the parsnips seemed to be having little effect, but when shame-faced Derek admitted he'd slapped a cleaner's bottom at work at Pendlebury Paper Products, a guilt-ridden Mavis knew her parsnips were to blame.

She rued the day she'd ever set eyes on the root vegetable when the molested cleaner threatened to take the company to a tribunal for sexual harassment. Appalled, Mavis begged the woman to change her mind, and after much persuasion managed to get the cleaner to drop the action against her husband. Needless to say, when the Wiltons discovered Bet had put parsnips in their hotpots a few days later they lost their appetite.

The skeletons in his closet of shiny suits came back to haunt Mike within weeks of his wedding to his business partner Jackie Ingram, making their marriage one of the shortest in Coronation Street history. Of course, Mike's attraction to Jackie was nothing to do with the fact he was down on his luck financially and that Jackie was a very wealthy woman, thanks to her husband (one of Mike's competitors) recently dropping dead and leaving his entire fortune to his wife.

Meet the wife: Mike introduces Jackie to his ex, Deirdre.

After spontaneously tying the knot, it only took a week for it to dawn on Jackie that cunning Mike was more interested in her bank balance than her. Finding out he was still involved with his ex, Alma Sedgwick (*see page 155*) – Mike had bought the café in secret using a fictitious company, Alcazar Holdings – and that her husband also had an illegitimate son he'd failed to mention, were the final nails in the coffin of their relationship. Feeling bitterly betrayed, Jackie threatened a petrified Mike with a loaded shotgun before leaving him for good.

If Mike thought things were bad for him, he could have looked to his love rival Ken for comfort, for when 1990 drew to a close Ken had reached rock bottom. He'd hoped for a reconciliation with his ex, Deirdre, but she'd fallen for the charms of dodgy amusement arcade owner Phil Jennings and the couple were spending New Year together in Paris. Meanwhile, maudlin Ken (who was now living in reduced circumstances over the corner shop) was spending New Year's Eve on his own and had let himself into Number 1 to drown his sorrows surrounded by memories of better times gone by.

With the party in full swing at the Rovers next door, a drunk and depressed Ken was on the verge of taking an overdose. He lined up twelve pills on the table and proceeded to pop them into his mouth one by one, interspersed by gulps of whisky. Fortunately he was interrupted by Bet, who'd assumed something was up when

'Smooth lecherous Cockney he might be. But there aren't many of the boss class left like him. Dedicated to grinding the faces of the working classes and laughing all the way to the bank. Now that's what I call job satisfaction.'

Alec

she saw the light on in the supposedly empty house. Quietly letting herself in by the back door, Bet caught a startled Ken in the act and went to call an ambulance. But on discovering Ken had only got to his third pill, she put the phone down and pulled up a chair to listen to his troubles.

Ken was tearful as he poured his heart out, explaining that he'd made a mess of his life and felt so desperately alone. The pills had seemed an easy way out. Taking Ken's hand, a concerned Bet admitted she once very nearly did exactly the same thing.

The next day Bet called in on an embarrassed Ken who told her he'd always be grateful for her kindness. Bet replied that she wasn't a saint and didn't need his gratitude – instead she suggested they carry on as normal: 'The next time you come in the Rovers, I want you to order your half a bitter as usual, pay your 44p and say thank you as you always do – just as if last night never happened.' Smiling for the first time in weeks, Ken promised he'd try.

In 1992 fresh-faced Carmel Finnan first set foot onto the cobbles and Gail couldn't believe her luck at finding such a considerate, caring babysitter to help look after her three children. On the surface, softly spoken Carmel seemed perfect nanny material, but beneath the sickly sweet smile it soon became apparent she was a total loon. She developed an unhealthy obsession with Martin and saw his son David as a way of getting closer to him.

Nanny-from-hell Carmel wants Martin all to herself.

There was no doubt that David was her favourite Platt child – because he was the only one that was biologically Martin's – and on a number of occasions the increasingly sinister Irish woman would pass him off as her own. One time she even whispered insanely to David that she loved his father more than life itself and intended to replace Gail as Martin's wife.

Carmel managed to fool everyone in the Platt household, but Sally wasn't quite so gullible. When the nanny implied, all faux concern, that perhaps the Platts' marriage of a year was on the rocks, a suspicious Sally became one of the first to spot that maybe Carmel wasn't the full shilling.

Her Martin-focussed obsession stepped up a gear when Gail stayed overnight at hospital with her mum Audrey, who was afraid Alf had suffered another heart attack – it turned out he'd merely been stuffing

Natalie Barnes

Played by **Denise Welch**

Natalie Horrocks sashayed into Weatherfield to take over the running of the garage from her mechanic son, Tony, but she seemed far more interested in giving co-owner Kevin Webster the come hither than the profit margins. As one of the show's most stable marriages fell apart, vampish Natalie became the most hated woman on Coronation Street.

But she wasn't as brassy as she liked to make out, and when Kevin crawled back to Sally, she dusted herself down, got a job at the pub and fell for bookie Des Barnes. Tragically, a month after they were married Des was murdered by thugs searching for her son Tony. There was more heartache for Natalie two years later, when her drug-dealer son was found dead and buried on a nearby building site.

By now Natalie had risen from much-gossiped-about man-eater to popular Rovers proprietor, having bought the boozer from Alec Gilroy. 'I was stunned and honoured when I found out I was going to be landlady of the Rovers. I thought, "My God, I used to watch this show when I was five or six years old and Annie Walker ran the place!" But as any fictitious barmaid will tell you, the reality of it is you're hours on end standing in the background without any dialogue. Roy Barraclough [who played Alec] and I used to invent our own little subplots behind the bar to relieve our boredom.'

Natalie began dating dashing Ian Bentley, only to discover he was about to marry Sharon Gaskell (who was Rita Sullivan's former foster child). So after being confronted by a livid Rita, she swiftly dumped him. In 2000 Natalie found herself pregnant by ex-boyfriend Vinny Sorrell, who'd cheated on her with her flirty younger sister, Debs Brownlow, and after much soul-searching Natalie decided to leave the heartbreak behind her and make a fresh start in the Cotswolds.

'I never expected to be in the show for so long because Natalie came in purely to break up the Websters' marriage and then I'd thought she'd be off. But the timing of the character was that the public were ready to have someone to love to hate, and as any actress will tell you, playing the bitch is much more satisfying than playing the nice guy.'

↑↑ Natalie gets passionate with Kevin.
↑ Wedding joy with husband Des and son Tony.
↘ Des dies after being attacked by a druggie gang.

Occupation: Rovers barmaid and landlady.
On screen: 1997–2000
Defining moment: Seducing mechanic Kevin into looking under her bonnet in 1997 and subsequently destroying the Websters' marriage.

50 CORONATION ST. ICON

It was ladies versus gents in the Rovers when the brewery ordered Bet (now on her own after Alec had walked out on her for a life on the ocean wave) to enter the Rovers in a local super quiz in order to boost trade. Lecherous Reg offered his services as team leader – in a bid to get into Bet's good books and potentially get his leg over – and organised a practice quiz night to prepare for the main event. With Reg as quizmaster and dumb-blonde barmaid Raquel as his glamorous assistant, the teams consisted of Curly, Derek, Jack and Martin versus Vera, Mavis, Gail and Deirdre. The event started well, but it soon descended into chaos when the women became convinced the men were trying to cheat them out of a point. All hell broke loose, with Gail and Vera getting particularly irate. All this took place under the disapproving eye of unimpressed brewery boss Richard Willmore, who told a downcast Bet she had a couple of months to get more custom in the pub, or she would be replaced.

his face with past their sell-by-date Christmas puddings. With Martin all to herself, Carmel made the most of the opportunity and climbed into his bed while he was out at a Christmas party. When he returned home he was so drunk that he didn't notice the woman in the bed next to him was Carmel, not Gail. The following morning poor Martin nearly jumped out of his skin when he woke up and discovered who it was that was spooning him. He was livid, whereas Carmel decided it was a good time to confess her undying love for him.

Her true colours were exposed for all to see when Martin finally snapped after yet another of her increasingly bizarre advances and prepared to throw her out. Fighting back, Carmel informed a bewildered Gail that she was far too old for Martin, that Gail had taken advantage of a younger man and that Martin was head over heels in love with Carmel, not Gail.

Gail just laughed in Carmel's barmy face, and with Martin's help she chucked her out into the street, thinking they'd seen the back of her once and for all. But the nanny from hell soon reappeared and went on to feign pregnancy and tried to abduct David. Only the arrival of her grandfather from Ireland put a stop to the proceedings. He told the Platts this had happened before, explaining that Carmel had needed hospital treatment for her obsessive tendencies before and he was taking her back to Ireland for more psychiatric help.

'Once I only had to walk in t' Ritz Ballroom and I'd be fighting 'em off. Now I could swan in in me nuddy and they'd not give a pause from swilling lager.'

Bet

A moment's happiness: Rita marries terminally ill Ted.

'I've had trifles last longer than some of her marriages.'

Vera on Rita

In June 1992 two very different Weatherfield weddings took place. Mike and Alma finally tied the knot at Weatherfield Registry Office with the bride glowing in canary yellow and a slap-up no-expense-spared reception afterwards. While the third Mrs Baldwin hoped for wedded bliss, fellow bride Rita, who had been married just two weeks earlier, already knew her marriage wasn't to have a happy ending.

When she began dating gentlemanly confectionary sales rep Ted Sullivan, Rita knew she'd met a kindred spirit. He asked her to retire to Florida with him and they holidayed there to see if Rita would take to a life in the sun. On their return Ted proposed, but then he shocked Rita with the revelation that he had an inoperable brain tumour and wanted to spend all the time he had left with her. Thinking it over, an emotional Rita agreed to marry him, but insisted they stayed in Weatherfield, near her friends and neighbours – much to Mavis and Derek's annoyance as they'd been hoping to buy The Kabin when Rita emigrated.

In the middle of her hen night Rita broke down and confided in Audrey the truth about Ted's condition, which deteriorated rapidly over the following weeks. Their marriage lasted just under three months and Ted passed away quietly on a park bench whilst watching Percy play in a bowls tournament.

Rita coped with the funeral thanks to the support of her friends, but it was the aftermath of her husband's death that proved to be more of an ordeal for the grieving newsagent. When Ted's will was read – leaving most of his estate to Rita – his family exploded, calling Rita a conniving gold-digger who'd married Ted for his money and vowing to contest the will.

Mortified, and not wanting any ill feeling, Rita met up with Ted's brother-in-law Philip Brookes, who upset her by suggesting that terminally ill Ted wasn't of sound mind when he'd married her. Meanwhile, Ted's sister Sarah wanted to come to an agreement with Rita without going to court, saying that Ted's house was full of memories of their childhood. This caused Rita to ponder how well she actually knew Ted – after all, they'd only been married a short time. Rita decided to come to an agreement with them, saying she only wanted one of Ted's watercolours and that they could have everything else. She also offered to split the money from the sale of the house, but that wasn't enough for Ted's greedy family and they told Rita they'd see her in court.

Fortunately, the judge was firmly on Rita's side and she won the entire estate. Back at The Kabin after the hearing, Rita was furious that Ted's memory had been dragged through the courts, and when his nephew Roger tried to apologise she threw him out. She was upset that his family's behaviour had forced her to question her relationship with Ted, because she knew that his last days with her had been his happiest...

Wide-eyed Lisa Horton also had little luck in love. She had only married criminal-minded Terry earlier in the year when she'd found out she was pregnant with his child, but with Terry imprisoned for GBH she struggled to bring up their son Tommy on her own. Realising Terry was never going to change his bad-boy ways, she dumped him and moved into Number 6 with bookie Des Barnes (whose marriage to flighty wife Steph had been shortlived) who was a much better father figure for her young son. Terry's mum Vera was furious at these developments, accusing Des of wrecking her son's marriage, until Des pointed out that Terry had managed that all by himself by getting locked up in the first place. Lisa and Des had planned a future together as a family away from

1990s Deaths

Katie McDonald (premature birth)	2 January 1992
Ted Sullivan (brain tumour)	9 September 1992
Lisa Duckworth (brain damage/car crash)	12 Feb 1993
Brendan Scott (heart attack)	20 August 1993
Samir Rachid (head injuries)	2 June 1995
Ivy Brennan (stroke)	23 August 1995
Joyce Smedley (run over by car)	21 February 1997
Derek Wilton (heart attack)	7 April 1997
Don Brennan (car crash)	8 October 1997
Billy Williams (heart attack)	3 November 1997
Shannon Tattersall (meningitis)	17 April 1998
Anne Malone (frozen to death)	9 October 1998
Des Barnes (heart attack)	18 November 1998
Alf Roberts (heart attack)	1 January 1999
Tony Horrocks (murdered)	4 February 1999
Judy Mallett (embolism)	24 September 1999

It was the end of an era – albeit briefly – for Alf when his wife Audrey finally convinced him to sell the corner shop, worried that working such long hours was affecting her Alfie's health. On his emotional last day of trading, the portly shopkeeper took home the bacon slicer as a memento (much to Audrey's annoyance) and was delighted to be made an honorary life member of WARTS (Weatherfield Association of Retail Traders). But his self-imposed retirement didn't last long, and after the corner shop's unpopular new owner, Brendan Scott, had a heart attack, Alf couldn't resist buying his beloved premises back at auction, telling an exasperated Audrey he simply couldn't live without it.

Weatherfield, but tragically in 1993 Lisa was knocked down by a speeding car as she fumbled on the ground for her dropped purse on her way home from the Rovers. She died later in hospital, her death affecting a heartbroken Des much more than her estranged husband Terry.

Vera agreed to give up her job at the factory to care for Tommy until Terry completed his prison sentence, when she'd expected her son would play the loving father and take over full parental responsibilities. Instead, to Vera's horror, two days after his release Terry sold Tommy to Lisa's parents, the Hortons. He said he wasn't the fathering type and that Vera was too old to raise a child, but in reality the dodgy Duckworth just saw Tommy as a way of getting his hands on some easy cash. Vera was stunned that her own flesh and blood could be so heartless, and as the Hortons arrived to take Tommy back to Blackpool with them, she broke down completely.

Lisa and Des plan a future with baby Tommy.
Vera is forced to hand Tommy over to Geoff Horton.

Tyrone Dobbs

Played by **Alan Halsall**

When Deirdre Barlow's light-fingered, ex-cell mate Jackie Dobbs and her seemingly bad-lad son Tyrone began squatting at Number 7 the neighbours must've feared for the safety of their best cutlery. With jailbird Jackie as a role model, Tyrone hadn't had the best start in life, but he wasn't cut from the same cloth. So when his mouthy mother was hauled back to her native Liverpool by his thuggish dad, Tyrone opted to bed down in the bins at Freshco instead.

Soon Kevin Webster took him on as an apprentice at the garage, while Jack and Vera Duckworth treated him as a surrogate son and welcomed him into their home. His transition from potential delinquent to teen with a dream was almost complete – all he needed now was a girlfriend. First came dowdy dog-obsessed Maria Sutherland, as they bonded sweetly over his pet greyhound, Monica, who was followed by stalker-ish troublemaker Fiz Brown. Finally he met the love of his life, shop assistant Molly Compton.

'What people forget is that Tyrone was a really bad lad when he came into the show, which was obviously his mother's influence. But deep down all he wanted was to be loved and to have some sense of family, which he eventually got from Jack and Vera, who helped him grow up.'

With real life mirroring the *Street*, Alan also credits his screen 'dad' Bill Tarmey for helping him find his feet as a young actor.

'Bill took me under his wing from a very early age and I was so thankful for him, because if anyone's got a level head on their shoulders it's Bill. What you have to understand is that I was a sixteen-year-old kid and I was in the biggest show on British television. I was being recognised everywhere I went and when you're that young you can be very easily influenced. I was going down that road of thinking I was invincible and going out all the time instead of focusing on being an actor. So Bill sat me down and gave me a good talking to, using some quite colourful language, and I still try to thank him every day for doing that. Because I really love my job, and without him I'm not sure I'd still be doing it.'

Finger-wagging Jackie sets Tyrone a bad example.

Doggy-doings: Maria and Tyrone bond over Monica.

Jack is proud as punch when Tyrone and Molly wed.

Current occupation: Mechanic.
On screen: 1998–
Defining moment: His romantic wedding to Molly Compton in 2009 – they get hitched despite the big day nearly being ruined due to one of Auntie Pam's dodgy deals and his mum robbing their Paris honeymoon tickets.

50 CORONATION ST. ICON

Warring barmaids Tanya and Raquel are the best of enemies.

After years of defending him, an exhausted Vera finally saw the light – her son was bad news and even she couldn't justify his behaviour this time.

Over at the Rovers, newcomer ditzy barmaid Raquel Wolstenhulme (*see page 174*) and vampish new pint puller Tanya Pooley were at war. The rivals were chalk and cheese and manipulative Tanya knew just how to hit childlike Raquel where it hurt, regularly mocking her featherbrained nature and supermodel aspirations. One time Tanya took great delight in setting Raquel up on a fake modelling assignment, which resulted in the sweet-natured blonde standing alone in a deserted fruit and veg market until she'd realised it was just a cruel trick. Des found out and rescued teary Raquel, then spent the night comforting her. The pair began dating, which led to Tanya deciding her next trick would be to have an affair with Des behind Raquel's back.

At Bettabuys, wannabe ladies man Reg Holdsworth (*see page 158*) couldn't believe his eyes when he discovered his first love, Maureen Naylor, had started working at the store. Twenty-five years earlier, Maureen's domineering mother, Maud Grimes, had split the couple up after taken an instant dislike to Reg's smarminess. But it wasn't long before the eccentric pair, older but maybe not wiser, rekindled their romance down the aisles in Bettabuys, despite Maud's attempts to ruin their relationship second time around.

'If you want to scratch each other's eyes out you do it outside of working hours. Because while you're behind this bar, there are no barmaids and there are no models. There are only bloody ladies. Alright?'

Bet to Tanya and Raquel

OVERHEARD

Ken gives Raquel her first French lesson, 1993

THE ROVERS BACK ROOM. KEN IS SITTING AT THE TABLE WITH A PILE OF FRENCH TEXT BOOKS. RAQUEL TOTTERS IN WITH TWO CUPS AND SAUCERS.

RAQUEL: (HANDING KEN HIS TEA) It's very exciting for me this. Cos there's summut about French people I like. I find them sort of...

SHE SITS DOWN.

KEN: Sympatique?

RAQUEL: (NOT UNDERSTANDING) Yer what?

KEN: Sympatique. It means you get on. You feel an affinity.

RAQUEL: Oh yeah. Sympatique. Like I should've been born French, you know. Instead of in Eccles.

KEN: Oh well, never mind. I'm sure there's a lot of Frenchmen wishing they'd been born in Eccles.

RAQUEL: (LAUGHING NERVOUSLY) There aren't Ken. I mean, I can't prove it. I just feel it in me water.

KEN: So, how much French do you know?

RAQUEL: Well, I know what baguettes are. Coffee's café. Red wine's vin rouge. Oh, I met a French man in Corfu who taught me how to say isn't it a lovely day today.

KEN: I think you'll find there are lot of words you know as we go on. Okay, let's start at the beginning. Bonjour Raquel.

RAQUEL: (ENTHUSIASTIC) Oh yeah I know that. Bonjour Ken.

KEN: Je m'appelle Ken...

RAQUEL: (THINKING ABOUT IT) Oh right, yeah. Je m'appelle...Je m'appelle Raquel!

KEN: Excellent. That's very good. Right, now, let's put a sentence together. I want you to say to me in French: Hello Ken. My name is Raquel. Isn't it a lovely day today.

RAQUEL: (CONCENTRATING) Ooh, clever. Right, here goes. (DEEP BREATH) Bonjour Ken, Je m'appelle Raquel. Voulez vous coucher avec moi ce soir?

KEN IS LOST FOR WORDS.

RAQUEL: (HAPPY). Oh Ken, isn't it important. Communication. Oh I feel dead sympathique, me.

Three's a crowd for Maud, Maureen and Reg.

A major handicap for the furthering of Reg and Maureen's relationship was that the skittish shelf-stacker lived at home with her disapproving mother. Fed up of Maud's presence thwarting any attempts at passionate lovemaking, an exasperated Reg informed Maureen they were taking the afternoon off for some highly-anticipated hanky panky at his bachelor pad.

Back at his flat over The Kabin, Reg proudly revealed his shiny new waterbed to Maureen, who was giddy with excitement at the prospect. Sloshing about on the bed's satin sheets the giggling pair whispered sweet nothings in each other's ears – and Reg even removed his trademark spectacles for the occasion.

Meanwhile, downstairs in the shop Derek was up a stepladder repairing a faulty light fitting for Mavis. But as he drilled into the ceiling, water began to drip through the hole and Mavis panicked that he'd hit a water pipe by mistake. Trying to remain calm, Derek suggested it was more likely the tub in Reg's bathroom had overflowed.

The couple dashed upstairs and banged on the door, only to be confronted by Reg, naked but for a striped towel around his waist. It was difficult to tell who was more startled, Reg or the Wiltons. Derek began explaining they thought Reg's bathtub had brimmed-over, but he was interrupted by an ear-piercing scream.

Reg rushed to the bedroom, closely followed by Mavis and Derek who were flabbergasted to see water all over the floor and

TOP FIVE Christmas Crackers

The season of goodwill is often anything but festive in Weatherfield...

1961 Ena had a nasty surprise when she accidentally swallowed a sixpence buried inside Minnie's Christmas pud. After a lengthy choking fit, Ena jabbed at the remainder with a fork – only to find she had three more sixpences on her plate while Minnie and Martha had none!

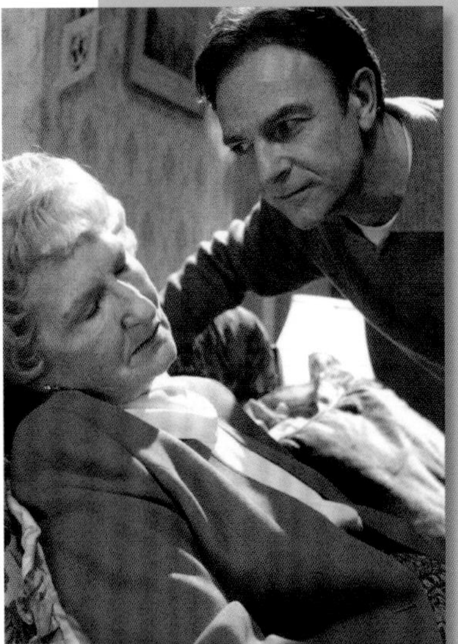

1991 Angry that husband Alec was working away on a cruise over Christmas, Bet invited old flame Des Foster to have dinner with her. Des took this as an invitation for some rumpy-pumpy under the mistletoe, and when Bet fended off his advances, he accused Bet of teasing him and punched her in the face.

2002 Norris knocked himself unconscious trying to light the Christmas pudding in the dark and was rushed to hospital an ambulance. Meanwhile, on hearing Emily was home alone, Richard called round and waited for his elderly investor to fall asleep before smothering her with a cushion. Fortunately his murderous intentions came to nothing when Rita interrupted him.

2005 When the Battersby-Browns' oven broke down they attempted to cook their Christmas turkey on Cilla's sunbed. When that didn't work, Cilla and best-mate Yana bunged the bird in the deep-fat fryer at Mr Wong's where they worked. Unfortunately, while they were in the pub congratulating themselves on their handiwork, the chippy was blown to smithereens!

2006 Dastardly David ruined the combined festivities for the Platts and the Websters by confronting his mother Gail about her wanting to have an abortion when she'd realised she was pregnant with him. Not content with that, he went on to reveal his grandmother Audrey's raunchy affair with Bill Webster to Bill's devastated wife Maureen.

The Wiltons interrupt Maureen and Reg's waterbed frolics.
Ken and newcomer Denise get romantic over dinner.

'Some things never change – a pillock's always a pillock... and a muckheap's always a muckheap!'
Maud on Reg

a distraught Maureen, hyperventilating because the bed seemed to be collapsing around her. She then suddenly became aware of Mavis and Derek standing in the doorway and let out another hysterical scream. 'I can't get up – I haven't got any clothes on!' she shrieked, clutching a sopping sheet to her cleavage. Flustered, Reg handed her a dressing gown and an embarrassed Mavis attempted to explain that Derek had been drilling in the ceiling below. But all sobbing Maureen wanted to do was get out of there – reflecting that maybe her mother had been right about Reg after all!

In 1994 Ken began dating feisty newcomer Denise Osbourne, but true to form, despite bedding the charismatic hairdresser, he continued to hold a torch for his ex Deirdre, who was away looking after her ill mother, Blanche. When Deirdre popped back to Weatherfield on a flying visit she admitted to Ken that she was surprised at how much she'd missed him, and as a result her former husband failed to mention his latest flame.

With a spring in his step, Ken headed for the Rovers, only to find out from Denise that she was pregnant and intended to keep the baby. She asked Ken to keep mum until she'd had her three-month scan, but a few weeks later, when Deirdre returned to Number 1, Ken came clean that he was seeing pregnant Denise. Upset, Deirdre threw him out saying she'd always wanted to have a child with him but he'd refused.

Denise then went through the trauma of miscarriage, but as she mourned the loss of her baby she discovered she had been pregnant with twins and one baby had miraculously survived. Feeling he had to do the right thing, Ken dutifully suggested tying the knot with Denise, but with five broken marriages between them, the independent hair stylist didn't want to go down that road and told him their relationship was over.

Fred Elliott

Played by **John Savident**

With a gleam in his eye as well as on his butcher's knife, a salivating Fred Elliott once boomed to his son Ashley: 'I'm going to hack up a cold carcass. It's one of life's under-rated pleasures.' Whether it was eating it or manhandling it there were few subjects guaranteed to get the redoubtable shopkeeper more misty-eyed than that of animal flesh. Indeed, the first time he turned up in *Coronation Street* he was part of the Weatherfield delegation competing in a black pudding competition in France. The contest ended in a fight after Fred attempted to bribe the judges into looking more favourably on his meaty offering.

The larger-than-life Square Dealer also became famed amongst the locals for his ability to make marriage proposals at the drop of a hat and his tendency to repeat himself in a fog-horned voice so loud and thunderous it could surely be heard in neighbouring Macclesfield. 'I based Fred's loudness on people I knew who really spoke like that. It was all to do with the Industrial Revolution and the Lancashire mills where people repeated themselves in order to be heard above the noise of the looms. It was still happening when I was at mixed infants. The girls would come out of the factories with cotton fluff everywhere and they used the repetition because it got into normal usage. So I began to put it into Fred's speech and people would say, "Are you allowed to do that?" I admit when I changed lines in my first episode to make them sound more authentic I did think I was going to be sacked. So when they asked me back I was most surprised.'

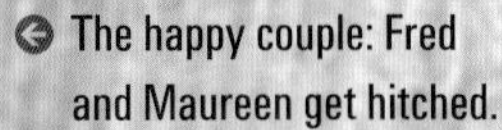

- The happy couple: Fred and Maureen get hitched.
- At loggerheads with daughter-in-law Claire.
- In the festive spirit with Ashley.
- All smiles, but Eve turns out to be a bigamist.
- Prospective Thai-bride Orchid wasn't all she seemed.
- Bev and Fred seal it with a kiss.
- Fred collapses from a heart attack at Audrey's.

It was to close friend Audrey Roberts that Fred first revealed that his nephew Ashley was actually his biological son. To do the right thing, at the time Fred had proposed to Ashley's mother, but she hadn't wanted to be tied down so the baby had been raised by Fred's childless sister, Beryl, instead. Fortunately, easy-going Ashley reacted well to the news and Fred was his rock in 2003 following his first wife Maxine's murder by Richard Hillman. Later, Fred actively encouraged Ashley to pursue a relationship with his grandson Joshua's sweet-natured nanny, Claire Casey.

50 CORONATION ST. ICON

'Steven Arnold, who played Ashley, and I became great friends and we had a lovely relationship. Although I have to say all the cast and crew were marvellous people and they are what I miss about not being there anymore. What's

so touching about everyone who works on the *Street* is that they have a tremendous loyalty to the programme.'

Fred's seemingly jinxed love life has often been the subject of ridicule – he married Maureen Holdsworth in 1997, but she quickly had a change of heart and absconded to Germany with builder Bill Webster. Next he tied the knot with gobby Eve Sykes, only to discover she was still married to someone else. Lonely Fred then opted for a Thai bride, but before they could make it down the aisle, Orchid (or Stacey as she was more commonly known) was exposed as a cash-hungry con artist.

The booming butcher also proposed unsuccessfully to Rita Sullivan, Doreen Heavey, Penny King and twice to Audrey Roberts. By 2006 he'd finally stuck gold and was due to marry Shelley's highly strung mum Bev Unwin: 'You can't play a randy old jack-the-lad forever and I liked the fact he was determined that this was the time in his life to settle down once and for all.'

'He's a man of a certain age. Put a gorilla in a short skirt and a blonde wig and he'd be cooing sweet nothings at it.'

Bev

However, before the wedding an emotional Audrey blurted out that she'd regretted turning him down. On the morning of the ceremony Fred went to see her saying he still intended to marry Bev, whom he loved, but he suffered a massive heart attack in Audrey's hallway, croaking his last words: 'Be happy, I say, be happy.' Audrey then faced having to explain to his bride-to-be why he had been at her house in the first place. A devastated Ashley and Claire later changed their son's name from Thomas to Freddie, in memory of his late grandfather.

A former policeman, John Savident got into professional acting after being a keen amateur and has appeared on stage and screen in the likes of *A Clockwork Orange* and created the role of Firmin in the original London production of *Phantom Of The Opera*.

'When I went into *Coronation Street* I knew I'd really have to work hard to establish Fred in order to make my mark. Because joining the *Street* at that time meant having to hold your own amongst a whole cast of wonderful characters – and now I'm proud to be able to look back and say that I managed it.'

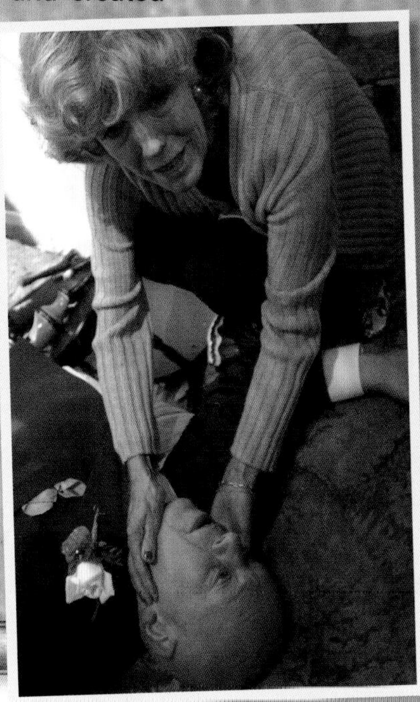

Occupations: Master butcher and Rovers landlord.
On screen: 1994, 1995, 1996–2006
Defining moment: In 1999 he dresses up as Santa and forces Ashley into an elf costume to sell Reindeer meat – but no-one buys it and he only succeeds in scaring children and making them cry.

When Audrey Roberts found out there was an official mayoral visit to France on the cards she'd pictured herself sipping vin rouge in sophisticated Paris – not judging a black pudding contest in Weatherfield's twin town of Charleville! As the competition was about to begin, Mayor Alf gave the Weatherfield butchers a pep talk, reminding them they were ambassadors for Great Britain and Weatherfield. Meanwhile, a bored Audrey was being fawned over by loudmouthed butcher Fred Elliott, who lasciviously informed the mortified mayoress that he wanted to buy her some lacy French lingerie. Fred later tried to bribe the judges into giving his pudding the top gong, which saw him disqualified and the beginnings of an almighty international row. Indignant, Alf vouched for devious Fred's innocence but the French mayor was unimpressed, sniffily insisting: 'Napoleon was right – you are nothing but a nation of shopkeepers.' Insulted to his very core, Alf maintained that shopkeepers were the very salt of the earth and found himself unexpectedly un-twinning the two towns!

Deirdre confided in good pal Liz that she'd half expected to get back together with Ken and now she felt a fool. Disheartened and in need of cheering herself up, Deirdre booked a last-minute package deal to Morocco to clear her head. On her return she revealed to an enthralled Liz that she'd had a holiday romance with a handsome young Moroccan and was like an excited schoolgirl when she received a letter from him. Loved-up, Deirdre sent Samir the money for a plane ticket to Manchester and introduced him to the regulars in the Rovers.

'She's just the sort men walk all over. Time and again she'll team up with rats and they'll treat her like dirt. Ask what she thinks of 'em, "Ooh, aren't they lovely?"'

Bet on Raquel

Deirdre couldn't have been happier when Samir decided to stay on in Manchester, although the only job he could find was as a waiter in a Moroccan restaurant, where he worked illegally without a permit. When immigration officials began sniffing around the restaurant the couple married so Samir could stay in the country. At the Rovers, Bet threw them a surprise wedding reception, but not everyone was so supportive – brattish Tracy made no secret of the fact she thought her mother was making a fool of herself, while Ken remained convinced that Samir was merely using Deirdre for a British passport. Emily didn't approve either, refusing to even attend the wedding.

Later that year at the Rovers, Raquel was ecstatic at landing a modelling contract involving an overnight stay in glamorous

Birmingham. With Raquel out of town, Tanya seized the opportunity to get her claws into her rival's boyfriend, Des. After flirtily plying Des with drinks all night in the Rovers, they took a takeaway to Tanya's flat when the pub closed and Des stayed the night. The next morning a guilty Des confessed that while he was attracted to Tanya, he didn't want to hurt Raquel either.

Des continued to see Tanya behind Raquel's back and when Raquel finally discovered what had been going on she fled in tears to the Rovers and an unimpressed Bet helped her collect her belongings from Number 6. Increasingly unbalanced Tanya then came up with a plan to get some sympathy of her own out of the situation and set about hitting herself around the face. Later at work she broke down in front of an appalled Raquel and Bet telling them how Des had blackmailed her and beaten her up. Yet again her extreme manipulation techniques had worked and she was comforted by Raquel.

Mean-spirited as ever, when Tanya got wind that Raquel had been dropped by her agency she wasted no time in letting the regulars know that the ditzy barmaid had failed as a model, which lead to angry Des telling Tanya she was a bitch. Bet sacked her on the spot and Tanya then took the opportunity to gleefully tell the landlady that she'd been sleeping with Bet's trucker boyfriend Charlie Whelan behind her back and that they were leaving together. Fuming and humiliated, Bet snapped at them both to get out, but Tanya just smirked back at her before turning to Charlie and pouting: 'Come on, we won't stay where we're not wanted...'

⬆ Raquel falls for Des but he's cheating on her.

⬇ Trucker Charlie takes Bet for a ride in more ways than one.

To cheer themselves up, the next day Bet and Raquel had a competition to see who could get the most tips, then after closing they got sloshed on cocktails and bemoaned the men in their lives. Raquel explained to Bet she put the names of those that had made life difficult for her in the kitchen knife drawer. She explained: 'People who've wronged you. You write their name on a bit of paper and stick 'em in the drawer. It's very therapeutic. Those you're not sure about you stick in the freezer – put them on ice and thaw them out if you change your mind. Des has been in and out of there more times than I can remember. You should try it. Got any names in mind?'

Bet laughed back at her: 'Any names? Only a rainforest's worth!'

Meanwhile, after a long list of misunderstandings and complaints, Curly (*see page 128*) was sacked from Bettabuys, but he soon landed himself another position as manager at Soopa Scoopa, a supermarket where he was forced to a wear a brightly coloured nylon uniform complete with a baseball cap. In a bid to impress his new boss, Curly lied and implied he was engaged – which left him in need of someone to pretend to be his fiancée at the staff Christmas party.

Bet had fun winding him up by offering to be his date, but in the end kind-hearted Raquel volunteered to go, as a favour for a friend. The evening was a roaring success, so much so that Curly suggested they make the engagement real. Deep down Raquel knew she didn't love Curly, but she also knew he was kind and would treat her well, unlike most of the blokes in Weatherfield. After much thought, and despite Bet advising her against it, Raquel decided to accept and a chuffed Curly bought her the best ring his meagre Soopa Scoopa pay packet would allow...

A shock announcement from Newton and Ridley marked the changing of the guard forever at the Rovers Return in 1995, when the company decided to sell off six of its pubs, including the Street's much-loved boozer. The brewery wrote to confirm the sell-off and gave manageress Bet first option to buy the premises for £68,000. But Bet was brassic, and when an unsuccessful meeting with the bank manager failed to secure her the necessary funds, she feared for her future.

'I'm forever saying sorry. If you tread on my foot I'll say I'm sorry. Like I've no right to be there at all really.'

Raquel

A sloshed Raquel bemoans the men in her life.

Raquel and fiancé Curly ring in the changes.

Roy Cropper

Played by David Neilson

With his love of historical re-enactments, model railways and bus timetables, socially inept Roy Cropper's loner life changed forever when he fell for shy and awkward transsexual Hayley Patterson – who proved to be just as much of an anorak as him. The loveable misfits were blessed by a local curate in Roy's Rolls in 1999, then eleven years later the kind-hearted Scrabble fanatics were delighted to have their partnership finally recognised in the eyes of the law.

However, when he first turned up in the Street in 1995 pestering newly widowed Deirdre Rachid, who'd just moved into his block of flats, Royston Cropper was an altogether different proposition.

'They wrote this character to freak Deirdre out, he was Creepy Cropper, a sitting tenant at the top of an old Victorian house and a bit like Norman Bates. At that time we didn't know if he was daft or dangerous, but he was right up my street because I've always loved playing quirky, eccentric characters and I remember he really made me laugh the very first time he went into the Rovers as he took his own flask. He turned out to be harmless and people began to care about Roy because they related to his struggles with everyday life – he means well but he does have a little dark cloud that follows him around.'

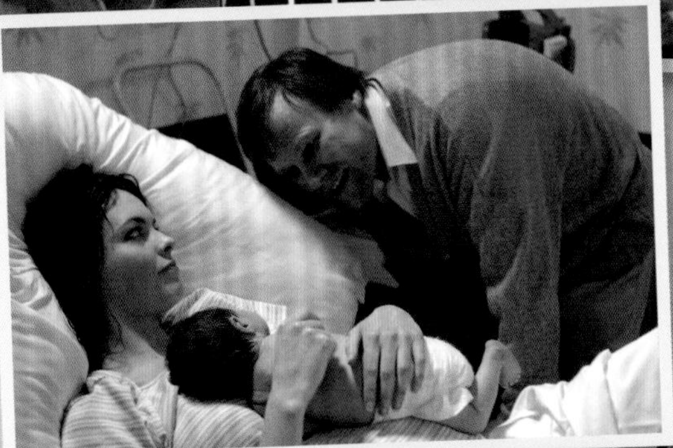

In 1997 Roy went into business with Gail Platt, buying Alma Baldwin's share of Jim's Cafe and renamed it Roy's Rolls. The following year he met timorous Hayley Patterson and was stunned to discover she was a pre-op transsexual, but he overcame his reservations. In 2003, conniving Tracy Barlow spiked poor Roy's drink and lied that he'd made her pregnant – although after much heartache Steve McDonald was revealed to be the father.

The public-spirited bat-watcher couldn't ever be described as a follower of fashion and it was David who put the finishing touches to Roy's unique trainspotter look:

'My mother died just before I joined the show so I was chucking stuff out and thought her key on a piece of elastic and her shopping bag would be good for Roy, because you see a certain type of man at bus stops with bags like that all the time. It must be thirty years old now and it's also very handy to carry my scripts around in!'

Who's the daddy? Roy falls for Tracy's lies.

He becomes a father-figure to employee Becky.

The Croppers' wedding dream finally becomes a reality.

Current occupation: Cafe owner.
On screen: 1995–
Defining moment: In 2001 Roy and Hayley refuse to return foster child Wayne Hayes to his violent stepfather. After going on the run they are arrested and charged with abduction.

The landlady's mood lifted when best mate Rita considered investing in the business and Bet, buoyed by this, persuaded the brewery to reduce the sale price by £2,000. But at the last minute Rita changed her mind when she discovered Bet had told everyone she was buying the pub before they'd even finalised the deal. When Bet found out about Rita's change of heart she lost the plot. Feeling like the ground was being pulled away from under her she confronted her friend in The Kabin and the pair had a vicious exchange. Bet accused 'clapped-out chorus girl' Rita of only having money because she'd married into it, whilst Rita snapped back that Bet had always been jealous of her because she'd wed Len. The brutal nature of their row effectively ended their friendship for good.

In desperation, Bet swallowed her pride and asked Alec's wealthy granddaughter Vicky McDonald to loan her the cash, but was again humiliated when Vicky refused, offering to buy her a small retirement house with a nominal rent instead. Raging, Bet pointed out she'd loved Vicky enough to house her rent-free for four years. She then stormed into the bar where the regulars were enjoying a lunchtime pint and chucked everyone out – confusing Alf who'd missed all the drama while having a sit down in the gents' and had reappeared to find the place deserted.

1990s Marriages

Steph Jones & Des Barnes	12 February 1990
Jackie Ingram & Mike Baldwin	5 July 1991
Gail Tilsley & Martin Platt	27 September 1991
Lisa Horton & Terry Duckworth	27 May 1992
Rita Fairclough & Ted Sullivan	5 June 1992
Alma Sedgewick & Mike Baldwin	19 June 1992
Maureen Naylor & Reg Holdsworth	26 January 1994
Deirdre Barlow & Samir Rachid	25 November 1994
Vicky Arden & Steve McDonald	9 August 1995
Betty Turpin & Billy Williams	20 October 1995
Raquel Wolstenhulme & Curly Watts	8 December 1995
Angela Hawthorne & Norris Cole	29 December 1995
Tracy Barlow & Robert Preston	13 November 1996
Maureen Holdsworth & Fred Elliott	22 September 1997
Leanne Battersby & Nick Tilsley	30 January 1998
Natalie Horrocks & Des Barnes	23 October 1998
Maxine Heavey & Ashley Peacock	24 September 1999
Sharon Gaskell & Ian Bentley	1 November 1999

The end of an era: Bet is forced out of her beloved Rovers.

OVERHEARD

Bet and Rita have a major fall-out over buying The Rovers, 1995

RITA IS UNSURE ABOUT INVESTING IN THE ROVERS. AS BET SWANS INTO THE KABIN WITH A BOTTLE OF CHAMPAGNE, RITA MAKES HER DECISION.

RITA: I've had the world and his wife in here today telling me what I'm going to be doing before I know what I'm going to be doing myself. I don't appreciate that.

BET: (TAKEN ABACK) But what's the big secret? You'd already said you'll back me.

RITA: (FLATLY) I said I'd think about it. And I have. I'm sorry Bet, it's not on.

BET'S FACE FALLS.

BET: Yer droppin' out?

RITA: I made no promises. I asked you to wait until I had a proper chance to look at the figures.

BET: I've got the books over the road.

RITA: I've done all the sums I need.

BET: (DEFENSIVE) Oh aye? Mrs High and Mighty all of a sudden...

RITA: Which is more than can be said of you.

BET: (SNAPPING) Excuse me. I've run that flamin' pub on my tod for years.

RITA: (ANGRY) Yes, and not made a penny from it. Well 'ave you? Unless you're keeping something from me.

BET: Don't you come the high and mighty with me, lady. You'd not be stood there with a bulging bank balance if you hadn't flamin' married it.

RITA: Yes, Len left me a tatty little shop but it was me that worked my guts out over there, me who opened this place.

BET: It was Len's cash what got you started. But for him you'd've been nowt but a clapped-out chorus girl!

RITA: Better than a clapped-out barmaid!

BET: Talk about fairweather pals, I should've known better than to turn to you.

RITA: Nobody pours thousands of pounds down the drain, no matter how good pals they are!

BET: (SPITTING WITH ANGER) Pals? Pals? You don't know the meaning of the word!

THE WOMEN PAUSE FOR A MOMENT. EMOTIONS RUNNING HIGH. RITA SOFTENS.

RITA: Bet. I'm sorry.

BET: (RESIGNED) But you won't change your mind?

RITA: No.

BET: Then I'm the one that's sorry, cock. Sorry I ever asked.

HEAD HELD HIGH, BET TURNS TO LEAVE THE SHOP.

Refusing to endure the humiliation of going down with a sinking ship, Bet packed her suitcases, slung on her finest leopardskin togs and took one last lingering look at the beloved pub that had been her home for the last 25 years. She cradled the keys in her hands for a moment, before leaving them on the bar and with a deep breath stepped into a cab, forced on her trademark barmaid's fixed grin and sped off to pastures new.

With Bet gone there was much speculation from the regulars as to who would be the new proprietors of the Rovers. The McDonalds,

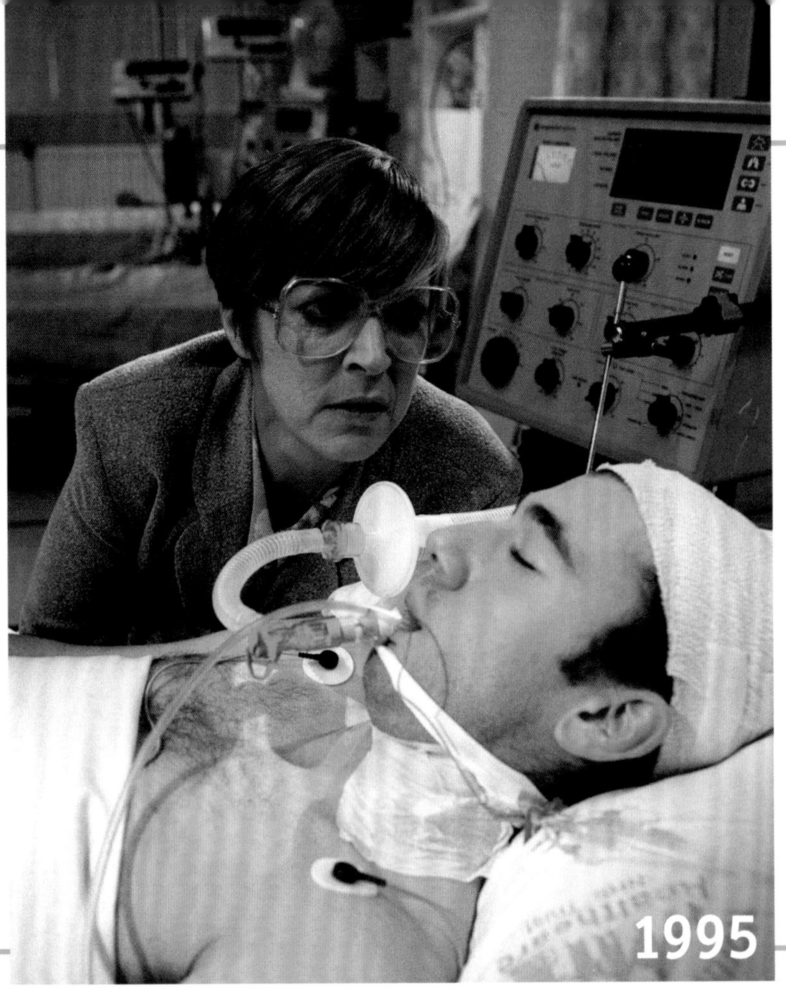

Tracy Barlow's life hung in the balance when she took ecstasy at a rave and ended up comatosed in intensive care with severe kidney damage. When she woke up she was told by the medics she had a choice: spend the rest of her life on dialysis or undergo a kidney transplant. Unsurprisingly, Tracy chose the transplant option. However, her mum's toy-boy husband Samir proved to be the only match, and much as Tracy had attempted to make his life a misery, the Moroccan do-gooder still offered to donate his organ, for Deirdre's sake. The last sighting of Samir was down by the canal on his way to the hospital when a gang of lads pushed past him and began making racist comments. The police informed a distraught Deirdre that Samir had been viciously attacked and he died in hospital later that day. When she visited a sleeping Tracy (who was recovering from the transplant operation using dying Samir's kidney), a choked-up Deirdre angrily threw a bunch of flowers onto her bed and stormed out. She blamed her daughter for Samir's death and it was left to Ken to tell a shocked Tracy what had happened.

desperate to run a pub of their own, were the likeliest candidates, but to everyone's amazement the Duckworths pipped them to the post, thanks to a surprise inheritance windfall on Jack's part. As Betty (who had by now married old flame Billy Williams) muttered: 'Mrs Walker must be turning in her grave.' But the Duckies would provide three years of comedy behind the bar – with poor Betty bearing much of the brunt of it.

First of all a jesting Jack pinched the hotpot queen's bum, and when landlady Vera – now full of her own self-importance – wound Betty up by asking her to clean as well as cook, Betty told Vera where she could stick her mop and promptly resigned, only to be begged by Jack to return. But the Duckworths struggled with the books and, with their accounts in the red, Jack sold a 50 per cent share of the business back to Alec at a bargain rate, much to Vera's fury, who locked them both out of the pub when she found out.

The Duckworths take over at the backstreet boozer.

Blanche Hunt

Played by Maggie Jones

In 2007 Blanche decided to organise her own wake while still alive, but she was disappointed by the low attendance. When her friends suggested that it could be down to her sharp tongue, she vowed to be nicer to people. However, it wasn't long before she reverted to type. She would have been heartened by the impressive turnout at her funeral after she'd died 'with the sun on her specs and the wind in her slacks' while holidaying in Portugal with secret fancy man, Arnold.

Sadly, Blanche's demise came after the sudden death of much-loved actress Maggie Jones, who after a period of illness passed away in December 2009, aged 75. *Corrie* fans had loved Blanche's stinging scene-stealing put-downs and Anne Kirkbride remains full of admiration for her screen mum: 'I don't think people realised just how much hard work she put into playing Blanche because she made it look so effortless. It wasn't an easy part to play, but when she delivered one of her brutal lines she'd hit it absolutely right and it would be wonderful.'

Born in Yorkshire, Maggie got a taste for acting at school and trained at the Royal Academy of Dramatic Art. She made her television debut in 1961 on *Coronation Street* playing a policewoman, then she appeared again six years later as a drunken shoplifter. She starred in *The Forsyte Saga* and Seventies' drama, *Sam*, before making her debut as razor-edged Blanche in 1974, when she slapped Deirdre's boss and future husband Ray Langton around the chops in the Rovers.

The veteran actress became a regular character in 1999 and won British Soap Awards for Best Comedy Performance in 2005 and 2008 for Blanche's countless crushing observations. She once told son-in-law Ken: 'I tell you, Kenneth, you'd better learn to enjoy other people's misfortunes or you'll have a very unhappy old age.' When Liz McDonald wore a low-cut outfit for an interview, Blanche didn't hesitate at suggesting the appropriate job: 'Prostitute.'

Says William Roache: 'She was very physically frail, had been for a long time, but mentally and spiritually she was very powerful. Maggie was a gentle, quiet person who had a lovely sense of humour which was as funny, if not funnier, than Blanche's.'

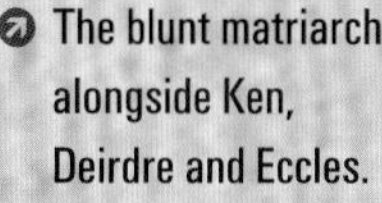

- The blunt matriarch alongside Ken, Deirdre and Eccles.
- Time for tea with Deirdre.
- Fruity Blanche celebrates the millennium with Emily and Betty.

Occupations: Retired corset maker, barmaid and corner-shop assistant.
On screen: 1974–1976, 1977, 1978, 1981, 1996, 1997, 1998, 1999–2009
Defining moment: On hearing about Peter and Leanne's new business venture in 2009: 'An alcoholic and an arsonist open a bar? Sounds like the start of a joke...'

50 CORONATION ST. ICON

By 1996 Jim and Liz's already volatile relationship had sunk to an all-time low. Feeling unloved and taken for granted, Liz bagged a job at the bookies, where it became clear there was a frisson between her and her manager, Des. But they only got as far as a quick snog before frizzy-haired Liz realised she still wanted to be with Jim after all. In order to escape Des's charms, Liz resigned, but she told Jim she'd been made redundant. However, Jim didn't believe her story when he saw her job being re-advertised and she eventually admitted the real reason she'd quit. Predictably, Jim flew into one of his rages.

Just when it seemed things couldn't get any worse for the couple, in the car on the way home from Jim's army reunion Liz owned up to another infidelity that had taken place years ago with one of his regimental pals. She explained she'd been feeling lonely with Jim away for such long periods and gave in to temptation. They pulled in at a service station and continued to argue, when Jim finally snapped and yanked Liz out of the car. Blind with anger, he knocked her to the ground and called her a whore before speeding off, leaving Liz sobbing on the wet garage forecourt, from where she had to hitch her way home.

After hiding away at Number 1 with Deirdre for a few days, Liz pulled herself together and chucked Jim's belongings out into the

Jim lashes out when Liz admits to an affair.
Curly and Kevin hold Jim back as he sees red.
Man-eater Natalie sets her sights on Kevin.

In November it was tissues at the ready at Number 7 when Raquel accepted a beautician position in Kuala Lumpur as a way of escaping her marriage of convenience. When she broke the news to husband Curly (who was now working at Firman's Freezers) the tears start to flow, but attempting to put on a brave face he told Raquel he was over her anyway and left for a sales conference in Wigan. At the conference, Curly opened up to Eric Firman about his true feelings for his wife and his boss suggested Curly immediately head home and tell Raquel how much he really loved her. But Curly refused, explaining that if he did go back he'd only break down and beg her not to leave him. Meanwhile, Raquel revealed to neighbour Judy Mallett, who provided a shoulder for her to cry on, that she should never have married Curly in the first place. Before leaving for Kuala Lumpur, Raquel left Curly a pile of freshly ironed shirts, on top of which she placed her wedding ring. After giving the Street a last sentimental glance she forced a smile and turned to Judy, saying: 'Look after him.'

street before changing the locks at Number 11. Furious, Jim tried to get Liz to speak to him, and when pounding on the front door failed to get her attention he started smashing the windows of the house instead. After being dragged away by Kevin and Curly, Jim was arrested and Liz, scared stiff of what his next move would be, took out a restraining order against her husband. Still Jim wouldn't leave Liz alone, and he ended up in prison after repeatedly breaking the restraining order.

In February 1997 the stilettoed heel of sassy blonde Natalie Horrocks (*see page 179*) first set foot on Coronation Street, when her mechanic son Tony suffered a breakdown after accidentally running over Judy Mallets' mother in his car. In Tony's absence she took over the day-to-day management of the garage and became attracted to married mechanic Kevin. Kevin couldn't resist Natalie's vampish charms, so while Sally was away in Scarborough looking after her ill mother, Natalie cranked up her seduction offensive a gear and the pair slept

Ken: The Loves and The Lies

Over fifty years there have been twenty-four women who've been unable to resist the floppy-haired Barlow charm...

1960–1961 **Susan Cunningham** The middle-class student was Ken's first girlfriend.

1961 **Marian Lund** A much older librarian who hid the fact she was engaged.

1961–1971 **Valerie Tatlock** Ken's first wife was tragically killed by a faulty hairdryer.

1973–1974 **Janet Reid** Ken's second wife was a career woman who didn't want to be a stepmother.

1973 **Rita Littlewood** Despite enjoying a one-night fling the pair went on to become lifelong friends.

1973 **Elaine Perkins** Ken asked the posh headmaster's daughter to marry him, but she didn't love him.

1974 **Gaynor Burton** The pair enjoyed a fumble at a party in the back room of the Rovers.

1974 **Peggy Barton** Ken and the warehouse shop steward managed one date, but a relationship never materialised.

1976 **Wendy Nightingale** The graduate left her husband to be with him, but after five weeks she'd had enough of Ken and life on the Street.

1978 **Sally Robson** Ken briefly dated Uncle Albert's chiropodist, but neither wanted a serious relationship.

1978 **Karen Barnes** Ken taught Karen to read and write, and although she kissed him on the cheek, he insisted nothing else happened.

2009 **Martha Fraser** Ken was about to leave Deirdre for the arty barge-living actress, but he jumped ship and changed his mind at the very last minute.

1997 **Sue Jeffers** Ken was seduced by his headmistress boss and Deirdre caught them in bed together at Number 1.

1994–1996 **Denise Osbourne** When she became pregnant with their son Daniel, the hair-stylist admitted she didn't love Ken enough to marry him, and they eventually split when he discovered that she was having an affair with her brother-in-law.

1992–1993 **Maggie Redman** The florist grew tired of Ken and her ex, Mike, scoring points off each other and dumped him.

1991 **Alma Sedgewick** Their relationship ended when Ken's arch-rival Mike sweet-talked the café owner back into bed with him.

1964 **Pip Mistral** Ken wanted to spend the night with the exotic dancer – she turned him down.

1966 **Jackie Marsh** Val briefly walked out on Ken when she discovered his affair with the newspaper reporter.

1972–1973 **Norma Ford** The affectionate shop assistant adored Ken, while he merely used her until he found someone else.

1971 **Yvonne Chappell** Widower Ken proposed to the receptionist, but she realised he was just looking for a Val replacement.

1981 **Sonia Price** Ken had one romantic rendezvous with the beautician before proposing to Deirdre.

1979–1990, 1996–1997, 1999 onwards **Deirdre Langton** After dating on and off for a couple of years, the gutsy single mum signed up to become the third Mrs Barlow in 1981. They divorced in 1992 and remarried thirteen years later.

1989–1990 **Wendy Crozier** When Deirdre discovered Ken's affair with his secretary she threw him out on New Year's Day.

1984 **Sally Waterman** Briefly his secretary at the *Weatherfield Recorder*, they had a passionate snog but there was no affair.

'By hell, lady – I've met some hard-faced bitches in my time, but you take the bloody gold medal!'

Rita to Natalie

together. But the next day, before Kevin got any romantic ideas, Natalie made it clear she wasn't looking for anything more serious than some no-strings rumpy pumpy.

Their secret affair continued and Natalie surprised herself by falling head over heels in love with Kevin and asking him to leave Sally and their daughters, Rosie and Sophie (who had been born in 1994), and live with her instead. When Sally was informed of Kevin's plans she hit the roof and stomped out of Number 13 to find Natalie. When she located her she slapped Kevin's bit on the side across the face with all her might. Thanks to her brazen attitude, marriage wrecker Natalie became the Street's public enemy number one, which inevitably put a strain on her relationship with Kevin.

By Christmas Kevin was missing his family and he came to his senses and returned home. Sally agreed to give their marriage another go for the sake of their children – unsuccessfully as it was to turn out, as they divorced two years later.

Later Natalie was to fall for Des and at last it was true love for both of them; in the following October they married in a whirlwind at Weatherfield Registry Office. The grand wedding was the event of the year, but tragically, after only a month of marriage, Des died of a heart attack after being hit on the head trying to help Natalie's son Tony, who was being beaten up by a gang looking for the drug money he owed them. A broken woman, Natalie threw herself into her business interests and at the end of the year became the new licensee of the Rovers when the doomed partnership of the Duckworths and Alec came to an end.

In 1997, with the song 'Tit Willow' from Gilbert & Sullivan's *The Mikado* blaring from his car radio and a giant paperclip attached to the roof of his car, there was another unexpected Weatherfield demise when stationery salesman Derek suffered a heart attack following a road-rage incident on the M6. Meanwhile, an oblivious Mavis busied herself with a houseful of guests attending her birthday party while tutting to herself about Derek's tardiness. His death hit her hard and she broke down completely when Derek's friend Norris Cole (*see page 206*) popped round with something that'd been found in Derek's glove compartment – Mavis's birthday present, a silver locket which her late husband had inscribed with the dedication: 'To my loving wife.'

↑ Derek meets his maker at the wheel of his car.

↓ Widowed Mavis says farewell at Derek's funeral.

At Derek's wake, Mavis overheard some of the mourners joking about Derek when they thought she was out of earshot and she surprised everyone by rallying against those

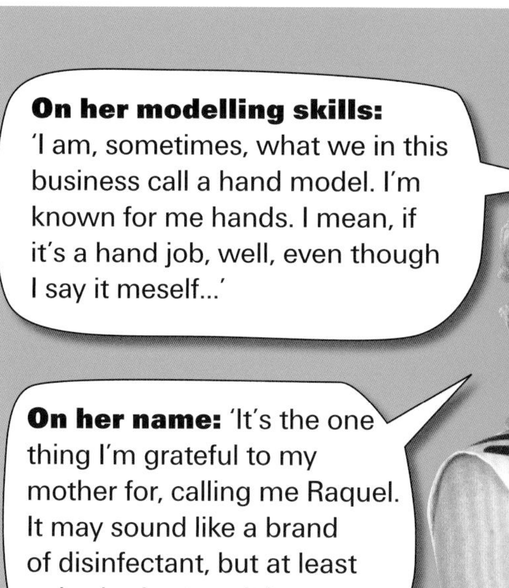

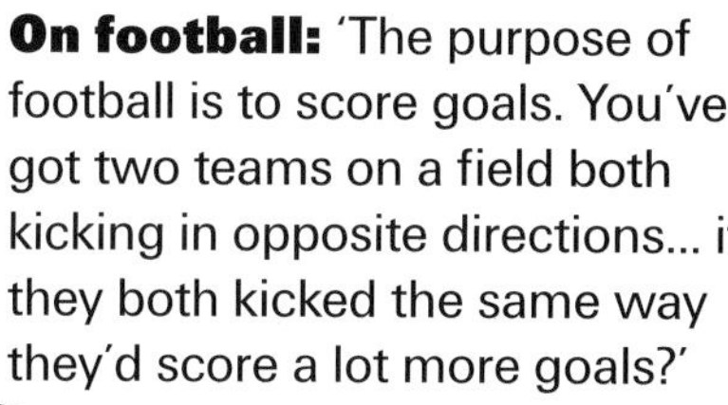

Raquel-isms: **The dizzy barmaid wasn't the brightest spark, but she had her own unique take on the world...**

who had considered him a joke. She made an incredibly moving speech, sneering that she didn't care what they thought because she'd loved Derek, Derek had loved her and they had shared a happiness that no one else could ever experience. Soon afterwards, a devastated Mavis left the Street to make a fresh start running a B&B in the Lake District – her farewell present from the residents was a framed photograph of Mavis and Rita in a typical pose behind the counter of The Kabin in the Seventies.

Norris Cole

Played by **Malcolm Hebden**

Crazed competition enthusiast Mary Taylor had been trying to get closer to Norris for a while, but even he couldn't have predicted the lengths the camper-van queen would go to in order to ensnare the pernickety pensioner during their jaunt into Brontë country. Trapped in their remote holiday cottage, Mary sabotaged the van's engine, cut the phone lines and crushed Norris's specs, while thrusting her ample bosom at him at every opportunity.

An increasingly alarmed Norris sprained his ankle trying to make a run for a phone box, but instead of heading for hospital, screwy Mary returned him to the confines of the cottage. By the time Norris saw her wielding an axe in the yard he was fearing for his life. When Mary demanded to know why he felt like that, Norris protested, 'Because you're a fruitbat, woman!' before escaping to the approaching police car he'd called after he'd discovered her hidden mobile phone.

'The viewers seem to love watching Norris when he's up against it and I'm relieved everyone enjoyed those scenes so much because they were way over the top with both comedy and drama. It was like Stephen's King's *Misery*, but with some quite outrageous innuendo thrown in for good measure.'

From the moment Norris first gave stranded fellow-salesman Derek Wilton a lift home from London, he's lurched from one scrape to another. After leaving his wife, Myrtle, Norris stayed with Derek, who had issued an open invitation without expecting it to be accepted. Mavis was furious, especially as Norris insisted on calling Derek 'Dirk' and went on to kidnap one of their beloved garden gnomes.

'I have no idea why Norris is so popular because he's not very pleasant and he's extremely nosy. I'm staggered he gets away with what he does. He's very popular with children as well, which also amazes me – maybe they just like to laugh at him? Because whatever Norris does he never wins. Even though he now owns The Kabin, Rita is working there and she still rules the roost, so he's still a loser.'

In 1999 a divorced Norris found lodgings at the Duckworths' B&B before moving into Number 3 with Emily Bishop. Meanwhile, Rita Sullivan found herself offering him a job at the The Kabin and the duo have been tolerating each other behind the sweetie counter ever since. In 2007 he even asked Rita to marry him; she replied that she was flattered but gently turned him down.

Famed for his busybody antics, Norris was on tenterhooks when Ken

- The Wiltons discover Norris is the gnome kidnapper.
- Getting pally with Rita in The Kabin.
- Norris models his shiny volunteer shell-suit.
- He refuses to call a truce with estranged brother Ramsay.
- Mary takes a shine to Norris.
- Norris wakes up to find scary Mary hovering.

Barlow informed him he'd been named as a beneficiary in Blanche Hunt's will – but her bequest was merely to allow him the chance to hear the gossip first-hand for once (and to cancel her magazine subscription). Occasionally Norris has found himself in the thick of it – in 2001 he ended up an unlikely midwife when he delivered Curly and Emma Watts's baby, Ben, and in 2009 he had a shock when his estranged half-brother, Ramsay Clegg, visited from Australia, whom he blamed for their mother's fatal heart attack.

A former shop assistant and window dresser, Lancashire-born Malcolm was an amateur performer before taking the plunge into the world of professional acting and directing at the age of thirty-one. The first time the *Street* came knocking was in 1974, with an offer to spend six months as Mavis Riley's waiter boyfriend, Carlos.

'I wasn't long out of drama school and, of course, I'm from the North, so I thought great, *Coronation Street*, I can use my own accent. And then he turned out to be Spanish. Well, I'd never been to Spain but at the local college there was a Spanish guy who would read the lines out for me and I'd just copy the way he said them. The accent was so successful the Spanish Embassy rang Granada to see if I'd got a work permit!

'Being in the show was extraordinary to me back then because, having seen it as a kid living in a two-up two-down in Burnley, long before I ever thought about being an actor, these people were real to me. As a working-class person, my mother was a cleaner and my father sold chemical lavatories, watching *Coronation Street* was like seeing our own lives on television for the very first time. So to walk in and to be sat with these people was almost other-worldly.

'I suppose I'm a bit of a romantic about this show – yes, sometimes I'm tired and I want to tell everyone to stuff it – then occasionally you walk out on those cobbles and you think: "A lot has gone on here." There are moments when you really do have a sense of being part of something quite magical...'

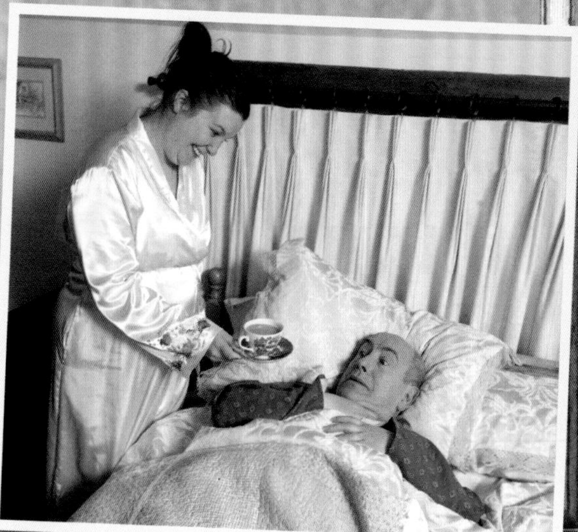

'When I first met you it was Norris Cole Competition Winner who enthralled me. Now I've got to know the real Norris. The essence of Norris. And I've fallen a little bit in love.'

Mary

Current occupation: Newsagent.
On screen: 1994–1997, 1999–
Defining moment: In 2002 he volunteers at Manchester's Commonwealth Games and is promoted to medal bearer – but his moment of glory is ruined when no-one sees him on TV.

The rough-and-ready Battersby clan gave the Street a wake-up call when they arrived in Weatherfield in the summer. Disapproving pensioner Percy started a petition to have them forcibly removed, while life became unbearable for next-door-neighbour Curly thanks to the loud music blaring from Number 5 in the early hours of the morning. At the end of his tether, Curly stormed into Chez Battersby and threw their CD player out of the window, smashing it onto the pavement. In response – and much to teenagers Leanne and Toyah's amusement – Les proved he was a class act by head-butting Curly to the ground and breaking his glasses. But the troublesome teens weren't smiling when the family attempted to kill Theresa the Turkey for their Christmas dinner. Before Les had a chance to stun the bird with a baseball bat, wily Theresa managed to escape, only to meet her untimely death under the wheels of the Battersby's car. When the family sat down to eat a squashed Theresa, Leanne and Toyah refused to tuck into the bird, insisting the tyre marks on it had put them off!

There was a downward spiral for an increasingly bitter and twisted Don that year, having had his leg amputated five years earlier after an unsuccessful suicide attempt. In his anger, he embarked on a terror campaign against the Baldwins, who he blamed for all his woes. Penniless, having lost all his money buying the overpriced garage from Mike, he'd been forced to sell the business at a loss to Kevin and Tony. To get back at Mike a frenzied Don abducted petrified Alma and drove at top speed into the canal, attempting to kill them both. Fortunately they both survived, but Don was sectioned under the Mental Health Act.

'Les Battersby's a beast in human form. Well, almost human form...'

Alec

Still determined to get his revenge on Mike, who continued to belittle him, Don hobbled into the deserted factory in October and whacked Mike around the head with a chair leg. It looked like he was about to finish Mike off there and then when he was interrupted by fashion designer Angie Freeman, who attacked him with her handbag. Don had now lost the plot. He grabbed the keys to Alma's sports car and, after furiously revving the engine, drove into the wall of the viaduct and was burnt to death when the car exploded on impact.

Mike tries to stop Don's bitter vendetta against him.

Janice Battersby

Played by Vicky Entwistle

Factory boss Danny Baldwin nicknamed her Lippy, on account of her extraordinary ability for backchat. Meanwhile, an incensed Claire Peacock went one further in 2005 when a sullen Janice ruined her 'Clean Up The Red Rec' campaign – she branded the litter-bug machinist a 'pug-faced scumbag' and the pair proceeded to mud wrestle each other to the ground.

'That mud fight was hilarious because it was a really hot sunny day so all the mud was rock hard and we had to get hoses out to make it wet again. Once I'd had a bit of slop thrown at me I really got a taste for it and Julia [Haworth, who plays Claire] and Steve Arnold [Ashley Peacock] and me didn't want the day to stop – by the end we were caked in it!'

The residents of Coronation Street didn't know what had hit them when the ballsy Battersby brood pitched up in 1997, with gobby mum Janice perhaps the most intimidating of them all. But the sly grin was wiped off her face eight years later when she realised she'd caught nits from Sophie Webster and was forced to shave her hair off.

'I quite liked having a shaved head, but I would never have told my bosses that, because I wanted them to think I was this amazing martyr for razoring my hair for a ridiculously daft three-week nits storyline. I wouldn't say I'm a bonny woman anyway, but after that I certainly looked like a big bruiser.'

Lonesome Janice hasn't had much luck in the romance department either – she left layabout husband Les for biker Dennis Stringer, but Les attempted suicide and she was distraught when heroic Dennis was killed rushing him to hospital. After failed relationships with policeman Mick Hopwood and nice-guy plumber Roger Stiles, Janice had high hopes for handsome bin man Trevor Dean, who became her flatmate in 2010 – but he only had eyes for her boss, Carla Connor.

'It's funny because when Janice went off with Dennis, Bruce [Jones, who played Les] got really jealous, like a bitter ex-husband. Then, even though our characters had split up a few years before, when Les got together with Cilla I felt pangs too – sometimes it would feel as if we'd been married in real life as well...'

- Janice offers Toyah a shoulder to cry on.
- Jealous Les flies at her new love Dennis.
- It's nit funny! Janice is forced to shave her head.

Current occupation: Underworld machinist.
On screen: 1997–
Defining moment: In 2008 Janice cons her workmates out of their lottery winnings – she stands trial, is given community service and is dumped by boyfriend Roger as a result.

50 CORONATION ST. ICON

When it came to her love life Deirdre Rachid hadn't had much happiness, and her last marriage to Moroccan toyboy Samir had been cruelly cut short when he died after being viciously attacked by a group of thugs. So when Deirdre met pilot Jon Lindsay in a bar while on a girlie night out with Liz she thought at last her luck was in. Handsome, courteous and dashing in his airline pilot uniform, Deirdre couldn't believe she'd landed herself such a catch. And, more importantly, he seemed to be a straightforward, easygoing type and free of any emotional baggage. He courted her in a lavish, extravagant way that Deirdre had never experienced before and she soon moved into his luxury house in the leafy Didsbury suburb of Manchester.

However, it turned out that Jon wasn't the high flier he'd claimed to be when Ken spotted him working at Manchester Airport's tie shop and told Deirdre. When she confronted Jon, he insisted he'd only deceived her to impress her and together they continued to live the high life. But unbeknown to Deirdre, Jon was financing it with forged credit cards and a stolen identity.

One by one his other misdemeanours began to be exposed. Deirdre was shocked to discover Jon was already married with children, who he lived with whilst pretending to be away on business trips. Realising Jon was no good, Deirdre set about recovering the money she had lent him by withdrawing cash from their joint account, but as she did so, Deirdre was arrested for fraud.

- ❶ Deirdre is smitten with fake pilot Jon Lindsay.
- ❷ Deirdre finds herself on trial for Jon's fraud.
- ❸ Cell-mates: Jackie Dobbs bunks up with 'The Weatherfield One'.

'If Deirdre's guilty of these preposterous allegations then... I'm a banana!'

Emily

With her friends and neighbours supporting her in the gallery, a bewildered Deirdre stood trial, convinced that Jon would be exposed as the real fraudster. But the prosecution managed to make Deirdre look like the brains of the operation and her supporters gasped when the judge deemed her to be a manipulative woman who had tricked a naive Jon into securing her a mortgage. He sentenced a distressed Deirdre to eighteen months' imprisonment while Jon was let off with a suspended sentence.

Back at the Rovers the whole Street was in shock at the verdict. Arch-enemies Ken and Mike put their differences aside to get together to prove her innocence and Emily organised the printing of t-shirts featuring a photo of Deirdre and the slogan, 'Free The Weatherfield One'. In the meantime Deirdre was finding her time at Her Majesty's Pleasure far from pleasurable, not least because she had the coarse, gobby Jackie Dobbs as her cell-mate.

Fortunately, Mike and Ken's tireless investigations into Jon's life finally bore fruit when one of his ex-wives came forward and was able to confirm his conman credentials. After twenty-one days in captivity, Deirdre Rachid was a free woman again.

OVERHEARD

Hayley reveals her big secret to Roy, 1998

ROY HAS PREPARED A CANDLELIT TABLE FOR TWO AT ROY'S ROLLS. THEY HAVE FINISHED THE MAIN COURSE. HAYLEY IS STILL NERVOUSLY AWAITING HER MOMENT OF TRUTH TELLING. ROY IS CONTENT AND DARES TO PUT HIS HAND OVER HERS.

ROY: Do you think... shall we take coffee upstairs in my flat? Make ourselves comfortable.

HAYLEY GENTLY WITHDRAWS HER HAND, KNOWING NOW IS WHEN SHE MUST FORCE HERSELF TO CONFESS.

HAYLEY: I'm sorry, Roy...

ROY: (CONCERNED) Have I said something I shouldn't?

HAYLEY: No. No. It's me, Roy. I've not said something I should. I'm afraid it's quite big and I don't know how you're going to take it.

ROY: Why? What?

HAYLEY: I just want you to know first that, well, however much I've loved your company, Roy, I'll understand if you don't want to see me again...

ROY: (PUZZLED) Nothing could make me not want to see you again, Hayley.

HAYLEY: This might.

ROY: What is it?

HAYLEY: It's to do with my past, Roy. Several years past now, but...

ROY: What?

HAYLEY: (GULPS) I'm a transsexual. (HAYLEY FORCES HERSELF TO EXPLAIN) I mean, I'm not female by birth Roy, but by choice.

ROY STARES UNCOMPREHENDINGLY.

HAYLEY: Do you understand what I said?

ROY: Er... no... I don't think so.

HAYLEY: (DISMAL) I was born with the wrong body. I was one of those little boys who always felt...

ROY: Boys? Is this some kind of joke? Are you making fun of me?

HAYLEY: No.

ROY: Then, what... what... I don't... I...(LOOKING EARNESTLY AT HAYLEY) Are you ill?

HAYLEY: (MORE SURE OF HERSELF) No. I have been. But I'm not any more.

A whole new side to Emily was unleashed when her nephew Spider (real name Geoffrey Nugent) settled into Coronation Street. The pair became close and bonded over their joint passion for good causes, especially when (along with Toyah Battersby) they attempted to save the Red Rec from Alf's proposed Millennium Concert Bowl redevelopment. The gently spoken churchgoer turned eco-warrior, and even spent the night camped out in a tree in a bid to ensure the last remaining green space in Weatherfield was preserved. Much to Rita's amusement, the next day a photo of Emily in her camouflage combats and army boots was splashed all over the front page of the *Gazette*. Emily organised a sit-down protest in front of the bulldozers just as the archaeologists declared the site was an area of great historical interest, so Alf was forced to call off the bulldozers in front of a victorious Emily.

The residents may have been in the grip of 'Free The Weatherfield One' fever, but there was still plenty going on elsewhere to keep them tittle-tattling. One development that sent tongues into overdrive was when Ken was exposed as a male escort at Alec's Golden Years Escort Agency.

This unlikely turn of events came to light when one of Ken's dates, a nervy woman called Babs Fanshawe, died midway through their meal in a restaurant. Babs had gone to the ladies' loo complaining of hot flushes, and after she'd been in there for a worryingly long time Ken discovered she had collapsed and died. This led to all kinds of embarrassment for Ken when the police turned up and demanded to know the details of his relationship with the deceased. When the *Weatherfield Gazette* ran a news story implicating him in Babs's death, Ken was dubbed an 'ageing gigolo', although he was later cleared when medical reports revealed his client had suffered a heart attack.

'Hope? I feel like the world's poking fun at me, like it always has done. First, giving me the wrong body and now giving me a wedding and snatching it away from me at the last minute. If the world can do that to me, what have I got to hope for?'

Hayley

In 1999 the very first (and probably the last) wedding took place in Roy's Rolls when Roy Cropper (*see page 195*) and Hayley Patterson (*see page 218*) finally tied the knot, surrounded by a supportive group of friends and neighbours. Of course, the greasy spoon hadn't been their first choice of venue; they'd originally intended to have a more traditional ceremony in a local church, but because of Hayley's transsexual status their nuptials had divided opinion on the Street. On their big day, neighbour from hell Les Battersby – spotting the chance to make a quick buck – tipped off the tabloids about the upcoming 'freak show', which saw the bride and groom being hounded out of the church before the service had even begun.

Leanne Battersby

Played by **Jane Danson**

'A rebellious, thieving, gobby, feisty little madam' is how Jane Danson describes the Leanne that arrived in Weatherfield fourteen years ago as the eldest daughter of new common-as-muck clan, the Battersbys. Trashy Leanne and her stepsister Toyah were first spotted shoplifting at Firman's Freezers, then they went on to make their neighbours' lives hell alongside her boisterous dad Les and mouthy stepmum Janice. Matriarch Gail Platt in particular took an instant dislike to Leanne for leading her precious son Nick astray, and she flipped when the pair eloped to Gretna Green.

'The Battersbys were brought in by the new producer Brian Park to spice things up as this larger-than-life, rough-and-ready family, which was very exciting. When we first appeared the papers dubbed us the family from hell and there was uproar about the characters. I remember at the time there was a poll on Teletext where ninety-seven per cent of people wanted us axed. So for us as actors it was a really unnerving time as we were only doing what we'd been told. But thankfully the viewers came round in the end.'

In 1999 Leanne's teen marriage fell apart when Nick forced her to have an abortion, leading the Rovers barmaid on a downward spiral into cocaine addiction. When she backed out of drug dealer Jez Quigley's plan to rob the pub, she was hospitalised by his henchmen and fled Weatherfield. Four years later, Les was shocked to discover Leanne shimmying in a lap-dancing club, and brought her back home. In 2007, after sleeping with almost every male member of the Baldwin family (apart from Mike), Leanne secretly started working as a prostitute.

'When I found out she was going to be a prostitute I thought, "Oh, is this the end now?" I wasn't sure how you could redeem the character after that. But it was written really well and there was a reason behind it, she'd gone through so much in her life – early marriage, abortion, drug addiction – and I think she was just punishing herself for all those things. When that storyline came to an end it was a relief, if I'm honest, but the writers managed to move Leanne onwards and upwards and now she's with Peter Barlow and for the first time in her life she stands a chance of happiness.'

Leanne's marriage to Nick ended in tears.

She beds Danny, as well as his son Jamie.

Leanne and Peter seem to be the perfect match.

Current occupation: Bookies' assistant.
On screen: 1997–2000, 2004–
Defining moment: She breaks nice-guy Jamie Baldwin's heart by cheating on him with his father Danny in 2005.

There was tear-jerking drama in September when Judy Mallett pegged out while pegging out the washing in the backyard of Number 9. Her death took place on the same day as Ashley and Maxine's wedding, when warmhearted Judy had stayed at home with her baby twins. Judy was still suffering from pains in her leg after being injured during an accident as a passenger in Vera's car – it turned out that Vera had unknowingly been driving a dodgy motor given to her by her equally dodgy son Terry. Meanwhile, just as her easygoing husband Gary was singing the praises of his own marriage in his best man's speech, Judy was keeling over as the blood clot in her leg travelled to her lungs. Alerted by the crying twins, neighbour Emily discovered Judy on the ground in the yard and it was left to Ken to break the news to a shell-shocked Gary. It was later confirmed the young mum had died of a pulmonary embolism.

The broken-hearted couple returned to the café and a shaken Hayley hid herself away in the upstairs flat, where she was comforted by good friend Alma. But then Roy had an idea, and after drawing the cafe's blinds the lovebirds were married in Roy's Rolls in a suitably touching and dignified ceremony. Hayley then revealed she had already changed her surname by deed poll to Cropper and the newlyweds headed off for a highly romantic honeymoon touring the railway museums of York.

Roy was back in the thick of it at the end of the year when he chaired the organising committee for the highly anticipated Millennium Street Party. Under Roy's supervision the event was a huge success, with attractions such as a bouncy castle, a fairground ride and Steve McDonald (dressed as a spiv) running a tombola. But the highlight was seeing the residents in fancy dress – including Ken as Sherlock Holmes, Emily as Florence Nightingale, local butcher Ashley and his wife Maxine Peacock as Anthony and Cleopatra and Martin and Gail as Laurel and Hardy. Perhaps the most bizarre sighting of all was Blanche Hunt, who had now made a permanent return to the Street, dressed as Carmen Miranda – with what looked like the entire fresh fruit section of Freshco stuck to her head!

The new millennium is kicked off with a rousing chorus.

Bad Boys

Which Weatherfield rogue is the most evil of them all?

Alan Bradley

He attempted to suffocate girlfriend Rita with a cushion when she discovered he'd impersonated her dead husband Len in order to remortgage Number 7. She had a breakdown as Alan's sinister harassment continued, but her nightmare ended when he was mowed down by an oncoming Blackpool tram.

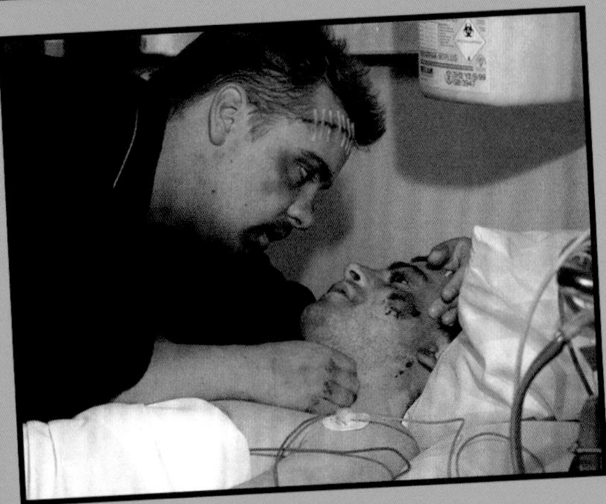

Jez Quigley

He killed mechanic Tony Horrocks, who owed him drug money. When Steve testified against Jez at Tony's murder trial he was nearly beaten to death by his gang in an underground car park. Steve's dad Jim battered Jez in a revenge attack and was later imprisoned when the gangster died of his injuries.

Richard Hillman

Having left Duggie for dead on a building site, Richard killed his ex-wife Patricia by smashing her around the head with a shovel, murdered young mum Maxine and also attempted to finish off Audrey and Emily. Perhaps he wasn't ideal husband material for Gail after all.

Tony Gordon

Tony arranged for his love rival Liam to be killed on his stag night and then, having suffered a heart attack, he tried to drown Roy having confessed all to him on what he thought was his deathbed. He escaped from custody and held Carla and Hayley at gunpoint before frying to death in the Underworld blaze.

Jon Lindsay

Deirdre's 'pilot' boyfriend actually turned out to be the airport's tie-shop manager, who also had another family he'd neglected to mention. A cold-hearted conman, Jon framed innocent Deirdre for fraud and she was sentenced to eighteen months in prison.

In the end it was trainee mechanic and the Duckworths' surrogate son Tyrone Dobbs (*see page 184*) dressed as an astronaut who won the fancy dress competition, while factory girls Janice Battersby (*see page 209*), Hayley, and Linda Sykes were joined by Deirdre as Abba tribute band 'Fabba', performing a floor-filling version of 'Waterloo'.

Later, as the celebrations continued in the Rovers, an elegant blonde figure walked silently up the ginnel and rapped on the back door of Number 7 – after three years away, Raquel was back in Weatherfield...

But her return was only a brief one. Raquel had come to tell a stunned Curly that he was a father – their daughter Alice had been born on 23 July 1997 – and to ask for a divorce. A more mature and sophisticated Raquel explained she now lived in France and had recently found out she was pregnant again and wanted to marry her French partner. Teary eyed, she apologised to Curly for not telling him about Alice and said she wanted him to be part of her life, suggesting he visit them at their château during the Easter holidays. She slipped out again by the back door, turning to Curly for a moment and softly adding: 'And I nearly forgot, Happy New Year, Happy New Life.'

The dawn of a new millennium had brought with it a shocking start for Curly, but it was nothing compared to the scandal in store for Gail, whose world was about to be turned upside down. Meanwhile, the new year would find Steve McDonald getting hitched again – this time for a bet...

A blast from the past: Raquel returns.

Hayley Cropper

Played by **Julie Hesmondhalgh**

It was Mike Baldwin who made big-hearted knicker-stitcher Hayley Patterson's double life public knowledge after he spotted that she was referred to as Harold on her tax-office paperwork – until that point the only people she'd confided in about her transgender status were loyal friend Alma Baldwin and sympathetic Roy Cropper.

Once the initial shock had subsided, she was gradually accepted by the residents. In return, community-spirited Hayley would do anything for them – taking in waifs and strays such as Chesney Brown, Craig Harris and reformed bad penny Becky Granger, whom she'd bumped into again whilst doing voluntary work with ex-offenders. She also proved to be a dab hand with a sewing needle and created Becky's first wedding gown, bridesmaids' dresses for Maxine and Karen's nuptials and also fashioned a booster bra for Sophie Webster!

'All I knew at first was there's a part going in *Coronation Street*, she's called Hayley, she's going to work in the factory and she's fun. That's all they told me. So I immediately imagined myself as a Bet Lynch-type character and I did literally pitch up for the audition with red lipstick and a leopard-skin coat. Then Judi Hayfield, the casting director, said to me: "I don't know how to begin to tell you what this part is or how you'll feel about it, but she's a transsexual and at the moment she's still in a male body. What do you think about that?" Well, I was gobsmacked, of course, but I thought it was a fantastic idea. So I went away to this great bookshop in Manchester and said I need every book you've got on transgender.'

> 'When you get down to it, she's even more of a misfit than I am.'
>
> **Roy on Hayley**

Back in 1999, geeky lovebirds Roy and Hayley were forced to abandon their plans for a church blessing when Les Battersby tipped off the tabloids, so instead a low-key ceremony took place in Roy's Rolls. But in 2010, the red-anoraked first-aider was finally legally able to have the enchantingly romantic wedding day she'd always dreamed about.

'I think in the beginning the original idea may have been pitched as a sort of joke –

Curly reprimands supervisor Hayley for being too nice.

The Croppers' first wedding takes place in the cafe.

Loved-up at the Street's millennium party.

Heartbroken Hayley is snubbed by Christian.

Robbie holds her at gunpoint in Underworld.

50 CORONATION ST. ICON

you know, give Roy a girlfriend and she turns out to be a man. But I was really conscious that I didn't want it to be making fun of her, and as it happened it was beautifully written and David [Neilson] and I played it, and continue to play it, as a delicate love story.

'I've always loved Hayley, but at first my dad was like: "Oh no, you get a part on the *Street* and it's this?" I think he was worried for me that I'd get loads of stick and abuse, which I didn't at all. Actually, I don't get recognised anywhere until I open my mouth. If truth be told, Hayley and Julie have merged more and more into one over the years. I'm a real do-gooder and I drive everyone mad – just like Hayley. Basically, I'm just playing me but with a wig on.'

In 2007 Hayley found out she fathered a son, Christian, before her sex change, but he lashed out and rejected her. The incident put considerable strain on her relationship with Roy and she left for Mozambique for a while to work on a charity project. More recently, Hayley found herself being held at gunpoint in the dramatic Underworld siege, having been lured there by evil Tony Gordon's accomplice, Robbie Sloane.

'I was very excited to be involved in some action drama because that's not my normal place in the show, I'm usually behind a knicker machine or serving butties. When I got the scripts for those episodes I read them like a novel, all five episodes back to back – I found it absolutely thrilling.

'For years I was working in London doing TV and fringe theatre, and although my mum and dad were very proud and were great at supporting me, there's a thing in Accrington where I'm from: no matter what you're doing – I mean, I could have been playing Juliet at the RSC – all people would ask was: "When are we going to see you on *Coronation Street*?" So it was the absolute ultimate for me to get it and I'm amazed my parents didn't set fireworks off the top of the town hall when they found out.

'A few weeks ago I was in a Rovers scene with Bill Roache, Anne Kirkbride and Barbara Knox and I just stood there and thought: "Blimey, it's like legend central in here today!" At times like that I genuinely do imagine myself as a little girl watching *Corrie* and saying to her: "You're going to be in that one day. You'll be there in the Rovers with those people." Back then it would've seemed an impossible dream and even now I'm still pinching myself.'

Current occupation: Underworld assistant manager.
On screen: 1998–
Defining moment: She travels to Amsterdam in 1998 for her final operation and is delighted when Roy goes after her, and she agrees to return to England with him.

2000s

For the first time since 1961, on 8 December 2000 *Coronation Street* went live to the nation as part of its fortieth-anniversary celebrations. The hour-long special was given the royal seal of approval by the Prince of Wales, who popped up in the only pre-recorded moment – a news bulletin that had been filmed earlier that day reporting his visit to Weatherfield, where he'd met awed Councillor Audrey Roberts in a line-up. The episode also featured the first appearance of Chris Gascoyne as the newly returned navy man Peter Barlow (Ken's son had last appeared in 1986 with David Lonsdale in the role). In the final scene, as the jubilant residents cracked open the champagne having saved the famous cobbles from being tarmacked, the relieved cast celebrated for real.

'We were all terrified about going live, and at the time I thought I needed the extra stress of meeting Prince Charles that morning like a hole in the head,' remembers Sue Nicholls. 'But actually meeting him helped me take my mind off the live show and I thanked him for that. The episode came over very well in the end. There were a few hiccups, but we got through it and there was a tremendous feeling of achievement afterwards.'

September 2002 saw the launch of a fifth weekly episode of the *Street* (turning Monday's outing into a double bill) and a year later soap history was made with the introduction of *Coronation Street*'s first regular gay character, as sensitive soul Todd Grimshaw began to question his sexuality. This was a groundbreaking moment that creator Tony Warren had fought for years to make happen.

The headline-grabbing storyline of the Noughties was the saga of financial advisor-turned-wacko-serial killer, Richard Hillman; and in February 2003 came the episode

millions of fans had been waiting for. In a memorably melodramatic moment, Hillman confessed his guilt to Gail before steering his bewildered wife and her petrified family into the canal – but only succeeding in killing himself. The underwater sequences were filmed over two days in a Royal Navy tank at Fleetwood, near Blackpool, for which plucky Helen Worth refused the offer of a stunt double and took some hurried swimming lessons in order to overcome her fear of water.

Says Jack P. Shepherd: 'They submerged the car 14 feet under water and divers pulled us to the bottom. It was scary, but I loved it. I remember thinking: "How will they know the difference between acting and drowning?"'

The plot line swept the board at that year's British Soap Awards and the man behind the monster, Brian Capron, took home the gongs for Best Actor and Villain of the Year. Kieran Roberts, the producer responsible for 'Hillmania', told the *Manchester Evening News*: 'The episode that got the greatest number of viewers, 19.48 million, the "Norman Bates with a briefcase" two-hander featuring Richard and Gail, was essentially an old-fashioned play. When we get it right in *Coronation Street*, it's the ability to tell a story that intense, dramatic and tragic, and still lace it with humour.'

In 2009 it was announced with sadness that Maggie Jones, the actress who played Blanche, had passed away at the age of seventy-five after a period of illness. When the terrible news reached the set the cast broke into several minutes of spontaneous applause and filming was suspended for the day as a tribute to their well-loved colleague.

Maggie's final scene was broadcast on 11 December 2009. In it, Deirdre and her formidable mother finally persuaded Ken to suspend hostilities with his recovering alcoholic son Peter over the Christmas period – which led Blanche, with her eggshell-thin patience being tested yet again, to roll her eyes skyward and utter what was to be her closing line: 'Hallelujah!'

- By royal appointment: Sue Nicholls rehearses with Prince Charles.
- 'Hillmania' takes the nation by storm.
- More than fifty cast members come together for the fortieth.

While most thirteen-year-old girls were learning the words to Atomic Kitten's latest chart-topper, in 2000 Sarah Louise Platt was trying to come to terms with being five months pregnant from a one-night-stand with a sullen schoolboy called Neil Fearns. With her stepdad Martin being a nurse you would've thought she'd know better, but Martin was too preoccupied having an affair with co-worker Rebecca Hopkins to teach her how to be careful.

When her baby girl was born a disinterested Sarah-Louise initially decided to call her Britney, much to the disapproval of grandma Audrey. After a family conference 'Bethany' was agreed to be far more suitable, and Britney was relegated to a middle name. But bad luck loomed large for the poor mite – when only hours out of the womb she was stolen by Kevin's second wife, Alison, who'd just lost her baby, Jake, at birth. Kevin persuaded Alison to hand over baby Bethany, but straight after she hurled herself under a passing truck and died instantly.

'It's times like this I can understand why some animals eat their young.'

Gail on Sarah Louise

Martin wasn't the only one on the Street with an adulterous secret – young buck Mark Redman was sneakily having it away with his dad Mike's wife-to-be, Linda Sykes. Mike should have known better than to trust the gobby machinist who had seduced him, but he couldn't help himself and he loved her feisty, tough attitude. The family affair was exposed on Mike and Linda's wedding day when a heartbroken Mark proposed to Linda outside the hotel. When the

Keeping it in the family: Linda and Mark give in to temptation.

When the Hortons invited the Duckworths to Blackpool for a week to look after their grandson Tommy, an ecstatic Vera asked half the Street to join them – and ended up tripping the light fantastic across the floor of the Tower Ballroom with Norris Cole. The unlikely duo even entered a dance competition, but when an exhausted Vera cried off from Norris's punishing rehearsal schedule, the shop assistant turned his attentions to Celeste, a flirty ballroom regular, and asked her to be his partner instead. However, elderly Celeste had a fall and Norris was forced to plead with an affronted Vera to partner up with him again – which she did, after he'd promised to buy her a new frock. In the final of the competition the Weatherfield hoofers drew with reigning champions the Kershaws and found themselves in a tense dance-off. However, thanks to loyal Jack's interference, Norris and Vera snagged the winner's gong – he'd spiked Mrs Kershaw's drink with vodka, which meant she was barely able to stand, never mind dance!

bolshie bride told him where to get off, Mark took his dad to one side at the wedding reception and told him the stomach-turning truth. Mike was horrified by the revelation but, blinded by love, accepted his wife's explanation that it was just a brief fling and that his infatuated son wouldn't leave her alone. Mike disowned poor Mark and left for his honeymoon with the triumphant Linda.

Another cheating son, Terry Duckworth – the proverbial bad penny – turned up again in Weatherfield in November. Even though his dad Jack had just won £60,000 on an accumulator bet on the horses, it wasn't the *Weatherfield Gazette* photo of him and Vera kissing a giant cheque that had lured Terry back – it was Jack who had tracked him down.

Desperate for help, Terry's ex-girlfriend Andrea Clayton had arrived at the Duckworths' with the news that their grandson Paul was in dire need of a kidney transplant and she needed to find Terry, quick. Vera was shocked, not least because she'd been told that Paul had been adopted.

Unbeknown to Vera, Jack and lodger Tyrone Dobbs managed to track down Terry, but he was his usual charmless self and refused to help his dying son, until Jack offered him money. Before you could say 'organ donor', the greedy bad lad had agreed a fee of £25,000 for his kidney.

2000s Births

Bethany (Sarah Platt & Neil Fearns)	4 June 2000
Jake (Alison & Kevin Webster)	5 June 2000
Ben (Emma & Curly Watts)	26 Dec 2001
Joshua (Maxine Peacock & Matt Ramsden)	8 April 2002
Simon (Lucy Richards & Peter Barlow)	6 July 2003
Amy (Tracy Barlow & Steve McDonald)	9 Feb 2004
Billy (Sarah Platt & Todd Grimshaw)	31 May 2004
Asha (Sunita & Dev Alahan)	13 Jan 2006
Aadi (Sunita & Dev Alahan)	13 Jan 2006
Freddie Thomas (Claire & Ashley Peacock)	17 July 2006
Dylan James (Violet Wilson & Sean Tully)	22 Feb 2008
Liam (Maria & Liam Connor)	30 June 2009

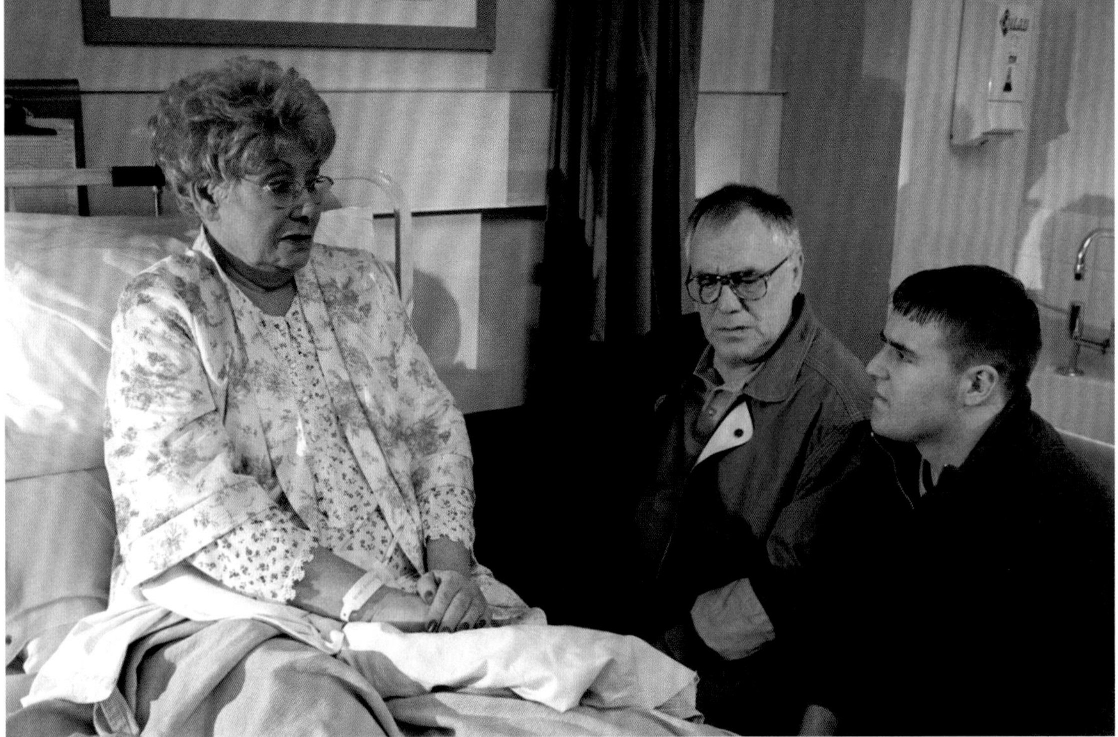

Meanwhile, Terry swaggered into Number 9 and pretended to a thrilled Vera that it was all his idea and he was doing it from the goodness of his heart. However, just as the operation was about to go ahead, a proud as punch Vera went to check on Terry, only to find an empty hospital bed. She raced out of the building to see him jumping into a cab bleating about how he couldn't go through with it. Vera then learned he had also run off with the money. Left with no other option, Vera decided to donate her own kidney.

This brave and selfless act was a success for Paul but nearly cost Vera her life when she had an allergic reaction to the drugs used for the operation. In a rare glimpse of the more caring side of Terry, he slipped back unnoticed to check on his mother, but when he knew she'd be okay, he quietly snuck away. Still taking the cash with him, of course.

Sassy and sexy Underworld machinist Karen Phillips (*see page 238*) had already had a fling with Street Cars co-owner Vikram Desai and a one-night stand with craggily handsome Peter Barlow by the time she started seeing Steve McDonald in 2001. Unable to resist a wind-up, Janice had teased Karen about her disastrous dating history and bet her she'd never be able to get Steve to propose. Karen, unable to resist the challenge, told Steve of the dare and persuaded him to ask her to marry him in front of everyone at the Rovers. However, Janice then upped the stakes and wagered Karen two days' pay that she'd never be able to actually get him up the aisle.

Brave Vera prepares to donate her kidney.

Steve is intrigued by Karen's proposition.

'Half the street think you're a slag, the other half think you're a nutter – I think you're both!'

Steve to Karen

TOP FIVE

Cobble Clashes

When the women of Weatherfield want to let off steam there's only one place to do it...

'That woman's tongue – if it was a bit longer she could shave with it!'

Ena and Elsie, 1961
The Weatherfield grand dames enjoy a no-holds-barred slanging match after Elsie accuses Ena of sending a poison-pen letter.

'You like showing yourself up in the street, don't you? It comes second nature to you...'

Sally and Natalie, 1997
The nation cheers as Sally right hooks Kevin's mistress to the ground.

Gail and Eileen, 2004
The rival matriarchs claw at each other following the revelation that Todd is gay and has been cheating on Sarah.

'Oh, here's the other one... the rest of the Village People!'

Cilla and Janice, 2006
Les Battersby's complicated love life turns into a street brawl when former wife Janice accuses his current partner Cilla of looking like she works in a massage parlour.

Michelle and Rosie, 2009
After being attacked by Rosie in the middle of a canoodle with Luke Strong, no-nonsense Michelle throws the troublesome teen out into the street.

'You always look like you work in some dodgy massage parlour!'

David Platt

Played by **Jack P. Shepherd**

Dastardly David Platt has always been more concerned with mind games and manipulation than actually doing anything constructive with his life. That seems to be his lot – along with aimlessly sweeping up clumps of Emily Bishop's barnet at his gran's hair salon. But unlike his alter ego, Jack P. Shepherd has always had a grand plan.

'I've wanted to be an actor since I was a really little kid, that's all I dreamt about doing. I used to watch films all day and just wanted to grow up to be like Jack Nicholson. That was my goal in life at five years old. So when you see David being unhinged, that's who I've based it on...'

After a spell at drama school and small roles in the likes of *Where The Heart Is* and *Clocking Off*, twelve-year-old Jack joined the Street, taking over the role from Thomas Ormson, who'd played David ever since he was first seen in Gail's arms the day after he was born.

'I remember I walked into the kids' green room and Johnny Briggs was in there sitting on a chair, because when there were no child actors in the older cast members used to use it for some peace and quiet. So Johnny Briggs was sat there watching Sky News and he was like, "You must be the new David?" I'd never watched the programme before so I just went, "Yeah, who are you?" My mum just gasped and went, "That's Johnny Briggs – that's Mike Baldwin!", in a really embarrassed voice. She was mortified.'

Despite only having three lines in his first episode (the scene took place in Roy's Rolls and involved ordering an Eccles cake), it went down a storm with Jack's family who'd gathered around the TV set to witness his debut.

'First of all you saw Roy and then you could make out a bit of me in the background at the side and my brother started shouting, "There's his arm! There's his arm!" The first time you actually saw my face on screen it was like there'd been an earthquake in our living room, everyone was screaming and my mum was in bits. It was a brilliant moment, though, and I bet most people who've joined the show have been through something similar.'

For any parent David would be the child from hell – his crime sheet includes ruining his mum's relationship with reflexologist Phil Nail by sending her eerie cards from

her dead ex, Richard Hillman, and nearly killing niece Bethany, who ate one of the ecstasy pills he'd hidden in her doll. Not forgetting the time he was sentenced to four months in a young offenders' institution when, having discovered she'd advised his girlfriend Tina to have a termination, he shoved his mum down the stairs and proceeded to smash up the street with a metal pole.

'That was great fun to do and I really went for it. I may have gone a bit too far as unfortunately I ended up injuring Bill Roache. I was supposed to just tell Ken to keep away from me, but we decided David would be angrier than that, so I gave him a shove and Bill fell and hurt his arm. Like the true gentleman he is, he insisted it wasn't my fault. But I felt really bad. I also smashed a few windows I shouldn't have.

'The way I look at it is if anyone had been through what David has been through it's possible they would've turned out the same way. He changed when his dad Martin left and started acting more mental after Richard Hillman tried to kill him, which is bound to screw with your head. He's not as evil as people think and that's why he's fun to play, because he's volatile and swings between being quite nice and a totally nasty deviant.'

'I want to believe you're not rotten to the core. I want to believe you with all my heart. But I'm not stupid. I know what you're like.'

Gail

By David's side, even at his most despicable moments, has been his long-suffering mother Gail, played by Helen Worth. 'She's been like a mum to me at work as well. I literally see Helen more than my own mum, which is slightly weird. Coming into the show aged twelve you don't know about the technical side of being on a set, so it was brilliant to have a permanent mentor like Helen to guide me. It's like she's been my Jedi master, you know, teaching me the ways of the force.'

So can Jack ever see David changing his manipulative ways and settling down?

'Definitely. He's only nineteen now. That's what everyone forgets. He's still a teenager and has got his whole life ahead of him. So he could be running Audrey's salon when she pops her clogs or even the Rovers. Or maybe he'll just end up as a total loon? The possibilities are endless...'

- Barney the rabbit arrives at the Platts'.
- Tina is unimpressed by David's tattoo.
- Mum Gail confronts David about her fall.
- David loses the plot and attacks Ken.
- He supports Gail after Joe's disappearance.

Current occupation: Hair salon assistant.
On screen: 2000–
Defining moment: Pushing Gail down the stairs during a row and leaving her for dead in 2008.

OVERHEARD

Jack and Vera celebrate their wedding anniversary in style, 2001.

JACK HAS SURPRISED VERA WITH A ROMANTIC ANNIVERSARY MEAL IN HIS ALLOTMENT SHED. VERA SITS IN A DECK CHAIR, JACK ON AN OLD DINING CHAIR. THEY'RE EATING FISH AND CHIPS WRAPPED IN PAPER AND DRINKING ALE.

VERA: This is a nice bit of fish.

JACK: Haddock. I splashed out. Remember that night? After we took your mate home I bought us chips and we went back to your old man's place.

VERA: It started to rain so I said 'let's go into shed'. I remember the look in your eyes. Lust.

JACK: (SMILING AT MEMORY) You kept giggling.

VERA: I were nervous. It was my first time.

JACK: Aye. It were my first time too.

VERA: Oh I know.

JACK: (INDIGNANT) What do you mean? You thought I were a lady killer.

VERA: I never.

JACK: You did. I remember you saying. We were laying on some potato sacks, you looked up and said: 'You're a real lady killer, be gentle with me.'

VERA: I never! I said: 'You've a look of that lady killer, be gentle with me.' It were the lighting down there. Made you look like that Christie chap. Him that wallpapered all them women into his kitchen.

SHE SEES JACK'S HURT EXPRESSION.

VERA: Oh, have I bruised your ego? I'm sorry. Have me pickled onion...

JACK TAKES THE OFFERED ONION, IN A SULK.

VERA: You were very good though, considering it were your first time. If it weren't for you shouting 'at last!' at end I'd have never known.

Neither Karen nor Steve was prepared to back down and admit the whole thing had been a joke, even though most of the Street knew it was a prank by now, and in May they suddenly found themselves at Weatherfield Registry Office saying 'I do', followed by a reception at the Rovers.

The shell-shocked newlyweds decided to arrange a honeymoon to Florida six weeks later, which is when they woke up to the fact that the arrangement wasn't a nightmare after all, but they were in fact love's young dream. That is, until they got divorced two years later when Karen got it into her head she wanted to remarry Steve properly in the wedding of her dreams. Despite marrying again, their union wasn't to last, and a second divorce soon became a reality.

Toyah Battersby's life was to change in a traumatic, dramatic and terrifying way at Easter when she was coming home from a gig with male stripper, Sam Kingston. The young student insisted she'd be all right walking back to her door alone, but in fact she was raped and left for dead in the ginnel. Jason found her there the next morning, semi-conscious and with no recollection of her assailant. Many of the male residents were accused of the attack, including innocent Sam and Peter Barlow, but the rapist was revealed to be a friend called Phil Simmonds, who she'd met through ex-boyfriend Spider. Creepy Phil came round to check on her, but when he said her name, Toyah had a flashback to him attacking her. She tried to leave the house under the pretence of needing biscuits, but he realised her memory had returned and grabbed her round the throat. He told her the attack was all her fault and how he'd thought they were friends. Fortunately, Peter heard the screams, kicked down the front door and caught Phil as he tried to flee, dealing him an almighty right hook.

Later that year there were tears aplenty when much-loved former café owner Alma discovered that due to a missed smear test and a further misdiagnosis, she had inoperable cervical cancer. Initially the only person she confided in was best pal Audrey, who ended up relaying the terrible news to Alma's shocked ex-husband Mike. Wanting to be with Alma in her time of need, Mike tracked her down to the Lake District where she'd gone to get away from it all, mull over her past and come to terms with her limited future.

Alma and Mike are reconciled at the Lakes.

Full of regrets and apologies, Mike confessed he had made a huge mistake in leaving her. The pair sweetly reminisced over their time together, but Alma insisted he should now make every effort to make a go of his marriage to Linda.

On their return to Coronation Street Mike discovered that charmless Linda – jealous of the time Mike had been spending with his dying ex – had been playing away from home with one of his

business rivals. Disgusted by her behaviour, Mike rushed to be with Alma, who was spending her last few days on earth at Audrey's. Together they listened to Perry Como and recollected how they'd seen him live at the Royal Albert Hall. Another ex of Alma's, Ken, joined them and then, as Alma slipped away, a weeping Mike begged for her to know he had never loved anyone like he loved her. For Mike, Alma's death finally rammed home the fact that he'd made a huge mistake in marrying Linda and he filed for divorce.

By 2002, with her daughter Bethany now two years old, Sarah had left most of the mothering duties to Granny Gail. She was more interested in running amok with bad boy Aidan Critchley, who not only had she stolen from best friend Candice Stowe but for whom she had also dumped sensible, safe Todd Grimshaw.

Aidan thought that showing a girl a good time meant a joyride in Ken's car. He then cranked up the excitement a gear by deliberately zooming past speed cameras to get Ken points on his license, but by this stage Sarah had had enough and tried to get him to stop. When that failed, she opened the car door and the car flipped over. With Sarah unconscious, Aidan scarpered, leaving her for dead.

Sarah was discovered and rushed to hospital where she stayed in a coma for several days and Gail was told she was likely to have brain damage. But after Todd told Sarah he loved her at her hospital bedside, she came round with just some nasty bumps. Luckily these had knocked some sense into her and she realised that not only did she have to be a better mother to Bethany, but Todd was the one for her. Everyone was chuffed to bits, except for Todd's feisty mum Eileen (*see page 247*), who was dismayed to see her son throw away his Oxford University place for the Platt 'floozy'.

▲ Mike leads the mourners at Alma's funeral.
▼ A tender moment for Todd and Sarah.

Dev Alahan

Played by **Jimmi Harkishin**

Life probably hit an all-time low for Dev when deranged spurned lover Maya Sharma sought revenge. She was so enraged that Dev had chosen Sunita Parekh over her that she framed her rival for an illegal-immigration scam, which saw the innocent shopgirl being arrested for bigamy on her wedding day. When this evil plan failed, the looney-tune lawyer attempted to burn down the shop with Dev and Sunita both gagged and bound in the flat upstairs.

'He seems to have a strange effect on women,' laughs Jimmi Harkishin. 'I'd describe Dev as a bruised romantic and a reluctant heart-throb – he doesn't necessarily want to be a heart-throb and a flirt, but he just can't help himself. He feels he owes it to the ladies of Weatherfield...'

Medallion-wearing dandy Dev Alahan arrived from Birmingham to help out his cousin, Nita Desai, in the corner shop when her brother Vikram went missing. He ended up buying the business, adding it to the chain of shops he already owned. In 2001 he took in sweet-natured Sunita, who'd been fleeing an arranged marriage, but by the time it finally dawned on Dev that she was the woman for him, she'd fallen for the charms of chiselled Irish barman, Ciaran McCarthy.

Two years later the couple were reconciled and Sunita fell pregnant with their twins, Asha and Aadi, but she ditched Dev after making the shocking discovery that he had at least four secret offspring by other women, one of whom was his down-to-earth fourteen-year-old daughter Amber Kalirai, who in time came to live with him. When her narcissistic dad began singing the praises of his own sex appeal, Amber once sarcastically retorted: 'They can't resist that Seventies' crooner style, man. No wonder you haven't changed your look...'

In 2008 Dev surpassed himself by having an affair with Nina, the wife of his friend Prem Mandal, before falling for their daughter, Tara. When Tara in turn found out he'd cheated on her with solicitor Lisa Dalton, she publicly humiliated him by unveiling an enormous photograph of the shopkeeper stark naked.

'With Sunita now back in his life he's realising it's time he settled down and behaved. Ultimately, Dev is inches away from being a really good guy and he never acts with any malice or any forethought – he's just a bit ridiculous and stupid at times!' admits Jimmi.

Sunita and Dev tie the knot in style.

Amber is stuck between the warring Alahans.

Dev tries to keep his affair from Tara.

Current occupation: Owner of Alahan's corner shop and Prima Doner take-away.
On screen: 1999–
Defining moment: In 2001 he proposes to barmaid girlfriend Geena Gregory but cheats on her by bedding Deirdre Rachid.

Rita decided to take on Mr Woo, a Shi-Tzu formerly owned by a customer, but the day the dog arrived she was due to leave for a Mediterranean cruise. Emily volunteered to look after him for those three weeks, but her allergic lodger Norris hated the hound and it seemed the feeling was mutual – whenever the snivelling shop assistant came near, the pampered pooch would growl menacingly. About a week before Rita was due to return, a panicked Norris discovered Mr Woo had carked it in the stock room of The Kabin. Much to his relief, after a long and expensive search with the help of dog expert Kirk Sutherland, Norris managed to find an identical-looking replacement. The purchase left him a cool £450 out of pocket, but as he confided to Emily, it was money well spent if it meant avoiding the wrath of Rita. When she walked into the shop a suntanned Rita was pleased to see Mr Woo again, but she became upset that he didn't seem to recognise her. Later, in the Rovers, Emily and Norris's faces fell as Rita casually informed them she'd sold the dog to a breeder and was chuffed to have got a whopping £300 for him!

At Number 4, Ashley and his flighty but adored wife Maxine were having trouble conceiving, so she did what any young woman would do in her position – she went to see her local doctor, Dr Matt Ramsden. However, where most doctors would refer their patients to a specialist, Dr Ramsden slept with Maxine one drunken night and managed to get her pregnant.

When Matt's furious wife Charlie discovered the truth about the pregnancy and threw him out, an oblivious Ashley took pity on him and, much to Maxine's horror, told him he could stay with them. Just as Maxine's labour pains started, the truth came spilling out. Matt told poor Ashley the baby was his and that he and Maxine had feelings for each other. A panicking Maxine admitted to the one-night-stand but desperately insisted the baby was Ashley's and she only loved him.

Ashley was in turmoil as he supported his wife while she gave birth to the boy he hoped was his. Baby Joshua spent the first few

- Maxine gives into Dr Matt's bedside manner.
- Ashley gets physical with love rival Matt.
- While Duggie lay dying, Richard raided his house.

days of his life in an incubator while Ashley fell apart, unable to accept Maxine's betrayal. After Dr Matt left the Street, Ashley decided they needed to do a DNA test, but at the last moment he softly told Maxine he couldn't turn his love off like a tap for either her or baby Joshua and it was time they went home as a family. A blood test several years later, after Maxine's death, proved that Dr Matt was indeed Joshua's biological father, but despite a custody battle the little boy remained in doting Ashley's care.

Elsewhere, amiable financial advisor Richard Hillman first appeared in the Street at the funeral of his long-lost cousin Alma, and Gail was instantly taken with him. It wasn't long before he moved into Number 8, and while Sarah and David were initially wary of the new man in their mum's life, he soon won them over with expensive gifts and nice holidays. Richard had revealed to Gail that he was unable to have children of his own, which was a factor in the break-up of both his previous marriages, and he genuinely seemed to dote on Gail's ready-made family.

But Richard's other great love was money, and so he went into business with Rovers proprietor Duggie Ferguson, converting an old building into luxury flats. However, straight from the off things went wrong; costs soared and an application for a bail hostel to be built next door threatened any future development. Richard and Duggie argued one night in one of the half-finished flats and Duggie fell through the banisters, due to the poor building work, but instead of helping him, Richard raced off to steal money from Duggie's house, leaving him to die.

To add to Richard's woes, his ex-wife Patricia turned up demanding a share of his business. By now Richard and Gail had planned a summer wedding, but with no cashflow, Richard was panicking. He agreed to give Patricia a cheque but instead lured her to the construction site, smacked her over the head with a shovel and buried her body.

The lavish wedding went ahead at the five-star Aston Manor Hotel in July but Richard's debts kept spiralling. He even embezzled the Duckworths' life savings to try and keep afloat.

The Write Stuff: How Sir Ian McKellen joined the *Street* and introduced the residents to the pleasure of *Hard Grinding*, before ripping them off...

Sir Ian McKellen may be best known for Hollywood blockbusters such as *The Lord Of The Rings*, but he is also a fan of the cobbles. So much so that the award-winning Shakespeare aficianado jumped at the chance to play Mel Hutchwright, a dubious author with conman credentials.

In 2005 Norris had set up a reading club along with Rita, Emily, Blanche, Ken, Roy and Liz. The group's first read was *Hard Grinding*, a steamy bodice-ripper by Mel Hutchwright. An argument over the gender of the author led to Blanche writing to the publisher, followed by the appearance of Mel himself.

He breezed into the cafe looking for 'Blanche Hunch' and then enthralled the group with his stories of how he told Spielberg off for wanting to set his novel in Baltimore not Bolton. An awed Norris invited Mel to stay at Emily's while he researched his new novel. Mel waxed lyrical about his new work in progress, *The Canary's Last Song*, a saga of mining folk set in the north, all the while cadging free food and booze from the starry-eyed residents, each of whom he told would be taking leading roles in his book. Only Ken remained sceptical.

After Mel feigned depression with heavy sighs and hints about his publisher rejecting his idea, the book club finally suggested they could help him self-publish, each paying £200 in return for a share of the profits. When Norris broke the news to a delighted Mel, he was about to flit with Emily's porcelain figurines in a Freshco carrier bag.

However, a suspicious Ken did some digging, and just as Mel was accepting the cheques made out to the alleged printer 'Mr Hipkis', Ken unmasked Mel as Lionel Hipkis, a fraudster who regularly ripped off book clubs with the same con.

Roy was about to call the police when nasty Lionel sneered that he could poke fun at each and every one of them in the press. Feeling stupid, they let him go with their dosh in his pockets, the nail in the coffin of the Street's first-ever book club.

Sir Ian, who had once turned down the chance to play Elsie's nephew, said that appearing on *Coronation Street* was his only remaining lifelong ambition, and he was sorry to let the role of Mel go: 'I would love to go back. Betty Driver only last week wrote me a letter asking me, "When are you coming back?" But I was playing a character that couldn't possibly go back – he wouldn't be welcome. People do go back and play different parts but I think I've only got one *Coronation Street* character inside me and that was Mel. I had a ball though!'

'I said to my agent: Tell Mr Spielberg the very foundation of the novel is its Lancashire identity. Setting it in Baltimore would suck and siphon the very lifeblood from it. It would be like E.T. being from Milton Keynes rather than outer space.'

On learning that Audrey was worth £250,000, he tried to make it look like the grandmother was losing her marbles so he could seize control of her assets. When that failed, he went straight for the kill and set fire to her house while she slept. Audrey survived and realised it was her dodgy son-in-law who had tried to murder her, but no one, least of all Gail, believed her.

Richard was by now on the verge of bankruptcy and desperate times called for desperate measures. His company had bought out Emily's house and Richard decided her early death would bring in some much-needed cash. So while Emily was babysitting Joshua, Richard dressed up in Sarah's boyfriend Aidan's clothes, whom he'd previously drugged, and snuck into Number 4. But just as he hit Emily on the head with a crow bar, Maxine unexpectedly returned home early from her mother's birthday party at the Rovers and Richard was forced to attack her as well. While Emily survived, Maxine sadly died and Richard was tortured by the unnecessary killing of the young mum. Ironically, her death was made all the more unnecessary as the flats were starting to find buyers.

'You should've stayed at the party, Maxine...'

Richard Hillman

Feeling uneasy, Gail began to suspect that all was not right, and when it was revealed that Aidan had been drugged with Audrey's tranquillisers it finally dawned on Gail that there was something very wrong with her husband's explanations. So she confronted him.

But the truth was far worse than Gail could have possibly imagined when, finally, an unhinged Richard confessed everything but claimed he'd done it for her. A horrified Gail accused him of

Poor Maxine arrives home at just the wrong time.

OVERHEARD

Richard Hillman reveals the terrible truth to Gail, 2003.

THE HILLMANS ARE IN THE KITCHEN AT NUMBER 8. IT'S EVENING. GAIL IS STILL REELING FROM RICHARD'S SHOCKING CONFESSION.

RICHARD: (PLEADING) Everything I've ever done is for you. I might be a killer, but I did it for you. I killed for you, Gail. Would any other man you've ever known do that? Did Brian or Martin love you that much? They didn't even love you enough to stay with you. They betrayed you. Like most men do (CONTEMPTUOUS) with their seedy little affairs. But I'll never do that. If you live for a thousand years, you won't find a man who loves you more than me.

GAIL: All that claptrap about how much you love me, how you did it all for me...

RICHARD: It's true.

GAIL: (DUMBFOUNDED) You tried to kill my mother.

RICHARD: I didn't.

GAIL: Come on. Admit it. You messed with her mind, then set fire to her house. Didn't you?

RICHARD: Her mind was going anyway.

GAIL: (SNEERING AT HIM) You're not just evil. You're sick. Do you know that?

RICHARD: Getting old these days – it's a nightmare. The pension system's had it. Care for the elderly's a joke. There's too many old people – not enough young people to support them.

GAIL: So you bump 'em off and steal their money?

RICHARD: I just put my family first. Like every other animal on the planet. It's natural instinct. Survival of the fittest. I know I scared you just then, but you can trust me, I swear. No one else will ever get hurt. And now it's all out in the open, there's no need for any more lies. I'll always be loyal to you.

GAIL: You'll never have a 'seedy little affair', but you might hit me in the face with a shovel?

RICHARD: No. Never.

GAIL: You think your dad running off with another woman's a worse crime than clubbing someone to death? (SHE TURNS ON HIM) You're twisted. You're Norman Bates with a brief case. And I don't want you living under the same roof as my family!

being deranged and broke down as he fled into the night. Trembling, she called the police and the hunt was on for Hillman.

Hounded by the press and hated by her neighbours, Gail's ordeal was far from over – a few weeks later she came home to find Richard had gagged and bound David and Sarah, and sedated granddaughter Bethany in the car in the garage. He calmly announced that the way forward was for them all to die together as a family. He was planning carbon-monoxide poisoning for them, but before he started the engine Richard allowed Gail to kiss the children goodbye. As she did so a resourceful Gail was able to pass Sarah some nail scissors to cut her ropes.

Meanwhile, a frantic Audrey could hear the car revving and ran for help. The garage door was forced open by Gail's ex, Martin, and mechanics Kevin and Tommy Harris. With barking-mad Richard at the wheel, the car came speeding out towards them then wildly careered through the streets of Weatherfield towards the canal, with Hillman screaming 'This is it! I love you!' as he drove straight into the murky waters. Sarah, David, Bethany and Gail managed to escape and for one moment it looked as if Richard had too. However, his body was later dredged up and as a shocked Gail identified him by the side of the canal, she slipped off the rings he'd given her, threw them into the water and said: 'I'll sleep now.'

⬆ The Hillmans' car dives into the canal.

⬇ Safe at last: Gail and family recover from their ordeal.

There's not many that could manage to get married to one woman and have a baby by another in the same fortnight, but never underestimate the multi-tasking skills of Peter Barlow. It started in 2003 when he tied the knot with Lucy Richards, the florist boss of his sister Tracy. He was trying to do the honourable thing as she was expecting his baby at the time and they had a quickie registry office do in March that year.

However, somewhat dishonestly, he'd failed to mention to his new wife that he was also engaged to Rovers manageress Shelley Unwin (*see page 242*). Understandably, when Lucy found out she refused to see him again, but Peter wanted to have his wedding cake and eat it. So when Lucy went into labour he raced to the hospital, demanding to see his wife and son. Lucy was desperate to believe his claims that he wasn't seeing Shelley anymore and slowly let him into her and baby

Karen McDonald

Played by **Suranne Jones**

Considering the gob on her, Karen Phillips made a surprisingly subdued entrance when her mate Linda Sykes helped her bag a job as a knicker-stitcher at Underworld.

'When I joined they said to me, could you bring in a pair of your own jeans and a couple of t-shirts for your costume to kick you off. Three months later I was still wearing the clothes I'd brought in, so maybe they just didn't think I'd be hanging around. I was very much in the background at first but then the writers must've realised I was ballsy enough to play a ballsy character and next thing I knew I was married to Steve McDonald!'

Suddenly it was as if Karen was making up for lost time, and after a fling with co-owner of Street Cars, Vikram Desai, and a one-night stand with Peter Barlow, she tied the knot with Steve McDonald to get one over on Janice Battersby, who'd bet her two days' wages she couldn't get the cabbie boss down the aisle.

'Even though she was completely mad, Steve couldn't stay away from her – and the writers loved that. They were like one of those volatile couples that when they've had a few too many drinks in the local pub you just know it's going to kick off. That's what we tried to get across about them, but with an element of comedy.'

Stroppy Karen's nemesis was the equally deranged and jealous Tracy Barlow, who'd used every trick in the book to try and win back her baby's father, Steve. But after Karen kicked off a dramatic rooftop fight with Tracy (who thought she'd murdered Amy), Steve disowned his wife, which lead to Karen's exit on Boxing Day 2004.

'I loved Karen and Steve's second wedding which was really OTT and Tracy ruined it by turning up at the church with baby Amy. The episode where Karen got her own back and wrecked Amy's church christening was brilliant, too. Karen just did this weird Liam Gallagher-style walk down the aisle, punched Tracy, yelled "Now that is enough!" then stormed out again. When I left *Coronation Street* Anne Kirkbride made me a DVD with all the cast and crew dressed as me yelling, "Now that is enough!"' – even Bill Roache did it!'

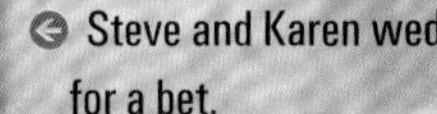

Steve and Karen wed for a bet.

Joe Carter beds Karen then uses her to embezzle from Underworld.

Karen brawls with Tracy at Amy's christening.

Occupation: Machinist at Underworld.
On screen: 2000–2004
Defining moment: In 2001 she marries Steve McDonald for a bet and then genuinely falls for him.

50 CORONATION ST. ICON

Lucy reveals Peter's double life to Shelley.

Simon's lives. So in between booking wedding cars and writing his speech for his big day with Shelley, Peter busied himself at Lucy's flat changing nappies.

Shelley's mum Bev smelled a rat when Peter's tales of spending time with his accountant didn't add up. She got the truth out of Peter's friend Ciaran McCarthy and told Shelley. When confronted, Peter admitted there had been an affair but said nothing of the wedding or the baby and a forgiving Shelley ended up marrying him.

Peter's bigamy wasn't uncovered until Jack made a throwaway comment to Lucy, who'd turned up in Coronation Street looking for Peter. Lucy went to the Rovers and met Shelley where they had a chat about weddings and exchanged pictures, until Shelley realised with horror that both of their big days had featured the same groom! For Shelley the agony was worse when she learned Peter also had a son with wife number one and she reacted by punching him in front of a packed pub. Lucy also cut him out of the picture by moving to Australia and a humiliated Peter packed his kit bag and left the cobbles.

'I can see from the photos you must have pushed the boat out. Wedding-and-a-half. Shame that in the eyes of the law it didn't really amount to much more than a fancy-dress party.'

Lucy to Shelley

Deirdre and Dev make it a night to remember.

Peter wasn't the only Barlow keeping a misdemeanour under wraps. His step-mum Deirdre was keeping schtum about her fling with her corner-shop boss Dev Alahan (*see page 231*) the previous Christmas. However, Dev was now sleeping with her newly returned daughter Tracy, who had walked out on her husband Robert claiming he'd had an affair, when in fact she'd been the one playing away. Deirdre found out about Tracy and Dev by walking in on them getting frisky in the back room of the shop and had difficulty disguising her disgust.

She tried to persuade Tracy to break off the relationship but was unable to tell her the real reason why. It was shop girl Sunita Parekh – later to be Dev's wife – who let slip to Tracy about her mother's one-night stand with the shop-owner smoothie. A furious Tracy confronted her mother and then spitefully revealed all to a devastated Ken. However, yet again the Barlows were reconciled and went on to fight another day.

2000s Marriages

Alison Wakefield & Kevin Webster	23 Jan 2000
Linda Sykes & Mike Baldwin	10 Sept 2000
Liz McDonald & Jim McDonald	30 Nov 2000
Emma Taylor & Curly Watts	24 Dec 2000
Karen Phillips & Steve McDonald	30 May 2001
Gail Platt & Richard Hillman	27 July 2002
Sally Webster & Kevin Webster	9 Dec 2002
Lucy Richards & Peter Barlow	24 March 2003
Tracy Barlow & Roy Cropper	17 Nov 2003
Karen McDonald & Steve McDonald	18 Feb 2004
Sunita Parekh & Dev Alahan	25 Oct 2004
Claire Casey & Ashley Peacock	25 Dec 2004
Deirdre Rachid & Ken Barlow	8 April 2005
Cilla Brown & Les Battersby	26 Nov 2005
Sarah Platt & Jason Grimshaw	31 Oct 2007
Liz McDonald & Vernon Tomlin	31 Dec 2007
Maria Sutherland & Liam Connor	11 Feb 2008
Carla Connor & Tony Gordon	3 Dec 2008
Molly Compton & Tyrone Dobbs	12 Jan 2009
Becky Granger & Steve McDonald	14 Aug 2009
Fiz Brown & John Stape	30 Sept 2009

Quietly whiling away his time in jail for the manslaughter of Jez Quigley was Big Jim McDonald – that was until he suspected his wife Elizabeth (known as Liz to everyone else) was having an affair with her boss in Blackpool. With the help of his son Steve he broke out of his open prison and together they sped off to the seaside where Liz was enjoying a Newton and Ridley brewery bash along with many residents of Weatherfield past and present, including landlady legend Bet, Fred Elliott, Ashley and Joshua Peacock and nanny Claire Casey.

Flattered by her escapee husband's foolhardy recklessness, Liz decided to spend the rest of her life on the run with Jim and, via a speedboat, the pair planned to disappear that very day to Northern Ireland. However, just as they set off, they spotted Ashley, Claire and Joshua adrift at sea in a broken-down boat. Seeing a family in need, Jim nobly gave up his dream of being a fugitive in the Emerald Isle and helped them to return to shore, where he was given a warm welcome and a tight embrace by the police.

2003

In 2004 a freshly divorced and pregnant Tracy had tricked poor Roy into believing he was the father of her unborn child, claiming they had slept together after she slipped him a date-rape drug at Shelley and Peter's wedding. In fact the real father was Steve, who was engaged to be married to Karen (again), but he wanted nothing to do with her or the baby. So Tracy persuaded the Croppers to buy her unborn baby. They were desperate for a family, but first they insisted Tracy marry Roy so he'd have some legal rights over the child and to stop her doing a runner with their cash.

'I could have any man I wanted. Well, any man but you, that is.'

Tracy to Hayley

In the meantime Tracy kept herself busy by ruining Karen's elaborate wedding plans. When Steve confronted Tracy about her meddling, she went into labour and he was forced to take her and Roy to the hospital. Roy stayed by Tracy's side during the labour and witnessed what he believed to be the birth of his daughter. Deep down in the mess that was Tracy's conscience, she felt something stir for the newborn, and attempted one last time to win over Steve. When she failed, Tracy reverted to her usual hard-faced self and handed the baby over to the delighted Croppers.

Shelley Unwin

Played by **Sally Lindsay**

When Shelley Unwin strode into Weatherfield full of brassy confidence and with a firm pint-pulling arm, thanks to her previous position at Duggie Ferguson's rugby club, there was no way she was going to take any nonsense from any of the Rovers regulars.

Having been spotted by Corrie producers playing Twiggy's trashy girlfriend in *The Royle Family*, Sally Lindsay was originally only contracted for a brief seven-episode stint and had no idea of the trauma that was in store for poor old Shelley. 'I think I was considered a comedy actress before *Coronation Street* and what playing Shelley proved to me was that I could really have a go at anything. It was the best learning curve as an actress you can have, it was phenomenal for me, really. I can still remember my first day as if it was yesterday. I was terrified. I had to get my mum to drop me off because I was too nervous to drive. It was very scary and when I finished the first day I threw up, because the first time you get to the *Corrie* studios it's like a northern Madam Tussauds in there, watching all these people you've grown up with coming to life.'

'I don't mean to be uncharitable but she's a proven basket case.'

Charlie

Cut to four years later when, after a bigamous marriage to Peter Barlow and a disastrous date with cellarman Eric Gartside (played in a guest cameo by off-screen friend Peter Kay), Shelley had fallen for the dubious charms of Charlie Stubbs and was now a simpering shadow of her former feisty self. The conniving builder slowly but surely chipped away at her self-esteem, self-confidence and self-worth, undermining her at every turn with comments about her weight, behaviour and personality. Shelley became increasingly isolated from everyone around her and even, on Charlie's cruellest instructions, disowned her own mother, Bev.

Watching Shelley reach her lowest ebb, an agrophobic mess of insecurities, was one of the show's most gut-wrenching storylines of recent years – a

50 CORONATION ST. ICON

vivid account of psychological abuse that seemed to strike a chord with viewers up and down the country. 'The reaction to the Charlie/Shelley storyline was colossal,' remembers Sally. 'It opened up a can of worms with some of the crew, people I didn't know and people I knew really well, and some of my best friends all coming up to me saying they'd been in a relationship just like it. I used to get the most moving letters saying how much certain scenes had affected people because exactly the same kinds of things had happened to them – especially the time when Charlie made Shelley change her outfit fourteen times and pulled her earrings off before a night out.

'By the end she was just a gibbering wreck. That was how low she'd sunk. The old Shelley would never have stood for that, she'd have told him where to go. But he chipped away at her. When we first met Shelley she was a laugh – and even though she wasn't the most beautiful or the most clever or successful person ever, she was very comfortable in herself. I think a lot of women liked her because of that and that was part of her success as a character.

- All smiles with two-timing fiancé Peter.
- Bullying Charlie reveals his darker side.
- Shelley wonders where it all went wrong.
- Bev fears for the safety of her daughter.
- Shelley finally sees the light and ditches Charlie.

'So when I was sat down by our producer he said, "Look we've come up with this idea and you're going to have to go with it because it's going to be really hard," I was like, "Oh dear, what is it? Am I going to be burying someone under the patio?" He told me it was going to be a very gradual mental-abuse storyline. I thought it was the most brilliant idea because Shelley was always happy in her own skin and she really thought she was quite fit actually. But when Charlie started to comment about her weight doors started to open in her head that she wasn't good enough and that's when she started to shut down. The strength of the storyline was that if this could happen to someone like Shelley, then it could happen to anyone.'

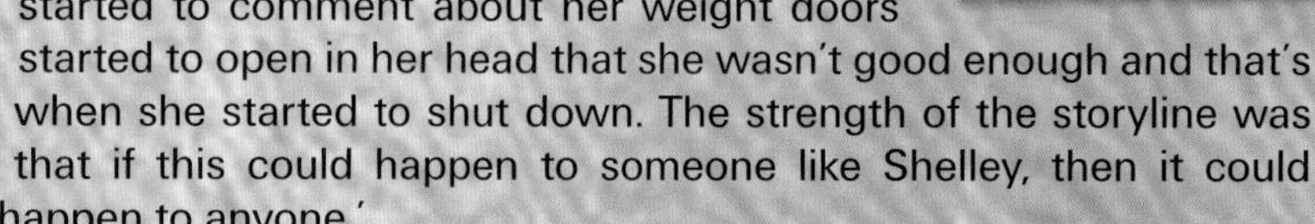

And there's no doubting the viewers' affection for 'everywoman' Shelley. Whether it was the dramatic moment she found out husband Peter was already married to florist Lucy or when she finally saw sense and dumped Charlie at the altar, the nation was rooting for the down-to-earth Rovers pint-puller. 'You could have Obama stood there with a massive megaphone but what he was saying would not affect people in this country as much as watching their favourite characters going through hell on *Coronation Street*. Because if people fall in love with a character they'll follow you to the end of the earth.'

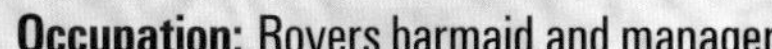

Occupation: Rovers barmaid and manager.
On screen: 2001–2006
Defining moment: Ditching cold-hearted manipulator Charlie Stubbs at the altar in September 2005.

'You could win the lottery and have a personality transplant and Steve still wouldn't wanna know! Okay?'

Karen to Tracy

But as soon as the baby was gone, Tracy broke down sobbing. After a heart-to-heart with her grandmother, Blanche, she realised she needed to get her baby back and tell the truth. The moment she chose for getting these things off her chest was the day of Karen and Steve's wedding. She stormed into the church and announced to the assembled congregation that Steve was the father of her baby. Despite the bride going ballistic and brandishing her red stilettos in Tracy's face, Steve did an amazing job of convincing Karen of how much he loved her and the wedding went ahead. Eventually and reluctantly, the Croppers realised they had to return the child to Tracy, and little Patience Cropper became baby Amy Barlow.

Another demented dame doing the rounds was foxy, smart lawyer Maya Sharma. She'd first become known to the residents as the brief advising Hayley and Roy about baby Amy, but slowly and surely it became clear she was a bit unstable when she started doing odd things like kidnapping Tyrone's dog Monica.

It wasn't until she was jilted by boyfriend Dev Alahan in favour of Sunita Parekh, who was recovering from a brain tumour, that the full force of her craziness was unleashed. In an effort to split them up, she married several illegal immigrants in Sunita's name and attempted to frame her sweet-natured love rival on her wedding day to Dev. But Maya was rumbled and then arrested. She was released on bail and set about using her time productively – first she blew up a couple of Dev's other shops, then she kidnapped Sunita and taunted Dev on the phone about killing her.

Dev tracked down Maya and Sunita to the Coronation Street shop but ended up being held hostage as well. Then Mad Maya turned on the gas, put a match to the Alahans' wedding photo and left them for dead as the shop exploded. Fortunately they were rescued from the fire by barman Ciaran and builder Charlie Stubbs, as a seething Maya sat in her sports car and watched. She revved up her engine and sped at the gathered crowd, crashing into a wall. She then reversed the car and tried to kill Sunita, but drove into the path of a passing truck instead. Maya survived and after a spell in intensive care she was sent for trial.

Bride Karen lays in to uninvited guest Tracy.
Dev came to rue the day he met Maya.
Maya leaves Dev and Sunita gagged and bound.

When the Barlow-McDonald clans were signed up by Blanche to appear in a new family game show *Top Of The Tree*, Steve fretted that their fifteen minutes of fame would have some serious repercussions for him. Having been duped into playing happy families on TV alongside Tracy, he just prayed his stroppy wife Karen, who was holidaying in Dublin, would never find out. After a touch-and-go first round, the families bagged the top prize of a swish new car, thanks to Karen being Steve's 'Phone-a-Friend' and providing the winning answer on the subject of designer shoes, thinking it was a pub quiz question and oblivious to the fact she was on TV. In the green room afterwards, while a mini-skirted Liz attempted unsuccessfully to snare the show's host, Steve made a smug Tracy promise on their daughter Amy's life that she wouldn't tell Karen about their TV outing together. But in the Rovers the next day Blanche was only too happy to spill the beans – which led to an incandescent Karen screaming blue murder and demanding the keys to the gleaming motor that she had won!

There was more action on the cobbles in May when rival overly-protective matriarchs Eileen and Gail slugged it out for all to see when Todd admitted to pregnant girlfriend Sarah that he was gay – and sleeping with a nurse called Karl.

On hearing the shock revelation, a horrified Gail decided the best plan of action was to have it out with Eileen. After a doorstep confrontation, it spilled out into the Street when Eileen slapped Gail round the chops. Gail responded by pulling Eileen's hair and the pair fell to the ground, wrestling, watched by a gaggle of bemused residents. After they were finally separated, Gail used the opportunity to tell everyone what Todd had done and the Grimshaw lad was well and truly outed.

'She's never had a ring on her finger but she has had two sons from different fathers. And one of them turned out to be a homosexual. Not the father, that is, the son.'

Blanche on Eileen

Nurse Karl can't take his eyes off Todd.

Eileen Grimshaw

Played by **Sue Cleaver**

It was as a passenger in the back of his taxi that no-nonsense single mum Eileen Grimshaw impressed new cab firm co-owner Vikram Desai with her local knowledge and talked him into giving her a job at Street Cars. Within a year she'd rented Number 11 from her other cabbie boss, Steve McDonald, and had moved in with her teenage sons, sensitive scholar Todd and athletics-mad beefcake, Jason.

However, sorting out her own love life wasn't quite so straightforward. Biker Dennis Stringer cheated on her with machinist Janice Battersby, Gail Platt won the battle for the affections of reflexologist Phil Nail, and things were going swimmingly with affable churchgoer Ed Jackson until Eileen discovered he'd killed Ernest Bishop in the violent factory raid in 1978.

Rotund kebab shop owner Jerry Morton's chaotic family life put paid to any romance between them, however in 2009 it looked like she'd finally settled down when bumbling kids entertainer General Custard, alias Jesse Chadwick, moved in. Then she dumped him when he chose to spend his bookie winnings on a holiday for his parents, rather than her. Jesse begged Eileen for a reconciliation but ruined his chances when he made a pass at Julie Carp, who Eileen had recently discovered was her half-sister, thanks to their father Colin's secret affair with her underage former school friend Paula.

'I think the women who watch *Coronation Street* can relate to Eileen's struggles and the disappointments in her life – things haven't necessarily gone the easy way for her but she's making the most of it. At the root of Eileen is a straight-talking honest woman with a sense of humour who is just battling on.'

Following the revelation that Todd was gay and had been cheating on girlfriend Sarah, a fiercely protective Eileen found herself brawling after being confronted on her doorstep by furious rival matriarch Gail Platt.

'Helen [Worth, who plays Gail] and I were in hysterics filming that. It peed down with rain all afternoon, we had shin pads and knee pads on and she was ripping my hair out at the roots. We were writhing around on the cobbles, soaking wet. The crew said all that was missing was the mud, because it looked like we were mud wrestling!'

Todd referees the brawling matriarchs.

Eileen and Julie fall out.

Lloyd and Steve apologise to Eileen.

50 CORONATION ST. ICON

Current occupation: Street Cars' switch operator.
On screen: 2000–
Defining moment: She defends the good name of gay son Todd by street-fighting with Gail in 2004.

In 2005 the Rovers saw its second-ever corpse in the form of Ray, the biological father of Tracy, who had returned to find his daughter on the day Ken and Deirdre were supposed to be getting married for the second time. He ended up bumping into her, quite literally, by accidentally knocking Amy's buggy with his car. An exaggerating Tracy insisted Amy was taken to hospital, and still unaware of their connection, Ray accused her of trying to con him out of money.

Meanwhile, Ken and Deirdre halted the ceremony to rush to Amy and were stunned to find Deirdre's ex-husband Ray, who'd previously been living in Holland, quarrelling with his long-lost daughter. Relations didn't exactly thaw immediately, as ice-maiden Tracy kept her dad out in the cold despite knowing he was dying of stomach cancer. However, slowly but surely she began to warm to him and the reunited pair shared a tender moment in April, at Ken and Deirdre's rescheduled wedding reception, when they danced together and she apologised for behaving like a bitch.

Just as former mother-in-law Blanche revealed she'd never liked him, but admitted perhaps she'd been a bit harsh in the past, Ray clutched his chest in pain and let out a groan. The wedding party was alerted to Ray's demise and they gathered around in a deadly hush, while Tracy held Ray and wept, begging him not to go yet.

↑ Look who's back! Ray's return shocks them all.
↓ The Barlows remarry surrounded by friends and family.
→ It's decision time for confused bride Shelley.

'I live in a very funny area, me. I'm quite normal compared to most of them who live round our way...'

Vera

Over at the Rovers, another woman preparing to say 'I do' was Shelley – even though all her friends and family were begging her to say 'I don't', as her betrothed was manipulative, mind-game playing, bully-boy builder Charlie. The night before her wedding Shelley was forced to listen to a few home truths about her intended, including the revelation that he'd recently tried to kiss pretty young barmaid Violet Wilson. In the meantime Charlie was spending his pre-wedding night in the arms of another woman he'd met in a bar.

At the church it looked like it was going to be a no-show for the pair of them, but first Charlie swaggered in, followed by unsure-looking Shelley. Just as the vicar got to the part about 'Do you take this man?', Shelley blurted, 'No, I'm sorry, I don't.' The congregation gasped as she continued: 'I can't trust you! I can't marry you!'

Charlie didn't take this public humiliation well and drove off in the vintage wedding car with a petrified Shelley as a hostage in the back. He threatened to give her a good kicking and then accused her of being mentally ill. But this time Shelley stayed strong and ended their destructive relationship, running away from him through the streets of Weatherfield, free as a bird at last.

2005

When nurse Martin fell in love with sixteen-year-old schoolgirl Katy Harris he was branded a pervert, but he was determined to prove the detractors wrong. However, Katy's despairing parents, mechanic Tommy and machinist Angela, were even more determined to split them up and wrongly convinced their daughter that Martin was having an affair with Sally. Katy was pregnant with Martin's child at the time and, in a state of shock and betrayal, she had the baby aborted. Martin was devastated and because she hadn't trusted him he refused to have anything more to do with her. Meanwhile, when Katy confronted her father at the garage about his lies, Tommy showed no remorse or sympathy. He revealed that he couldn't have got her to the clinic fast enough because he'd known once the baby was gone, their sordid relationship would have been over too. In fury, Katy lashed out at her dad with a handy monkey wrench and killed him. The tragic events were witnessed by Angela, who tried to cover up the murder by first letting Martin be a suspect and then taking the blame herself. After her mother went to jail, Katy, who was a diabetic, fell into a depression and a month later committed suicide by feeding herself spoonfuls of sugar. Meanwhile, Martin found love again and moved to Liverpool with new girlfriend Robyn.

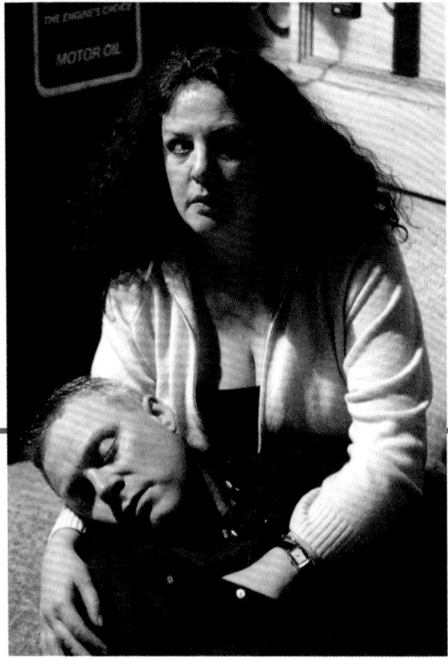

However, when Charlie teamed up with Tracy later that year he'd finally met his match. Both amoral, selfish and cruel, the duo enjoyed a fiery courtship before she moved into his flat and immediately the manipulative mind games began anew. She brought her daughter Amy with her, but Charlie threw them both out, saying a child wasn't part of the deal. So, much to her parents' disgust, Tracy deposited Amy with them and went back to Charlie's.

However, Tracy was already scheming and a few weeks later she pretended she was pregnant and allowed Charlie to talk her into having an abortion. He gave her the money to go private, which she spent on designer shoes whilst pretending to be grieving for her lost baby. In the belief it would help her recover, Charlie allowed Amy to move in with them. He later found out she had faked being

'Tracy Barlow? Even her initials spell a killer disease!'

Eileen

pregnant, but to her surprise and relief, he didn't end the relationship, instead he merely destroyed one of her much-loved new designer shoes and warned her never to cross him again.

Even though Tracy thought she'd won that battle, there were bigger fights to be had. Charlie had managed to seduce his ex, Shelley, before she left Weatherfield to run a pub in Derbyshire, just to prove he could. Shelley told Tracy but then, unable to stomach what she'd done, said she'd been lying. However, when Shelley later returned, it was obvious their one-night stand had been a reproductive affair and Shelley was expecting his baby.

Jealous Tracy lashes out at Shelley.

Charlie's days are numbered as Tracy plots the ultimate revenge.

'If I didn't love you Tracy, I'd be up them stairs. Dreaming of me and Rod Stewart running through the surf. But I'm not, am I? I'm down here with you. Going out of my mind.'

Deirdre to Tracy

This time it was Tracy's turn to forgive Charlie, but soon he started sniffing round young hairdresser Maria Sutherland, to whom he'd let his flat while he, Tracy and Amy moved into Number 6. He sabotaged pipes and appliances in the flat and even staged a burglary so that Maria would be dependent on him. They started an affair, but when she found him dunking David in the bath because he had threatened to tell Tracy, a frightened Maria decided to tell Tracy herself.

Tracy left Charlie for a short while but returned claiming to have forgiven him, when really it was to carry out the ultimate revenge. She managed to convince her family and neighbours that Charlie was physically abusing her by provoking loud rows with him, pretending she'd been locked in her bedroom and even burning herself with an iron.

When her brother Peter came to stay, she allowed Charlie to think she'd brought a lover home. Charlie beat him up and was given community service. When he returned home, he ordered Tracy out, but she refused to go anywhere. Instead she smugly revealed the lengths she'd gone to in order to punish him and then proceeded to do a sexy lap dance for him, saying she didn't even care if there were other women. With that, she took hold of a heavy bronze figurine and swung it at his head. She hit him once more for good luck, taunting him all the while. She then made it look like there'd been a fight and placed a knife in his hand, before calling an ambulance. Much to her horror, Charlie hung on in a coma and Tracy could barely conceal her delight when he finally died three days later.

Fiz Stape

Played by **Jennie McAlpine**

When her mother swanned off on holiday leaving her sixteen-year-old daughter home alone, flame-haired Fiz Brown was scooped up by social services and put in the care of kind-hearted Roy and Hayley Cropper, who fostered her. No one had met Cilla at that point, but when her loathsome mum did turn up in Weatherfield two years later, the reason for Fiz's issues with law abidance soon became apparent.

During her stay at the Croppers, Fiz was a loud-mouthed troublemaker and even falsely accused poor Roy of slapping her. When she returned to the Street three months later she still had a big mouth, but her true good-natured outlook had become more evident. After spotting an advert in The Kabin for vacancies at Underworld she sought out Mike Baldwin and demanded a job. 'How old are you?' he asked. Fiz replied, 'Old enough to know me way around a cotton gusset.' Amused by her boldness, Mike took her on for a week's trial...

When it comes to relationships Fiz tends to let her heart rule her head. None more so than with John Stape, her first love who'd reappeared in her life when she discovered him teaching at Weatherfield Comp, where Chesney went to school. Their love was soon rekindled, but all he gave her was heartache. Despite his affair with flirty pupil Rosie Webster (who he also held hostage in his granny's attic), Fiz forgave the shamed teacher and married him in prison.

'People I meet really think I am Fiz and they're always warning me off John. I don't have many days when I'm not called Fiz, but I quite like it. You can't get big for your boots and start moaning about things like that. I remember once I was doing an autograph signing and this little girl turned up with her mum and she burst into tears when she saw me. I have never seen anyone so hysterical in all my life, she was absolutely inconsolable. I was petrified I'd done something to upset her, but her mum apologised and said, "I'm so sorry, I told her she was coming to see Fiz... but she thought I meant Fizz from the *Tweenies*!" That really made me laugh – how could I possibly compete with that?'

Cilla, Chesney and Fiz smile gingerly for the camera.
Getting frisky with Kirk.
Fiz visits John in prison.

Current occupation: Machinist at Underworld.
On screen: 2001–
Defining moment: After Chesney was placed in a foster home in 2008, she moved in with ex-boyfriend Kirk in order to provide the care and secure homelife Social Services demanded he needed.

When the murky family affair between doe-eyed Jamie Baldwin and his glamorous stepmum Frankie became public knowledge, the local gossips had a field day. Even though she'd brought him up from an early age, Jamie found himself falling in love with Frankie, who'd split from his dad Danny after discovering his affair with Jamie's ex-girlfriend Leanne Battersby. The floppy-haired van driver tried to ignore his feelings by concentrating on his relationship with barmaid Violet, but when Danny and Frankie were reunited he was overwhelmed with jealousy and told Frankie how he felt. She reacted by giving him a kiss, and after various furtive glances and attempts at avoiding each other, they finally gave in to their passion. Danny came home one day to find them in bed together and like a man possessed he half-beat his son to death before leaving him to drown in the canal. Thankfully, at the last minute Danny came to his senses and saved Jamie, but he disappeared soon after, unable to cope with their betrayal. Frankie and Jamie's relationship spluttered on as they arranged to start afresh in Spain, but at the last minute Frankie got cold feet, bid Jamie adios and left Weatherfield all on her own.

2006

'No husband. No children. No grandchildren. Twenty-eight years of lying in an empty bed. Do you think that gets any easier as time passes?'

Emily to Ed

Emily is sickened by Ed's confession.

However, her joy was shortlived when she was charged with his murder. The night before the trial Tracy confessed to an appalled Deirdre that Charlie had never hit her, but she remained determined to plead self-defence. Her case quickly unravelled, though, as her witnesses fell apart and the evidence started stacking up against her. She was found guilty of murder and sentenced to life imprisonment, but as the deluded murderess was led down from the docks she could still be heard protesting her innocence.

In 2006 Emily had a crisis of faith when she was asked to forgive the man who'd shot her husband, Ernest, during the factory robbery back in 1978. Ed Jackson was now a reformed character, having found God during his time in jail. First he became a member of Emily's church and struck up a friendship with her, then he soon became a regular visitor to Number 3, helping with odd jobs and attending bible classes. When he did finally reveal his killer identity, Emily was far from forgiving and was furious at the way he had snaked into her life.

She later admitted to Eileen, who had started up a brief romance with Ed, that she'd rather have her revenge for the loss of her husband than turn the other cheek. Shocked by her feelings of hate, Emily stopped going to church and sank into a depression.

It took the divine intervention of the vicar, who warned her Ed was considering taking his own life, to change her mind. She went round to see Ed and finally freed them both from their torment by accepting that he was truly sorry for what he had done – and she forgave him. Weeping, she gave him Ernest's old camera and told him she never wanted to see him again, but asked that he send a photo of himself once a year so she'd know he hadn't done anything stupid.

In April, after thirty years of wheeling and dealing, cockney rag-trade boss Mike bade a sad farewell; his once razor-sharp mind having been dulled by Alzheimer's disease. In the run-up to his death he began to appear increasingly confused and lost and he even asked a concerned Rita how Len was, forgetting he had died twenty years ago.

Taking advantage of his vulnerable state was Danny Baldwin (who'd only found out a year earlier that Mike was his father, not his uncle as he'd previously thought) and his new girlfriend Leanne Battersby. The pair schemed to fleece Mike of his empire by making him sign documents that handed Danny control of all his assets.

Mike was admitted to hospital for pneumonia but ran off, believing he had some urgent business to attend to – Ken spotted him by the factory in a fragile and disorientated state and called for an ambulance. He then wrapped his coat around the ailing man and gently cradled him. But a confused Mike demanded to know what

Patricia Routledge 1961
Decades before *Keeping Up Appearances*, Patricia was Sylvia Snape, a café owner based in Rosamund Street. Sylvia was created as a long-term character, but after a handful of episodes the actress chose to spread her wings.

Mollie Sugden 1965–1976
The much-loved *Are You Being Served?* star often popped up as Annie's friend and long-time adversary Nellie, landlady of the Laughing Donkey.

Sir Ben Kingsley 1966
The future Oscar winner spent seven episodes as Ron Jenkins, a handsome stranger who chatted up married Irma at the cinema and pestered her for a date.

Star turns

Do you remember these famous faces passing through the Street?

Joanna Lumley 1973
In the Seventies Joanna Lumley made a career playing posh upper-class types, here as headmaster's daughter, Elaine Perkins, who went on to break Ken's heart.

Martin Shaw 1967
The star of *The Professionals* and *Judge John Deed* made five appearances as hippy commune leader Robert Croft, the subject of a major crush for Lucille.

Sue Johnston 1982
A matter of months after filming her three-episode stint, Sue became a household name in *Brookside*. In the Street she played Mrs Chadwick, who'd been loaned Annie Walker's car as payment of a debt to her husband.

Sir Patrick Stewart 1967
Long before he'd set foot on the Starship Enterprise the young actor appeared as a fireman when Dennis accidentally set Len's living room ablaze.

Michael Ball 1985
The fresh-faced West End star played Malcolm Nuttall, a tennis coach who was Kevin's rival for the affections of pretty Michelle Robinson.

Gorden Kaye 1969–1970
He became a household name as Rene in Eighties' sitcom *'Allo 'Allo!* but Gorden Kaye also played the fool as Elsie's permanently lovesick nephew Bernard Butler.

Peter Kay 1997, 2004
His first fleeting appearance was as a builder refurbishing the corner shop. Seven years later Peter returned as Eric Gartside, the dithering drayman who plucked up the courage to ask Rovers manager Shelley out on a date.

June Brown 1970–1971
The future *EastEnders* star played Mrs Parsons for three episodes – Ena was teaching her son to play the harmonium.

Barlow was doing there and proceeded to tell him how Deirdre and little Tracy were going to move in with him. Ken softly told him that was a long time ago but Mike was adamant, insisting, 'You're finished, Barlow. Deirdre loves me. She's mine.' And with that he died on the cobbles in the arms of his nemesis.

Dodgy clients are an occupational hazard for most prostitutes but when Weatherfield businessman Paul Connor booked high-class hooker Leanne, things got very dark for this lap-dancer turned lady of the night. New factory owner Paul was the brother of Leanne's new boyfriend Liam, and despite being a regular user of prostitutes himself, Paul didn't want his nice-guy brother dating one. He tried to split them up without revealing what he knew about her, and it was only when his ballsy wife Carla (*see page 264*) announced she was opening a restaurant with Leanne that he revealed the truth about her night job. However, in doing so he also exposed his own preference for paying for sex.

A disgusted Carla promptly dumped Paul and in fury he blamed Leanne and kidnapped her in his car. He tore around the streets of Manchester shouting abuse at Leanne, who was locked in his boot, before careering through a red light and straight into the path of an HGV. Leanne was unhurt in the crash but Paul later died in intensive care without regaining consciousness. Liam refused to have anything more to do with Leanne and for a while the Connors held her solely responsible for Paul's death.

Paul and working girl Leanne rendezvous in a hotel room.
Carla, Michelle and Liam are devastated by Paul's death.
Devious David plots to ruin his sister's big day.

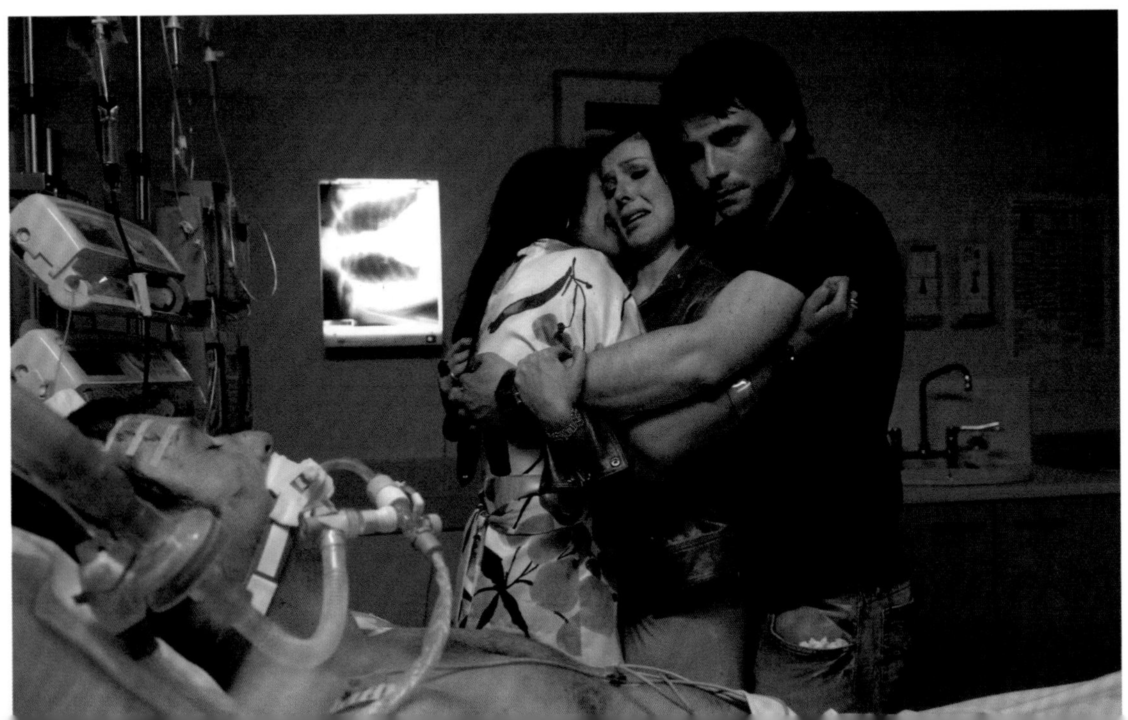

Sally Webster was chuffed to bits when she persuaded her wild-child daughter Rosie to return to Weatherfield High to take her A-levels. However, she wasn't quite so pleased to discover the little minx was enjoying one-on-one sessions which definitely weren't on the syllabus with her infatuated English teacher John Stape – who also happened to be Fiz Brown's boyfriend. Their affair was exposed on Christmas Day and a seething Kevin punched John to the ground and was arrested. Sally was beside herself, but her stress levels were to increase ten-fold when nearly a year later Rosie completely disappeared. Blaming the sultry schoolgirl for his sacking and not wanting her to ruin his renewed relationship with Fiz, an unstable John kidnapped his former pupil and held her hostage in the attic of his dead grandmother's remote cottage. After five weeks Rosie was freed unharmed by a horrified Fiz and John was jailed. In a bid to make amends, the shamed teacher sold the cottage and gave Rosie £150,000 compensation. After splashing out on a flashy sports car (which she couldn't drive), she thought she'd invested the rest of her cash in Underworld – but unfortunately the shares didn't exist and she realised she'd been scammed by her double-crossing former squeeze, Luke Strong.

Sally: 'I blame it all on that Christina Aguilera.'
Kevin: 'Is she in our Rosie's class?'

2007

For many years the Platt siblings Sarah and David had been at war, but 2007 saw their nastiest battle yet when David stupidly hid some ecstasy tablets in his niece Bethany's doll. Unfortunately, the child found them and swallowed some, but a panicking David refused to tell anyone about what had happened.

Even when she later started fitting and was rushed to hospital, he kept quiet about the pills. Finally he told all to Sarah's fiancé, Jason Grimshaw, and the doctors were able to take the appropriate action, saving Bethany's life.

Despite the shocking near-death of his niece, who he really did love, David refused to change his wicked ways as he planned his biggest act of spite ever. As Sarah and Jason's nuptials loomed, he plotted and schemed ways in which he could ruin it. One tactic was to invite Jason's estranged brother and Sarah's ex, Todd, to the wedding, and he also sabotaged some scaffolding, causing builder Jason to fall.

Sean Tully

Played by **Antony Cotton**

If you want something badly enough you'll do anything to make it happen. When sperm donor Sean Tully decided he wanted to trace his long-lost son, Dylan, he posed as leggy landlady Liz McDonald on a social-networking website and contacted former barmaid Violet Wilson. When she found out, Liz sacked him, but after Sean broke down at his enforced separation from Dylan she softened and offered to act as a go-between. The overjoyed knicker-stitcher couldn't thank her enough when her shrewd peacemaking led to Violet's agreement to give him access to their son. Similarly, Antony Cotton took an unorthodox route when it came to pursuing his own Weatherfield dream.

'I was a huge fan of *Corrie* and realised there was a gap in the market, because in some ways it's the campest show on television. It can be very dramatic and larger than life, so it's a perfect world for a gay man to inhabit, but there wasn't a gay character in the show. I knew it would only be a matter of time before that character would have to be represented and by hook or by crook I was determined I was going to be the one playing him!

'So I sent this greeting card with a dog in a pair of sunglasses on it to the producer, Tony Wood, literally saying give me a job. Coincidentally it arrived just as he'd had an initial conversation about giving Todd a gay coming-out storyline and was about to go out for a lunch meeting with Tony Warren to discuss it. Over lunch Tony Warren made the point that there had never been a gay character in the show before and added: 'If you do it there's only one Manchester queen that I know of and he's called Antony Cotton.' And Tony Wood replied: 'Well, I've just had a card from him today!' So that's how it all happened. I'm not someone who believes in fate especially, but it was very spooky how it all panned out.'

Camper than Ken Barlow's kimono, Sean made his first appearance at a hospital disco as a friend of Martin Platt's colleague, Karl Foster, the handsome nurse who ended up dating new gay on the block, Todd Grimshaw. After flattering Todd's mum Eileen with his beauty tips and palm-readings, Sean was invited to become a lodger at Number 11, much to her older son Jason's disapproval.

'From the moment he arrived Sean was a big, flaming homosexual and he became

50 CORONATION ST. ICON

everyone's friend. But he was very wary of Jason and Jason was very wary of him. I remember Jason's first line ever about Sean was 'You are joking?' to Eileen. He totally ignored Sean in the beginning, but now they're like brothers.

'As Sean is *Coronation Street*'s first out and proud gay man (although I think there was a toupee fitter who once vaguely alluded to being homosexual years ago) some of the show's more old-school writers weren't especially well versed in how to script a gay character. So, interestingly, Tony Wood told them to write him as if they were writing for Raquel, which I can understand because they are both similarly wide-eyed souls.

'In a way I sometimes think I'm partly playing Tony Warren; part of it is in honour to him because men like him were never represented on television in his day. I am very lucky that they are now, so I'm forever indebted to Tony...' reveals Antony, who had already made a name for himself in another ground-breaking Manchester-based drama, Russell T. Davies's *Queer As Folk*.

'You are a good boy, you know. I'm surprised you've never been snapped up before now – you'd make some lass a smashing husband.'

Betty

In 2007 Sean was surprised to discover his ex, Sonny Dhillon, was dating fellow bar-staff member, Michelle Connor. When Sean and Sonny became secretly involved again he was forced to reveal all to Michelle, who felt used and humiliated, but she eventually forgave him. Once machinist Kelly Crabtree tried to seduce Sean – convinced he was lying about his sexuality – but when he fought her off she claimed assault and he was briefly fired from Underworld.

Sean met his boyfriend, Marcus Dent, a sonographer, when his best mate Violet Wilson was having an ultra-sound. Sean had initially agreed to be her sperm donor but his more hands-on meddling led to Violet taking baby Dylan and disappearing with boyfriend Jamie Baldwin. Meanwhile, Marcus dumped Sean for being too jealous.

'Sean is an archetype in soap because he's not worried about coming out, not involved in an HIV storyline, he's not bisexual and confused, he's not got troubles with his parents about being gay and, despite all he has been through, he's a really happy and content man who fits into the community. Not only have we got this unapologetically gay character but he also has a child. How refreshing is that?'

Jason doesn't welcome their new lodger with open arms.
Sean enjoys a brief stint as a bingo-caller.
Sean bumps into Marcus at the hospital.
Sean and Michelle have romeo Sonny in common.
Proud dad Sean with Violet and baby Dylan.

Current occupation: Underworld machinist and Rovers barman.
On screen: 2003, 2004–
Defining moment: In 2006 he finds his estranged dad, Brian, who abandoned him as a child, but discovers that he isn't his biological father after all – his mum had a fling with a truck driver.

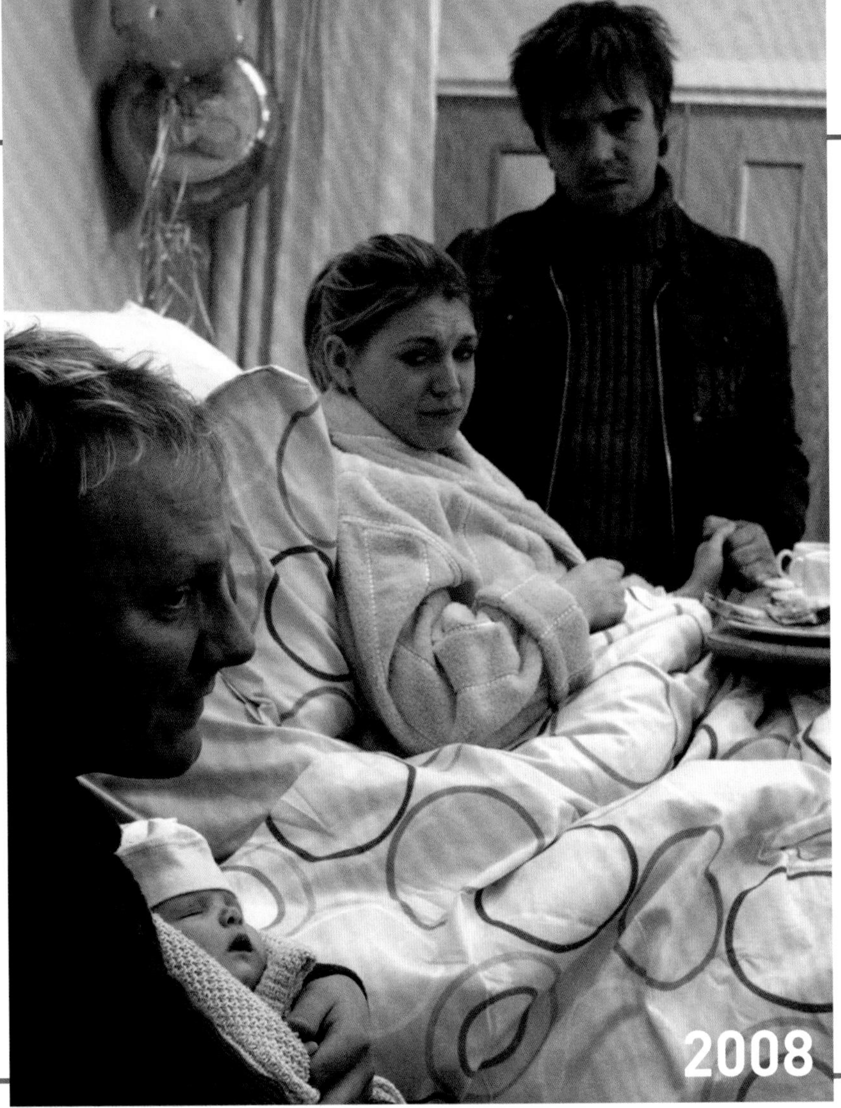

A new life entered the street in the shape of Dylan James Wilson, the product of an arrangement between barmaid Violet Wilson and her gay best friend Sean Tully. Violet was desperate to have a baby following an ectopic pregnancy and after being told her chances of having children were greatly diminished, a nervous but excited Sean agreed to be the donor by means of artificial insemination. Violet fell pregnant immediately and Sean was thrilled, but his exuberance and enthusiasm started to get on Violet's nerves, especially when she was reunited with her ex-boyfriend Jamie. Without telling Sean, the pair plotted to escape to a new life in London where they could pretend Jamie was the baby's father. But on the day they were due to leave, Violet went into labour in the Rovers and Sean was on hand to bring his son into the world. He immediately bonded with the little mite but his joy was short-lived when, just a few days later, Violet and Jamie ran off with the baby, leaving poor Sean with no means of seeing his son Dylan ever again. However, after a spot of online Miss Marple-style detective work, Sean located Violet two years later and the estranged father and son were finally reunited.

However, all this was small fry compared to the actual show-stopper – just as Sarah and Jason were about to take their vows, the police interrupted the ceremony with the news that David's car had been seen being driven into the canal. A sceptical Sarah, who had already found and destroyed a suicide note from him, hissed at worried Jason to ignore it all and continue.

Sarah's steely and grim-faced determination to not let her brother's possible death get in the way of her wedding did not put her in a good light. Even when a bedraggled David turned up alive, Sarah's insistence that it had all been faked had everyone tutting at her and feeling sorry for the smirking David. He then went on to try and ruin her marriage by stealing tarty ex-con Becky Granger's (*see page 274*) phone, using it to send Jason cheeky messages, but he was caught out by Jason.

There looked to be an escape for David and his self-inflicted misery when Gail's businessman brother, Uncle Stephen, arrived with talk of a job offer in Milan. Sarah was incensed by her bad brother's good luck and wreaked her revenge. She planted drugs in David's drawer at the hair salon where their grandmother Audrey

Sarah and Jason refuse to let David spoil their day.
All by himself: Jack mourns at Vera's funeral.

'It's as though there hasn't been two lives, hers and mine. There's been just the one, that we've shared. And that's the best kind of life you can have. So what I really wanted to say was... thanks, Vera. Thank you, love.'

Jack on Vera

found them. After the Bethany incident, no one believed his innocence and the Milan job offer was withdrawn.

Sarah wasted no time swooping in and picking up the job for herself, but just as she was about to board the train to the airport with Jason and Bethany, she confessed to Jason that she had framed David. Her husband of two months was shocked that she had stooped so low and walked off, leaving Sarah and her little girl to go to Italy on their own.

In 2008 everyone was stunned when long-time residents Jack and Vera announced their plans to move away from the Street. Blackpool was Vera's dream destination and Jack felt she finally deserved some reward for sticking by him all these years. After returning from measuring up the new Blackpool house, Vera talked about how much she still loved Jack and prompted him to say the same. A reluctant Jack finally admitted he never loved anybody else except her and then scuttled off to the pub for a quick half.

When he came back home he found Vera asleep in the chair. He then noticed the tea hadn't been started and tried to wake her. On failing to do so, he checked her pulse and Jack stumbled back from Vera, softly groaning as the dreadful truth sank in. He quietly whimpered, 'Oh Vee. Oh, you haven't left me have you?' before he started to cry.

He sat down, hugged Vera close and serenaded her with the song 'If You Were The Only Girl In The World'. Keeping the world at bay for just a few more minutes, he combed her hair and popped on her slippers before letting their neighbours, and his pigeons, know that his beautiful Vera had gone. The emergency services later confirmed she had died peacefully in her sleep of heart failure.

Tina reluctantly agrees to give boyfriend David an alibi.
As Gail fights for her life, David goes on a guilt trip.
Becky's too boozed-up to marry Steve first time around.
Second time lucky; the bride kisses the groom.

At Number 8 David was up to his usual tricks again, which typically involved no remorse. This time it was Gail who was at the receiving end of his wrath and the pair quarrelled when he learned his mother had secretly helped his girlfriend, Tina McIntyre (*see page 269*), get a termination. He went to pack, furious she had allowed his thirteen-year-old sister to have her child but arranged for his baby to be aborted. Gail desperately tried to explain that it was Tina's decision and tried to stop him leaving, but David pushed her down the stairs and left her for dead.

Panicking, he was forced to go and see his mum in hospital, but much to his relief, a confused Gail thought it was Jason who had pushed her. When Audrey began to suspect David was the real culprit, he asked Tina to give him an alibi. She did, because she felt so guilty about the abortion, but as Gail regained her memory, Tina realised she was doing the wrong thing and dumped David. When Gail confronted David, the tormented teen went on the rampage, smashing up the Street before being arrested.

'Sarah can have a child any time she likes. Thirteen years old, no problem. But the spawn of David? God forbid!'

David to Gail

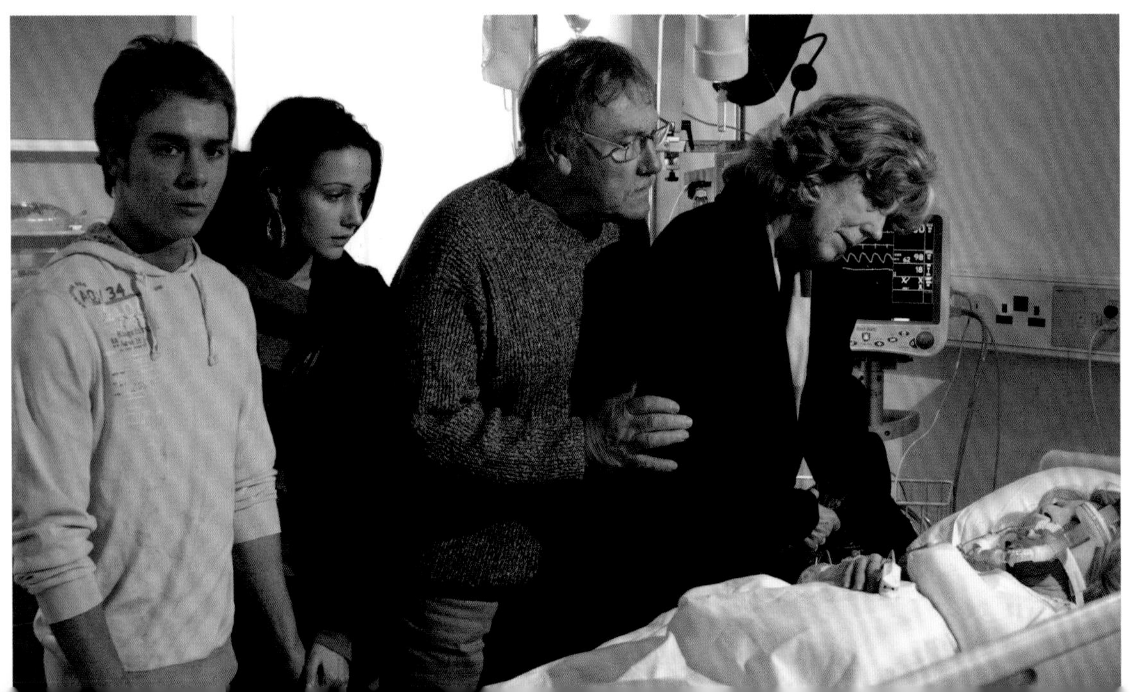

At the police station he confessed not just to attacking Gail but also to deliberately ruining Sarah's wedding day and trying to harm Jason. He shocked everyone by insisting he should be locked up for his own good and punished for his crimes. The magistrate took him at his word and David was sentenced to four months at a Young Offenders Institute, where he struck up a friendship with his oddball cellmate, Graeme Proctor.

There was no way tumultuous couple Becky and Steve would get hitched without a hitch in 2009 – not only was their wedding day on a Friday the 13th, but the bride-to-be was toasting herself with brandy and champagne over her breakfast. Blanche also sent over some celebratory Thunderclap Cider and Becky proceeded to get inebriated. At one point she was even on the factory roof, in her huge pink-blancmange dress, spraying the street with bubbly, Formula-One-driver-style. In this state Becky was dragged along to Weatherfield Registry Office by friends Roy and Hayley, but the sight of a slumped bride trying to slur a few words did not impress the registrar, who informed an exasperated Steve that the wedding couldn't happen.

Their second attempt at getting wed was even more disastrous. Even though they'd managed to become husband and wife this time, the riotous Rovers wedding reception saw the new Mrs McDonald being carted off by the police for possession of drugs.

Carla Connor

Played by **Alison King**

From the moment hard-as-nails Carla Connor swanned uninvited into her husband Paul's Christmas bash at Underworld and lorded it over the assembled throng, it was clear this was a broad who relished getting a few backs up – including that of her hubby. Theirs was a volatile relationship, none more so than when she discovered Paul had been cheating on her with prostitutes, and that one of them was her pal Leanne Battersby. She promptly ended their marriage, but was devastated when he was killed having crashed his car with Leanne in the boot.

However, Paul wasn't the only Connor brother to meet a sticky end as a result of a liaison with Carla. A year later, younger sibling Liam was killed by a hit and run and it turned out that his death had been organised by Carla's evil jealous husband-to-be Tony Gordon. The knicker-factory diva got her own back in 2010, though, by shooting her crazed ex before he burnt to death in the factory blaze.

'Any bloke she gets involved with seems to end up dead, so I'm amazed anyone goes near her. She's pretty damaged and she's not the most cuddly or warm person either, but she's a survivor and people do love a survivor.

'The interesting thing about Carla is she thinks she's a cut above the rest of them, with her designer clothes and warehouse apartment, but she comes from this really rough working-class background where her mum used to sell God knows what out of her pram and her brother's in prison for something like murder. So she's really fought and struggled to get on and has had to be tough as nails,' explains Alison, who made a fleeting appearance in 2004 as Mrs Fanshaw, a skimpily dressed housewife with the hots for builder Jason Grimshaw.

'It's so much fun when I'm playing Carla because I'm being given licence to shout in people's faces and slap them, things I wouldn't ever dare to do in my own life. What I find amazing is how many people actually believe she is real. I got a letter the other day asking me, in depth (it was about five pages long), to make four hundred pencil skirts, black, with all the details enclosed including the date they wanted the order delivered. You really couldn't make it up...'

Carla discovers Paul's prostitute shame.

Carla and Tony take their vows.

Tony goes in for the kill.

Current occupation: Underworld boss.
On screen: 2006–
Defining moment: On finding out Maria is pregnant she selflessly lies to Liam that she no longer loves him. He dies that evening in 2008.

The drugs had been planted by Becky's ex, the aptly named Slug, who was in the pay of bent copper Detective Hooch. The policeman believed it was Becky's troublesome past that was responsible for his failure to get promotion and he wanted to punish her, so instead of spending her wedding night in the arms of new hubby Steve, she spent it in a police cell. Eventually Steve managed to extract the truth from Slug about the set-up and threatened to expose Hooch. Under pressure, the dirty cop agreed to lose the evidence so the court case couldn't go ahead, and Becky was a free woman.

At Number 11 Eileen's father Colin turned up, and despite strained relations with his daughter his roguish charm quickly won her over. However, he was hiding a dark secret that was to tear Eileen apart.

The Grimshaw family and their friends were gathered at the Rovers to celebrate both Colin's seventieth birthday and his proposal of marriage to Rita. The happy events were interrupted by the arrival of Eileen's childhood friend Paula Carp, who had just learned that her ditzy daughter Julie had spent the previous night dating Eileen's son Jason.

All eyes are on Colin as his shocking secret is revealed.

As their friendship evolves, Ken omits to tell Martha he's married.

Absolutely horrified at the news, she drunkenly argued with her daughter, who couldn't understand why she objected so much until Paula announced the real reason to a gobsmacked Eileen – Jason and Julie were nephew and auntie. As everyone in the pub tried to process this information, Paula revealed that Colin had seduced and slept with her when she was just fourteen and he was thirty-eight. Shattered Eileen disowned her father, while Rita felt a fool for being taken in by him. Shunned by everyone except Jason and Julie, Colin suffered a stroke and later died of a heart attack just after Paula had reported him to the police.

Elsewhere, old dog Ken was up to some new tricks with an actress called Martha Fraser, who lived on a canal boat. They met when she fished the Barlows' dog Eccles out of the river and the pair soon bonded over a love of Radio 4, the arts and homemade leek and potato soup.

Ken initially let down-to-earth Martha believe that he was a widower, but eventually he was forced to admit that he was still married. Initially Martha wanted nothing to do with him, but Ken swore he was in love with her and pursued her until she took him

OVERHEARD

The Barlows at Peter's Alcoholic Support Group, 2009.

THE MEETING IS UNDER WAY. THE MEMBERS AND THEIR FAMILIES ALL SIT ROUND IN A CIRCLE IN THE COMMUNITY CENTRE. ROSS HAS BEEN TALKING ABOUT HIS DRINKING.

KEN: Well, Howard. Oh. I'm Ken by the way. I'm here supporting my son, Peter.

HOWARD: (+ MEMBERS) Hi Ken.

DEIRDRE: (A BIT LATE) Hi Ken.

KEN: I was fascinated listening to your story and it made me reflect on... well... how I want to help Peter from now on. I hope this doesn't offend you, Ross. But I think what was lacking from your life was trust.

ROSS: I think you're right, Ken.

KEN: Trust. In any family. Is vital.

DEIRDRE TUTS LOUDLY. THE ROOM TURNS AND LOOKS TO HER. KEN GLARES AT HER.

KEN: Deirdre, I'm trying to be honest here.

DEIRDRE: Honesty and trust. Two things you're a world expert on, hey Ken.

KEN WANTS TO GROAN. BLANCHE FEELS SHE SHOULD EXPLAIN.

BLANCHE: Ken recently had an affair with an actress.

KEN IS MORTIFIED BUT THE GROUP ARE CLEARLY INTRIGUED.

BLANCHE: Oh, it wasn't Nicole Kidman or… Glenda Jackson. She lived on a tug boat.

KEN: It was a barge.

PETER: Is it any wonder I drink?

back. He plotted to run off with Martha on her boat, but at the last minute he jumped ship and returned to life on land with Deirdre.

He had left a goodbye 'Dear Deirdre' letter on the table at Number 1, but this had been taken by son Peter who knew of the affair and suspected correctly that his dad wouldn't go through with leaving. However, a guilty Ken decided to show Deirdre the letter anyway and come clean about his extra-curricular activities. At first it looked like Deirdre was going to end their marriage, but then she admitted that Ken had forgiven her fling with Dev Alahan some years before so she decided bitterly that she could do the same.

The year before it looked like Maria Sutherland had reached her happy-ever-after when she married handsome factory boss Liam Connor. However, deep down Maria was plagued by insecurities that it was his sexy, sassy sister-in-law Carla to whom he was really attracted. Her instincts were right; Liam and Carla had a love/hate relationship which finally culminated in a love/love affair. Rosie spotted them kissing and brought the evidence to Tony Gordon, who was about to marry the now widowed Carla.

Liam and Maria seem to be the perfect match.

Forbidden love: Liam and Carla do the deed.

'The only person Morticia likes is the one that's looking back at her as she brushes her fangs in the morning.'

Janice on Carla

Tina McIntyre

Played by **Michelle Keegan**

Headstrong and wilful, Tina follows in the footsteps of Bet Lynch and Karen McDonald as the latest in a long line of feisty young Coronation Street women.

'She fits into that *Corrie* tradition because she's strong, she's independent, and she speaks her mind. The thing with Tina is one minute you could be crying, the next you could be having a massive argument and the next you could be really happy. She's an A to Z of emotion and I love that when I'm playing her.'

Tina's very first appearance was at the medical centre where she was rowing insolently with receptionist Gail over her appointment time. In retrospect she may have come to regret that incident, as it drew her to the attention of future boyfriend David Platt, who thought he'd spotted a kindred spirit.

But unlike David, Tina knew the difference between right and wrong, so she eventually retracted her statement that gave David an alibi for shoving Gail down the stairs at Number 8 after he'd discovered she'd encouraged Tina to abort his baby. A year later, sensing a pattern, she refused again to lie in court for David over his row with Gary Windass and promptly ditched him. The future looked more cheery for Tina when she moved in with easy-going builder Jason Grimshaw, but she was left devastated when her dad Joe McInytre died in suspicious circumstances while holidaying in the Lakes and she became convinced Gail had murdered him.

Michelle's own life was turned upside down when she went from working on a make-up counter at Manchester's Trafford Centre to filming her first scenes as Tina – all within a week.

'It was my second-ever audition and I only did it as an experience. I thought, I'm never going to get the part but I'll go and see what the audition process is like. When the producer Steve Frost told me I'd got it I literally started screaming. Then everything is a bit of a haze. All I remember is being taken down the corridor, being given scripts and being told I was starting in a week's time. In one week I had to leave my job and get my head round it all. I remember driving home from that meeting with *Coronation Street* scripts next to me on the passenger seat in stunned silence, it was totally overwhelming.'

- Tough times for Joe and Tina.
- Fooling around with David in the salon.
- Graeme and Tina become an item.

Current occupation: Shop assistant in The Kabin.
On screen: 2008–
Defining moment: Admitting she lied in order to give David an alibi for pushing Gail down the stairs in 2008.

Blanche-isms: no one delivered acid-tongued one-liners better than the formidable Blanche Hunt...

The sinister Underworld boss then arranged a hit and run on Liam on his own stag night and cradled the dying man in his arms, weeping crocodile tears. Maria, who had just found out she was pregnant, was devastated but began to suspect her husband's death was no accident. When she discovered the truth about Liam and Carla's affair, she accused Tony of killing Liam, but everyone thought the widow was just demented with grief.

↑ The face of a monster: Tony's ill-fated stag night.
↓ Carla and Michelle lead the mourners at Liam's burial.

⊖ The murderous truth dawns on Carla.
⊖ Tony attempts to drown Roy in the canal.

Carla did later marry Tony, but she also began to suspect that Tony may have had something to do with Liam's accident and finally got him to confess. Stunned and still grieving, she then felt so guilty at her part in it all that Carla left for LA without telling anyone Tony was a murderer. Meanwhile, Tony was so bereft without Carla that Maria started to identify with him and also felt sorry for him. Slowly, he snaked his way into her life and into her affections. Believing him to be a misunderstood good guy, she asked him to move in with her for the last few weeks of her pregnancy.

On a deserted beach walk with Tony, Maria went into labour and he helped deliver Liam Connor into the world, the son of the man he had killed. This moving moment brought them even closer together, and within a few months they were engaged. On the surface Tony had it all, but deep down his conscience was weighing heavy and the constant guilt and stress brought on a heart attack.

Roy took him to the hospital, and believing he was on his death bed, evil Tony came clean about his part in Liam's death. When he didn't die after all, he attempted to throw a terrified Roy into the

2000s Deaths

Jake Webster (Group B Strep)	5 June 2000
Alison Webster (suicide)	7 June 2000
Jez Quigley (internal injuries)	15 September 2000
Susan Barlow (car crash)	11 February 2001
Alma Halliwell (cervical cancer)	17 June 2001
Dennis Stringer (car crash)	2 January 2002
Duggie Ferguson (fell to death)	4 February 2002
Patricia Hillman (murdered)	20 May 2002
Maxine Peacock (murdered)	13 January 2003
Richard Hillman (drowned)	11 March 2003
Billy Platt (premature birth)	2 June 2004
Tommy Harris (murdered)	2 March 2005
Ray Langton (stomach cancer)	10 April 2005
Katy Harris (suicide)	20 April 2005
Mike Baldwin (heart attack)	7 April 2006
Fred Elliott (stroke)	9 October 2006
Charlie Stubbs (murdered)	15 January 2007
Paul Connor (car crash)	6 June 2007
Vera Duckworth (heart attack)	18 January 2008
Liam Connor (run over by a car)	16 October 2008
Colin Grimshaw (heart attack)	18 May 2009
Ramsay Clegg (brain tumour)	26 August 2009

canal, but at the last minute he saved him. Realising the game was up, Tony then went to the police and confessed everything.

It was Hayley who had to tell a stunned Maria the truth about her fiendish fiancé. Heartbroken and horrified by the twisted events, Maria took baby Liam to Ireland. Tony, meanwhile, remained in prison, plotting his next move...

After finding a box of yellowing photographs from past productions starring the likes of Annie and the Ogdens, landlord Steve, along with wife Becky and Claire, decided to revive the Rovers Amateur Dramatic Association (RADA) and bring some festive cheer to the pub by staging their own twenty-first-century charity panto. Shamed ex-teacher John was chosen as the director, with kids entertainer Jesse Chadwick and knicker-factory machinist Sean in dress-up heaven as the ugly sisters. Meanwhile, Betty was a suitably wise fairy godmother and hapless Graeme Proctor spruced himself up to play Buttons, performing with his leg in plaster having just fallen off his window-cleaning ladder. After battling Becky for the title role, competitive Claire won out to play Cinders opposite Steve's Prince Charming. But ultimately it was wide-eyed little Amy who stole the show by blurting out an inappropriate swear word while standing centre stage. 'Maybe they can give some of the money to the Tourette's Trust?' suggested amused audience member, Eileen.

2009

'You kiss her like that again and the turkey won't be the only thing getting stuffed this year.'

Becky to Steve about Claire

Becky McDonald

Played by **Katherine Kelly**

No one has gone from loathed to loved quite as successfully as Weatherfield's chain-smoking chav Becky Granger. The homeless ex-drug addict and ex-con first appeared in the Street when she tracked down former cell-mate Kelly Crabtree and begged her to put in a good word for her at Underworld. She then thanked Kelly by framing her mini-skirted mate for stealing at the factory, before fleeing with her ill-gotten gains. She turned up later in the year when she bumped into Hayley Cropper, who was teaching at an ex-offenders' literary class. She promised to reform, leading a sympathetic Hayley to offer Becky a job at Roy's Rolls. She repaid the Croppers' kindness by stealing their car with her equally criminally minded lover, Slug.

'I always think people will be a bit disappointed when they meet me because Becky is such a firecracker and they probably find me a bit tame by comparison. But I don't mind, I quite like the fact that I'm overshadowed by Becky. The thing with her is you could sit her down with anyone and she'd get on with them, even if it was the Queen or Tony Blair. She wouldn't be fazed by that.

'What I love most of all about her is she's not aspirational. I know people like that in my own life who just live for the here and now and I think that's such an attractive quality that seems to be disappearing nowadays. As long as Becky's got food in her stomach and enough money in her back pocket for a pint of cider and a packet of cigs, then she's happy.'

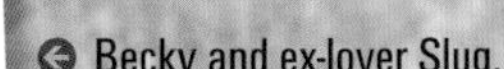

Becky and ex-lover Slug.
Becky makes her move on Kelly's boyfriend Lloyd.
Roy supervises Becky in the cafe.
Banged to rights on her wedding day.
Becky hangs on to Steve.
Sweetly playing mum with Amy.

Under the Croppers' guidance, loose-cannon Becky's priorities did slowly begin to change. She became fiercely protective of the oddball couple and even confronted Hayley's estranged son as revenge for his aggressive attitude towards her friend.

'The public seemed to warm to her when Hayley and Roy had a falling out over Hayley's son and you saw her non-judgmental side, which I think is a very redeeming factor in Becky. She didn't bat an eyelid when Hayley opened her heart and was very loyal throughout.

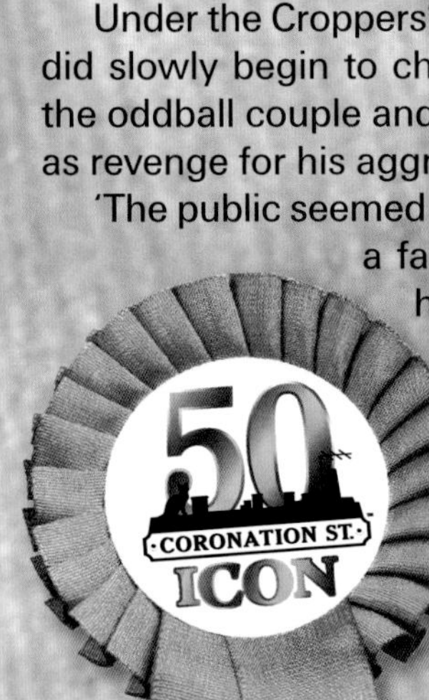

'When Slug arrived people began to understand her even more, because you could see this darkness

that was her past which she was trying to pull against. But she's one of those people who swings with the tide – if she's with good people then she'll be good, but if she's with bad people... then watch out.

'The big change in the public's attitude to Becky was when she was living with Roy in the café while Hayley was in Africa; it was like a teenager with an old dad who was trying to teach her the right way to go about life. That was the turning point for Becky, that was when her character became set in stone and you realised that actually she was all front. Theirs was such a beautiful relationship and it only happened by default really because Julie Hesmondhalgh [who plays Hayley] went off for a year. Honestly, if you asked Becky who her most favourite person was in the world she'd probably say Roy Cropper.'

The reformed bad girl's past reared its ugly head when she discovered her boyfriend Jason Grimshaw was still pining for his ex-wife, Sarah. She went on a drunken rampage and was arrested by her old foe, DC Hooch, a dodgy detective aggrieved that his previous dealings with Becky had cost him a promotion. Steve McDonald gave her an alibi, sparking the beginnings of their love affair. But at the McDonalds' wedding reception at the Rovers in 2009 she was arrested for drug dealing – set up by both her ex, Slug, and Hooch, who eventually let her off the hook.

'The fact she's now Mrs Steve McDonald the third is unbelievable. I would never have thought that in a million years; even when they started off with the affair I didn't think it would happen. The changes in Becky from that greasy unwashed character we first saw are really quite drastic, I mean, I only came into the show for one storyline and that was as Kelly Crabtree's sidekick. But the character seems to constantly re-invent herself and the pregnancy and adoption storylines opened up a whole other can of worms and showed a different side to her again. Honestly, if you'd said to me a few years ago I'd be the fiftieth barmaid in the Rovers and married to Steve McDonald I would've laughed in your face!'

'Half the time you seem that breakable I don't even want to let you step foot out the front door. The other half you're like a shook-up can of lager that no one's safe from...'

Steve

Current occupation: Rovers barmaid.
On screen: 2006–
Defining moment: When Hayley's long-lost son lashes out in 2007, Becky storms round to the record shop were he works and batters him.

2010

With its slickly redesigned opening titles, smooth re-recorded theme tune and high-definition picture quality, *Coronation Street* is in robust form as it marks its fiftieth anniversary. For the cast and crew the celebrations began in March when Tony Warren was presented with the prestigious Lifetime Achievement Award by the Royal Television Society. The judges who decided on this award described his creation as 'the most successful programme in the history of British television'. Says Warren: 'It was tremendous to get that recognition after all this time. I'm delighted it has lasted so long. By the time the first episode went out I was twenty-four. At twenty-four you don't think about next year, let alone fifty of them.'

Two months later the show's production team were awarded a special BAFTA, and other anniversary highlights included *Corrie!*, a humorous stage play written by Jonathan Harvey, and also *Florizel Street*, a one-off drama made by ITV Studios for the BBC which tells the story behind the show's complicated birth, penned by former archivist and scriptwriter, Daran Little.

Meanwhile, Tony Warren has his own theory about the continuing appeal of Weatherfield life: 'Our next-door neighbour was my Auntie Polly Duck, and whenever I behaved outrageously as a child, which was frequently, she said: "We know your faults but love you still." And that's really the motto of the show. Some of the people that live on Coronation Street get up to extraordinary things, but we know their foibles, we know their failings and we know the good deeds they've done, and the camera moves in very closely on all of that, and we love them still.'

In 2010 *Coronation Street* was voted Most Popular Serial Drama at the National TV Awards and at the end of July the producer's baton was passed from Kim Crowther to Phil Collinson, to steer the show through its on-screen birthday celebrations. But this wasn't Collinson's first foray into Weatherfield; a former actor, he'd popped up in 1997 as a mortgage advisor being duped by Deirdre Rachid's fake pilot boyfriend, Jon Lindsay.

Helen Worth accepts the special BAFTA.

Congratulations! The cast celebrate half a century on screen.

Self-confessed Corrie fan The Duchess of Cornwall meets Barbara Knox.

'I remember I sat nervously in the green room surrounded by legends like Roy Barraclough, Bev Callard and Annie Kirkbride and was as quiet as a mouse, which is very unlike me. The whole experience felt so daunting and I'm afraid if I'd been producing it back then I'd have recast and reshot it because I was truly awful as well. I'm much happier this side of the camera!'

Now firmly ensconced at the helm of the production, Collinson is clear about the task in hand: 'My first priority is to make the fiftieth anniversary a memorable and fitting tribute to all the cast and crew who have worked here over the last half a century. More importantly, though, we'll be laying the foundations for the next fifty years. I hope we'll continue to grip the nation with brilliant characters and storylines all mixed in with a big dose of northern humour, and bring a new generation of fans to the show...'

He may have been behind bars but Tony Gordon had been secretly plotting revenge on his estranged wife Carla and interfering neighbours, Roy and Hayley Cropper, for some time. The deranged former rag-trade boss escaped prison after faking a heart attack, meanwhile back in Weatherfield, he'd sent his ex-cellmate Robbie Sloane to pose as a potential business client in order to trick his way into the empty factory – and within minutes his henchman was pointing a loaded gun at Carla's head.

Poor Hayley also found herself taken prisoner and, bound and gagged, the two women were chilled to the bone when at last a gloating Tony made an appearance. Events swiftly spiralled out of control and after a row about money, he killed Robbie at point blank range.

Tony's plan to burn down the factory was further interrupted when Maria Connor returned unexpectedly from Ireland and visited Underworld. Even she couldn't reason with him, but he did at least let his petrified ex-fiancée escape before splashing petrol around the premises. It was Carla who persuaded him to release Hayley and in the burning building an almighty struggle ensued as the formidable factory boss fought for her life. When a gunshot rang out the crowd outside feared the worst, but it was Carla who had shot Tony's shoulder and using every ounce of her remaining strength she managed to escape through the flames, before a gigantic explosion destroyed the building with him in it.

When Gail Platt had first been wooed by playful kitchen fitter Joe McIntyre (behind the backs of their children Tina and David who were also dating at the time) she thought she'd finally met Mr Right – but once again she'd married someone she didn't know at

❶ Carla's life hangs in the balance as the factory blazes.
❷ Treacherous Tracy becomes Gail's cellmate.
❸ No jail for Gail: she celebrates freedom with Nick, Audrey and David.

'Is that it? You let a murdering psycho do a runner from his cell – and the best you can tell me to do is wrap up warm and cross your fingers?'

Carla

all and discovered he was broke and secretly addicted to painkillers.

While holidaying in the Lake District Gail was horrified as Joe revealed his intention to fake his own death by disappearing on a boat that very night, leaving her to cash in his life insurance and pay off his debts. Disaster struck, however, when Joe later drowned for real.

Even though her husband's death had been a horrible accident, grieving Gail found herself banged up on a murder charge. In court damning evidence was given against her by Joe's vengeful daughter Tina – who had become increasingly depressed after her dad's death. Then there was the testimony of surprise cell-mate Tracy Barlow, who – in a bid to be moved to an open prison where she'd have more access to daughter Amy – lied in court that her former-neighbour had confessed to the crime. To Gail's immense relief the jury saw through Tracy's fictional version of events and found her not guilty.

'No matter what he loaded onto her – the debts, the failing business, the tablets – she'd always come bouncing back with this big Stepford Wife smile on her face. All normal and loving on the surface, but inside . . . there's just this mess of crazy wiring.'

Tina on Gail

Tracy's court appearance hadn't been her first outing since her imprisonment in 2007, the previous month the twisted murderess had attended the funeral of her acid-tongued grandmother Blanche Hunt, who'd passed away unexpectedly while holidaying in Portugal. Not, as thought, soaking up the sun with her friend May from the one o'clock club, but courting a secret fancy-man called Arnold. At the funeral her daughter Deirdre Barlow's candid eulogy touched the hearts of everyone, but a handcuffed Tracy flipped when she saw Amy being cuddled by stepmother Becky McDonald and was bundled back in to the prison van when she aggresively threatened her rival.

At Number 6, kind-hearted cafe worker Anna Windass was at her wits' end when she discovered her gruff soldier son Gary had gone on the run during his basic army training. Eventually he turned up in Weatherfield and Anna and her cab-driver husband Eddie agreed to hide him when his warrant officer came calling. Afterwards, Gary confessed he'd gone AWOL because he was scared of what his future in the army may hold. In the meantime, Eddie had let the warrant officer know Gary's whereabouts and after a moral-boosting pep-talk from a teary Anna, he agreed to go back to the barracks.

While he'd been on the run, he'd bumped into machinist Izzy Armstrong, who liked the way he didn't cut her any slack just because she was in a wheelchair and there was a hint of chemistry between them. Despite his drunken one-night stand with Becky's chav half-sister Kylie Turner in September, which he regretted, Gary continued to have feelings for Izzy. On his last night before going to Afghanistan he slept with Izzy after admitting he'd been keeping her at arm's length because he was scared of getting too close to anyone in case he died.

Soldier boy Gary tucks in with proud parents Anna and Eddie.
When Sian's appendix bursts Sophie rushes to her bedside.
Tyrone shows off Molly's baby scan to Kevin, the real father.
Sally accepts her daughter's relationship with Sian.

Next door at Number 4, as Sally Webster recovered from her battle with breast cancer, younger daughter Sophie was going through her own turmoil. Having developed feelings for her best mate Sian

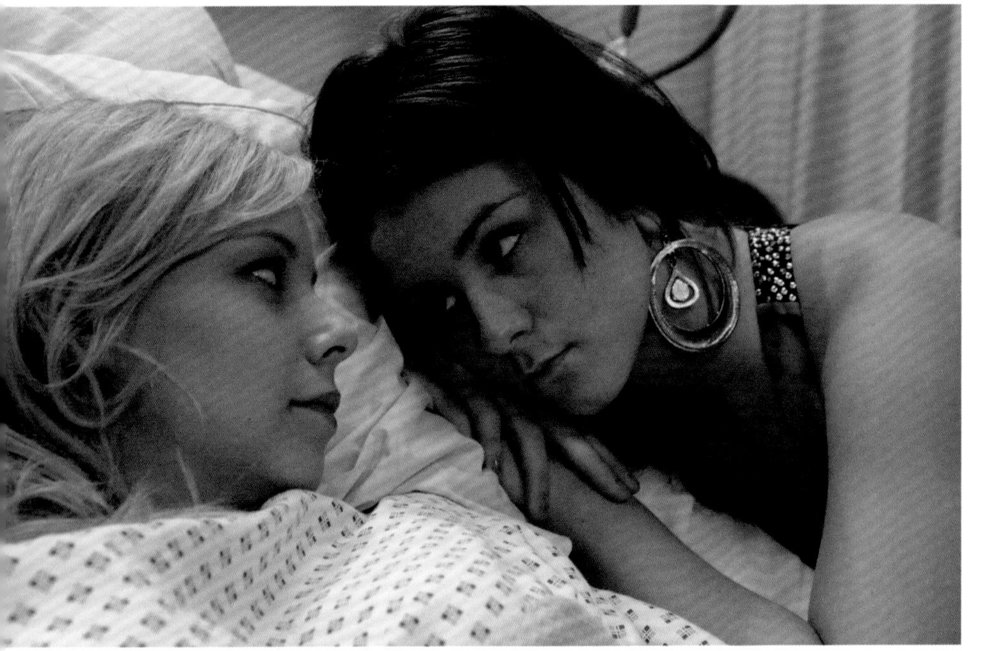

2010 Births

Jack (Molly Dobbs & Kevin Webster)	6 September 10

Marriages

Gail Platt & Joe McIntyre	8 January 10
Hayley Cropper & Roy Cropper	30 August 10

Deaths

Joe McIntyre (drowned)	8 February 10
Blanche Hunt (in her sleep)	3 May 10
Robbie Sloane (shot)	1 June 10
Tony Gordon (burned in fire)	1 June 10

Powers she told her startled pal, 'You are far more important to me than any lad,' and instinctively kissed her on the lips.

After an initial period of confusion the teenagers admitted their feelings for each other and eventually Sophie opened up to Kevin who promised to support his daughter. But when he insisted Sally should be told Sophie was aghast. Both girls were now terrified of their parents' reactions and ran away.

As the Websters blamed themselves for Sophie's flight, Kevin had other things on his mind as his former mistress Molly Dobbs was about to give birth to his child, whilst pretending husband Tyrone was the father. What he hadn't counted on was Molly unexpectedly going into labour while Tyrone was out on a breakdown job and, as the contractions came thick and fast, it was Kevin and Sally who ended up by Molly's side, until Tyrone rushed in just in time to see the baby being born.

Sally happily accepted when a grateful Tyrone asked the Websters to be godparents, while Kevin was horrified. But when Tyrone placed his 'godson' Jack into his arms Kevin was sideswiped and at that moment he knew he was going to struggle to keep away from his son...

'I know what you're thinking, what people are saying. But I tell you this: I'm proud of my daughter. Because whatever else she is, she's a good kid with a good heart.'
Sally

Meanwhile, Sophie and Sian had been crashing on the floor of a lad they met, but he'd tried it on with Sophie so they left and found themselves homeless and penniless. Deciding it was time to face the music, Sophie called her sister Rosie to pick them up. An emotional Sally and Kevin were overjoyed to see their daughter and – despite the challenges ahead – Sophie was relieved to be back home with her family on Coronation Street where she belonged...

Index

Page numbers in **bold** indicate the main entry for a character.

P

Q

R

S

T

U

V

W

Y

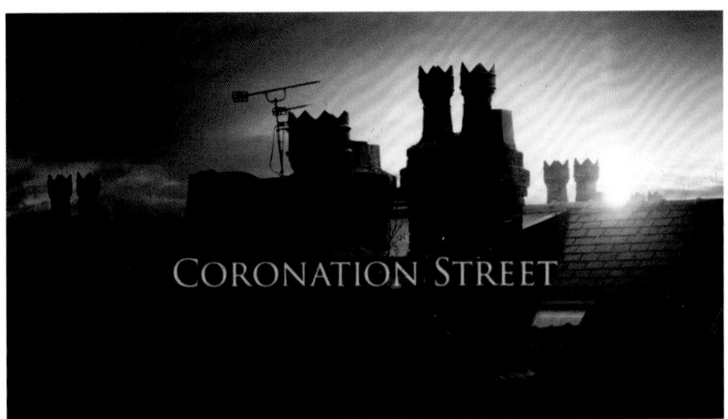